Tapestry Design Basics and Beyond

Planning and Weaving with Confidence

Tommye McClure Scanlin | *Foreword by* Rebecca Mezoff

SCHIFFER PUBLISHING

4880 Lower Valley Road · Atglen, PA 19310

All photographs and design examples are by the author unless otherwise noted in the captions.

Tapestry works shown are by permission of the artists and photographers noted.

"Horizon" from *The Art of Drowning* by Billy Collins, © 1995. Reprinted by permission of the University of Pittsburgh Press.

Permission for use of quotation and images from Silvia Heyden granted by Françoise Heyden, daughter.

Quotation from *Finding Freedom to Create* by Dianne Mize © 2014. Used with permission of the author.

Quotation from *Expressive Drawing: A Practical Guide to Freeing the Artist Within* by Steven Aimone © 2009. Used with permission of the author.

Quotation from "Tapestry, a 20th Century Art Form?," an essay by Archie Brennan, in *Tapestry: The Narrative Voice* exhibition catalog © 1989. Used with permission of Archie Brennan.

Designed by Brenda McCallum
Type set in Argus / Minion

ISBN: 978-0-7643-6156-2
Printed in China
5 4 3 2

Published by Schiffer Publishing, Ltd.
4880 Lower Valley Road
Atglen, PA 19310
Phone: (610) 593-1777; Fax: (610) 593-2002
E-mail: Info@schifferbooks.com
Web: www.schifferbooks.com

For our complete selection of fine books on this and related subjects, please visit our website at www.schifferbooks.com. You may also write for a free catalog.

Schiffer Publishing's titles are available at special discounts for bulk purchases for sales promotions or premiums. Special editions, including personalized covers, corporate imprints, and excerpts, can be created in large quantities for special needs. For more information, contact the publisher.

We are always looking for people to write books on new and related subjects. If you have an idea for a book, please contact us at proposals@schifferbooks.com.

For Mother—who always thought I could.
And for Thomas—who saw me do it and encouraged me all the way.

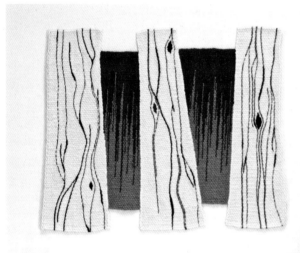

Contents

Opposite, details from: (clockwise from top L) Erin M. Riley, *Undressing 3* (Courtesy of Erin M. Riley and PPOW Gallery). Tommye McClure Scanlin, rya sample (Chris Dant, photographer). Tommye McClure Scanlin, sampler. Tommye McClure Scanlin, *Five Leaves for Miss Lillian.* Mary Jane Lord, *Triple Dog Joy* (Courtesy of Mary Jane Lord; photography by Randy Swing). Sue Weil, *New Growth Rising from the Ashes* (Courtesy of Sue Weil; photography by Jay Daniel / Black Cat Studio).

Foreword

by Rebecca Mezoff

The first time I visited Tommye Scanlin's tapestry studio, the last bit of winter was still hanging on. The lush southern greenery soon to come in Dahlonega, Georgia, had not yet filled the air with the scent of blooms. But inside, images of nature burst forth from several tapestries in progress on the looms filling every corner of her multiroom studio. I was fascinated by everything from the small teaching examples on the walls to the large-format tapestries being prepared for shows around the country.

I spotted a pair of small, vertically oriented landscape pieces tucked in a far corner. I doubt that Tommye realized my fascination with these small tapestry snippets. After all, there were huge, vibrant tapestries to marvel at everywhere. Those two narrow landscapes, though, offered a window into a different way of designing. Their small scale, simplicity, and narrative subject matter suggested a non-threatening way of practicing design along with technique. I knew my own students could also benefit from this approach. Large gorgeous tapestries are inspiring. Many of us will weave them. As Tommye encourages in this book, beginning with simple exercises and a small bit of weaving every day is a far less intimidating way to start.

Tommye's tapestries exude life in the same way her being is full of the wise knowledge and skill of a seasoned art professor. She has spent many decades teaching, both in the university and in workshops around the country, but my experience with Tommye's teaching is more personal. She became one of two important mentors to me after my teacher unexpectedly died, just as I was struggling to find my artistic path and eventually to become a tapestry instructor myself. A decade later, she has become a trusted friend and colleague. I owe much of my education and success to her generosity as a highly skilled teacher and her profound love for the medium of handwoven tapestry.

Finding my voice as an artist has been my biggest struggle. If you've picked up this book, it probably has been for you also. Tapestry is a medium that often appeals to its practitioners because of the texture and sensual nature of its primary material, yarn. It also appeals to many of us because there is an inherent structure to it. We can learn how the techniques work and then how to put them together to make a cloth that contains images. It is the designing of those images that can become a sticking point for those of us without formal training in art and design, because that is where the clear-cut rules seem to disappear.

My own start as a weaver came through my local guild and a pile of books. I found tapestry and picked up techniques through college classes and through an apprenticeship with the renowned tapestry artist James Koehler. Not all tapestry techniques are easy, but they are generally straightforward and I learned them readily. Designing for tapestry, on the other hand, presented its looming tangle of difficulty to me soon thereafter. I would bring my scribbled designs to James. He would look at them, point out the stronger design elements in my ideas, then leave me to try again. It turned out that trial and error, the process that works so well when learning the mechanics of tapestry technique, also works when learning tapestry design.

In the beginning, I desperately wanted some sort of template for designing. I took art classes at various colleges, but I felt inferior and not up to the task of creating successful designs because I didn't have an art degree. I soon learned that no one could do this thing for me. If I really loved tapestry and still wanted to express myself through this enchanting, sensual medium, I had to tackle design. Little by little I realized that there was no template. I was going to have to do some work to learn the elements of design and apply them to my chosen medium.

I wish Tommye's book had been available when I was first struggling with creating my own designs. This book is a much-needed addition to the scant literature on designing for tapestry weaving. Her explanations of the basic elements and "rules" of design, and the hands-on exercises she offers, provide a pathway through the twists and turns of finding your own voice. There is no person more qualified to teach these ideas than Tommye Scanlin.

Having taught a few thousand people both online and in workshops, I find that Tommye's assertion that many tapestry weavers feel they "can't make art" is true. In some ways, designing is a process of finding yourself. Maybe that is the scariest part of it all. Once the mechanics of weaving tapestry are learned, many of us struggle with the process of self-discovery that comes with the search for imagery that is both meaningful and can be rendered in the gridded medium of tapestry.

Tommye's answer to the struggle of finding your artistic voice is to encourage you to explore. The daily practice of weaving and the continuing discovery of ideas and design create a rhythm to this medium. She gives you the road map—paths to follow on this journey of discovery—and encourages you to keep at it every day. You don't have to master it all right now. You just need a few concepts and hands-on activities to get you started. Go explore. You're holding the guide you need right now.

Rebecca Mezoff
Founder of the online tapestry school Rebecca Mezoff Tapestry Studio, LLC; author of *The Art of Tapestry Weaving: A Complete Guide to Mastering the Techniques for Making Images with Yarn*

Rebecca Mezoff. *Emergence II*, 2009. Tapestry: 45" × 45".

Tommye Scanlin talks about color with her Penland School of Craft 2019 tapestry students.
Chris Dant, photographer

In my decades of teaching I've worked with students of all ages and skill levels, from children to adults, in many settings. I often met people who at first felt insecure about designing for tapestries. After all, some hadn't had art experiences since childhood, yet they'd become interested in tapestry and wanted to learn about the process. In every encounter, my goal has been to convey insights gained over many years both of learning about and teaching art concepts, often to those who felt that they couldn't "make art."

One thing about teaching that I began to understand in my first years with students was that the key to good instruction is having a passion for a subject and a desire to share what you know. That's what the best teachers I've had did for me, as well as for others. They shared their knowledge—but even more importantly, they were able to get across how passionately they felt about the subject. And they were encouraging of every honest effort their students made.

I discovered from those wise teachers that it's OK to say, "I don't know," then to follow up with "but I'll try to find out." The best instructors also often say to their students, "What do you think?" It's in the spirit of those wonderful teachers that I want to share with you some of what I've learned about design and how it can play a role in the making of tapestries.

In the discussions that follow, I will use the term "weaverly" to describe the approach to the fundamental components of design that are at work when weaving tapestries. I first heard this term from Silvia Heyden, who was an exceptional tapestry weaver. She also spoke about thinking of designs for tapestry with her "weaver's eye."[1] The more you weave tapestry, the better your own weaver's eye will become.

I will begin by presenting concepts about the fundamental elements and principles of design. I'll also suggest explorations to lead you through several of the design fundamentals and compositional considerations. Many of these explorations will be done with mediums other than weaving, but there will also be suggestions of approaches for interpreting these through tapestry methods.

Members of a tapestry study group in the Atlanta area undertook several design explorations in tapestry samples for this book. Examples from their work are included, along with their comments about the studies. Photos of designs and tapestries, along with remarks from several students from past workshops, are also included.

Silvia Heyden. *Weavers Dance,* 2002. Tapestry: 28" × 34".
Courtesy of Silvia Heyden Estate

How you put it all together—the subject or idea you want to use, the design you'll create, and your understanding of the medium (in this case, tapestry technique)—is determined by these three key factors that make up the WHAT, WHY, and HOW of any artwork. We often neglect to step back and take a critical look at our own work. Critical doesn't imply "negative" in this case. Instead, it means assessing visual impact on the basis of aspects of design fundamentals and expressive qualities seen within a composition. I'll address a method of critique that people of all ages and experience levels can use successfully when looking at artworks to help guide them in the process.

I'll describe many aspects of making cartoons for tapestry, all of which I've used at different times. Experience with each way of handling the translation of original design into a cartoon offers options for choosing the most successful method for a specific tapestry. Each approach has benefits; learning about them gives you the freedom to choose what may fit best with your way of working.

The making of a tapestry doesn't really stop with the last few passes of the weft. There are several more steps to take before it's ready to be called complete. I'll suggest a few finishing and presentation methods and make note of where additional information may be found about these important last steps.

LEFT Designing work underway at my studio

RIGHT Mary Jane Lea is one of the Atlanta-area tapestry study group members who worked through several tapestry technique explorations about design. One of her studies is still on the loom, along with a watercolor sketch and yarn color wrapping.
Courtesy of Mary Jane Lea; Kenneth J. Bryson, photographer

In an appendix there are a few basics about tapestry weaving noted. This is not intended as a primary techniques tutorial, but there are a few points to make about the process that may help as your tapestry-weaving skills develop. More experienced tapestry weavers may also find some of these ideas helpful. There will be a list of resources available at the time of the writing where you may find in-depth tapestry technique information.

Learning from others is important. Seeking out past, present, and future sources for information about art and design, inspiration, and creativity, and yes—tapestry making—can be a rewarding, never-ending pursuit. At the end of this book, print

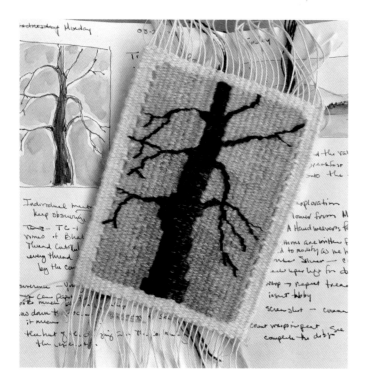

TOP LEFT Nancy Nordquist has been a student in several of my workshops. She often uses journal writing and watercolor sketching to plan tapestries. Many are inspired by location—Penland School of Craft, in this instance. *Courtesy of Nancy Nordquist*

TOP RIGHT Drawing a cartoon with Sharpie marker by placing Mylar over a watercolor painting. *Chris Dant, photographer*

BOTTOM Detail showing the back of a tapestry and a method I use to secure warp ends when I don't choose to do a turn-back or hem. This is done with half-Damascus warp finishing, followed by stitching small groups of warps together against the back. *Chris Dant, photographer*

and online resources are mentioned where you may continue your quest for guidance and inspiration.

Throughout the book are examples from tapestry artists whose work continues to inspire and amaze me. I've found in the tapestry world, small as it is, a tremendous spirit of sharing. Many thanks go to one and all for being part of this effort.

I once asked my husband, Thomas, what he would ask students to consider if he were teaching. He said that he'd ask them, *What do you hope someone who sees your work will "get" from it? What do you want to share with a viewer—something you saw? Something you felt? What do you want someone to take away from an interaction with your work? Work backward from those points.*

Those were good suggestions, and they relate to my hopes for this book, one that began as a compilation of assorted handouts developed in my years of teaching. I'll begin by paraphrasing his comments:

What do I hope someone will "get" from this book?

I hope someone would find in these pages a sense of the possibilities of the creative journey in tapestry for anyone and everyone.

What do I want to share with the reader?

I hope to be able to share many of the methods of searching for inspiration and designing tapestries that I've found to be both challenging and rewarding in my own work for over four decades.

Indeed, my greatest wish is that a few of these suggestions will lead someone to more clarity of process, or insight into their own best path to creativity.

How to use this book

- In Part One you'll find an overview of the fundamentals of design.
- Parts Two and Three hold an array of explorations to try out.
- In Part Four you'll learn to analyze your designs, find several ways to turn those into tapestries, and finally, consider several finishing methods.
- Appendixes hold useful information about resources and several helpful templates.

LEFT A sampler of a few basic tapestry techniques. *Chris Dant, photographer*

RIGHT Many books about art, design, tapestry technique, and creative process fill several bookshelves in my studio. Sitting down with coffee and a book is a great way to spend a bit of afternoon time. *Chris Dant, photographer*

Part One

Design Fundamentals

THE ELEMENTS OF VISUAL DESIGN | THE PRINCIPLES OF VISUAL DESIGN
TYING IT ALL TOGETHER INTO A UNIFIED COMPOSITION

I . . . have come to the conclusion that tapestry can indeed be an art form in its own right with its own specific mode of expression if the craft of weaving is allowed to influence the art of tapestry. In order to be meaningful, tapestry must find its own identity. It must not be a woven painting, but rather a composition that could only have been woven, not painted.

—Silvia Heyden, from *The Making of Modern Tapestry*

Silvia Heyden. *A Weaverly Path*, 2015. Tapestry: 35" × 40". This was Silvia Heyden's last tapestry, one she was not able to complete before her death. The exposed warp at the top shows that she had nearly finished it. *Courtesy of Silvia Heyden Estate; photographer, Charles Harris, Raleigh, NC*

The words of Silvia Heyden are important to begin with as we consider how design concepts may apply to tapestry. When one makes a tapestry, the images that are created are part and parcel of the making process. Her comment "*if* the craft of weaving is allowed to influence the art of tapestry" is key to effectively translating your ideas into tapestries you are happy with. I'll borrow a term from Silvia that you'll find many times in these pages: she wanted the tapestry images she created to be "weaverly." Let's first consider design concepts and then how these may be translated through the medium of tapestry in weaverly ways. Many artists have shared their tapestries in this book and these exemplify a few of the myriad weaverly ways there are to create beautiful compositions.

The notion that there may be a common visual "language" that can be broken down into fundamental components is relatively new when we consider that humans have been making visual works for many thousands of years without necessarily referring to guidelines for designing. In the late nineteenth and early twentieth centuries, Arthur Wesley Dow taught about composition and is often recognized as one whose teaching still echoes today. By the early twentieth century, it was generally thought in Western culture that there were ways to analyze art and craft by studying the visual components used in their creation. It also was widely recognized that aspiring artists/ craftspeople could be introduced to, learn from, and be able to use these guiding fundamentals for their own creative work.

The terms *elements* and *principles* came to be associated with two related basic aspects of art and design—in a sense as fundamentals. Edmund Burke Feldman says: "After we have learned to see them in art [the visual elements], we may discover the same constituents in nature. . . . Consequently, one of the indirect dividends of studying the structure of art is the added satisfaction we can get in perception of the real world."[2]

As a way to understand the relationship of the elements and principles to each other, you might compare the elements and principles of art and design to cooking, where you would use various ingredients and combine them in varying amounts and methods to create a variety of dishes. Think of the ingredients as counterparts of the visual elements and the principles as how they come together in the completed dish. Thus, the elements, as used with the principles of design, create the finished composition.

When you read about art and design fundamentals in different places, you may come across varying lists of elements and principles. A basic few will be all we need to consider when looking at ways in which design concepts and tapestry can interact successfully.

Line, shape and form, value (*light and dark*), *texture, space,* and *color* are often listed among the elements, and each may play important roles in tapestry weaving. *Balance, emphasis, repetition and rhythm, proportion,* and *variety* are among the principles that you'll often use in tapestry. The goal of working with the fundamental components of design is to create *unity* as you develop a composition for your tapestry that pleases your eye.

As we start to explore the elements and principles of art and design, perhaps we may wonder whether this study really matters. As with many things, in art there is always subjectivity. After all, self-taught, folk, or outsider artists make wonderfully exciting, expressive works yet usually have no formal art training. Those artists don't learn the "rules," and yet many make exceptional artworks. You might also consider the beauty of the artwork of children, especially very young ones, who make art with joy and abandon. Other cultures often have aesthetic traditions that are not the same as those that have developed in the Western world. In the end, all are right—none are wrong.

Design Fundamentals

ELEMENTS	PRINCIPLES
Line	Balance
Shape and Form or Volume	Emphasis
	Rhythm and Repetition
Value	Proportion
Texture	Variety
Space	
Color	

Where does that leave us? It seems we have the choice to make our designs, weave our tapestries, and not concern ourselves with ideas of art and design fundamentals as taught in the Western world's traditions. That way is certainly valid. On the other hand, we may choose to learn about design concepts and use them in our tapestry making. Assuming we do want to explore ideas about design fundaments and see if these may enhance our tapestry compositions, let's begin.

Since our goal is to apply design concepts to tapestry, let's first consider the elements and principles. Let's look at a few options for adapting in a weaverly approach. Then, in Part Two I'll suggest several explorations you may try on paper or in tapestry—or both. Definitions for unfamiliar terms are usually found in the glossary.

THE ELEMENTS OF VISUAL DESIGN

The elements of line, shape and form, value (or light and dark), texture, space, and color are usually important in every tapestry. Several useful ways to think about each of these will be mentioned in this section. We'll look at color last, because this element has so much complexity and many ways it can be applied in tapestry.

LINE

Line may be thought of as almost the simplest visual effect you can achieve. In art, line may be made by strokes from a marking tool, such as pencil, charcoal, pen nib, or marker. It may even be made with a brush and ink or paint. The line might flow smoothly, or it might be broken. It might vary in width. Lines may be measured and regular, or free flowing and organic. Line can lead us on a visual journey.

In tapestry, line may be made in several ways:
- Line may be broken, as made by a single pick, or half pass, of a contrasting color.
- Line may be narrow, as seen in two picks, or a single pass (two picks) of weft.
- Line may be horizontal (weft direction), vertical (warp direction), or diagonal (made as an edge is stepped back).
- Line may be seen in bands or stripes in a horizontal direction. These can be narrow, medium, or wide, depending on the number of passes used to make them.
- Vertical lines in tapestry may be done
  —with pick and pick
  —by wrapping up along one warp
  —by weaving over the same few warps in vertical direction
  —by another method, such as vertical twining, soumak, or flying shuttle.
- Curved lines are a bit more difficult to achieve in tapestry weaving because of the perpendicular grid nature of warp/weft. However, eccentric weft will travel over edges, moving out of the perpendicular. Soumak and twining may also move over edges to give curving effects. A contrasting color used

Assorted soumak and twining methods created outlining throughout this sampler.

for the method chosen for outlining will allow the linear effect to show more strongly.

Take a look at how several artists have used line in their tapestries. David Johnson has created lines in broad and narrow bands, as well as with areas of pick and pick and dots in his Echo series; this is #16 of those. Archie Brennan shows his mastery of tapestry technique in *Drawing Series VI- 3 × 3 Grid* to create an image in which outlines are the main means to define the simplified figures. Silvia Heyden used repeating patterns of flowing lines of all sizes and lengths in her tapestry *Rocks Form Water*. In her tapestry *Winter's Silence*, Becky Stevens used various weaverly ways to "draw" the lines of her abstracted barren landscape, including hatching for horizontal lines and thin woven diagonals. She then added stitched outlines for the tree limbs. In *casa espinosa*, Lyn Hart let delicate, eccentric lines define the cactus home for a nesting bird.

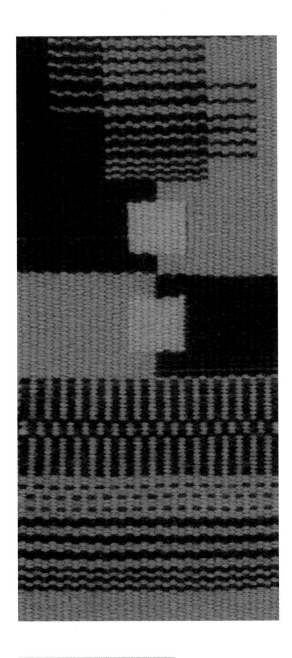

Lines in this sampler are made by several passes, pick and pick, hatching and hachure.

David Johnson. *Echo Series #16*, 2011. Tapestry: 60" × 30".
Courtesy of David Johnson

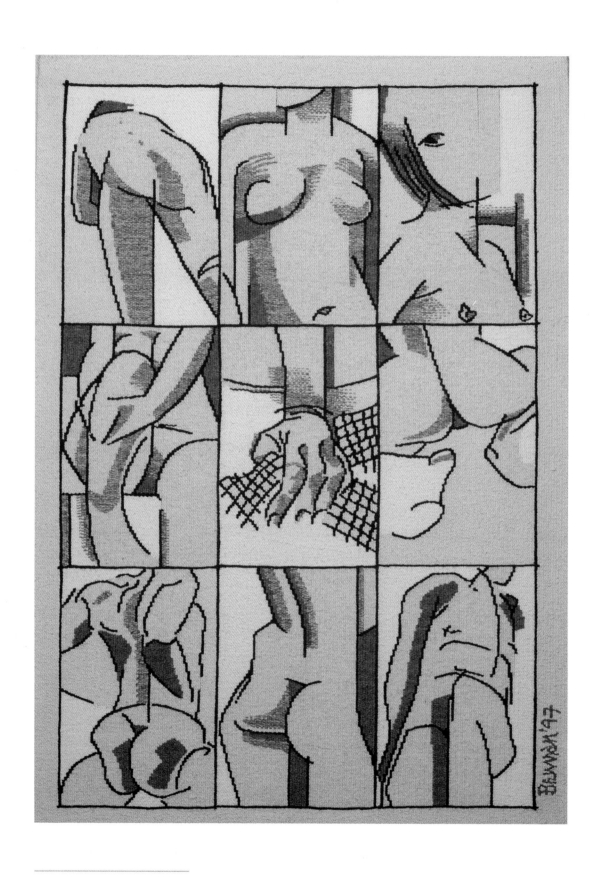

Archie Brennan. *Drawing Series VI-3 × 3 Grid*, 1997. Tapestry: 39" × 26.5".
Courtesy of Archie Brennan; Chris Dant, photographer

Silvia Heyden. *Rocks Form Water*, 2008. Tapestry: 39" × 32". *Courtesy of Silvia Heyden Estate*

TOP Becky Stevens. *Winter's Silence*, 2018. Tapestry: 15" × 15". *Courtesy of Becky Stevens*

BOTTOM Lyn Hart. *casa espinosa*, October 2016. Tapestry: 36" × 28.5". *Designed and woven by Lyn Hart; image courtesy of the artist*

SHAPE AND FORM OR VOLUME

Shapes are seen when there are boundaries. In some artwork, shapes are made when lines create edges that describe contours. Shapes may be organic and related to natural growth, or geometric, seen as more measured and often found in man-made things.

Shapes may have hard or soft edges—ones that are distinct in areas or more blurred, and indistinct, in others.

Shapes and the background in which they exist have a positive and negative visual relationship, sometimes also called *figure-ground relationship*.

We usually describe shape as being two-dimensional, with height and width. When depth is added, we usually define the results as having *three-dimensional form*, or *volume*.

In tapestry, shapes are created in many ways:

- Shape is created when an area is woven separately from another, even if in the same color. In breaking up an area with cutbacks, for instance, distinct shapes may be formed if changes are regular, as in a series of diagonal lines that zigzag back and forth.

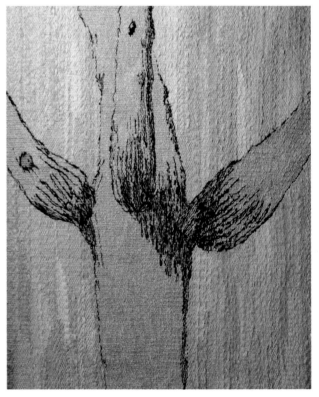

- Shape is also created when an area of color is outlined with a contrasting thread or small group of threads in a tiny stripe. Soumak and vertical twining may be useful for outlining shapes.
- Shapes may have geometric or hard edges. This is somewhat easier to achieve in tapestry than organic shapes because of the nature of the weave structure. For instance, a square or a rectangle may be made with a series of passes and another one woven beside it. Triangles and diamonds are made with regular steps of passes that move back and forth.
- Shapes may have soft edges. One way these may be made is by using hatching or hachure (see page 170) as transition between shapes.
- Shapes may be organic or flowing, although in tapestry the stairstep way of making a curving edge must always be considered. Factors playing a role in how smooth or how stepped the edge of the shape appears include warp size, sett, and the weft used.
- Shapes may have difference or contrast in scale (size), value (dark/light), texture, and color.
- Shape is also seen in the finished object itself and may be regular, as in a square or rectangle of any proportion. The tapestry may also be irregular or shaped at the edges. For instance, wedge weave causes irregular edges due to the way the technique is done.
- Tapestry may be three-dimensional, having form and volume. Various methods may be used to give volume to the tapestry, from pulled warps to weaving around a form.

Detail of *Oak Leaves,* tapestry by the author. Geometric shapes in the background are made by slightly pulling the weft turns so the slits are obvious. Organic shapes of the leaves contrast with the angles, although at 6 epi the steps of the curves are obvious. *Photo © Tim Barnwell*

TOP Sampler with several weaverly methods for making shapes by areas of passes, pick and pick, hatching and hachure. *Chris Dant, photographer*

BOTTOM Detail of *Five Leaves for Miss Lillian*, tapestry by the author. Background shapes are geometric triangles and diamonds, contrasting with the organic shapes of the leaves. The edges of these are smoother than in *Oak Leaves* (page 19) because the warp sett is closer, at 8 epi.

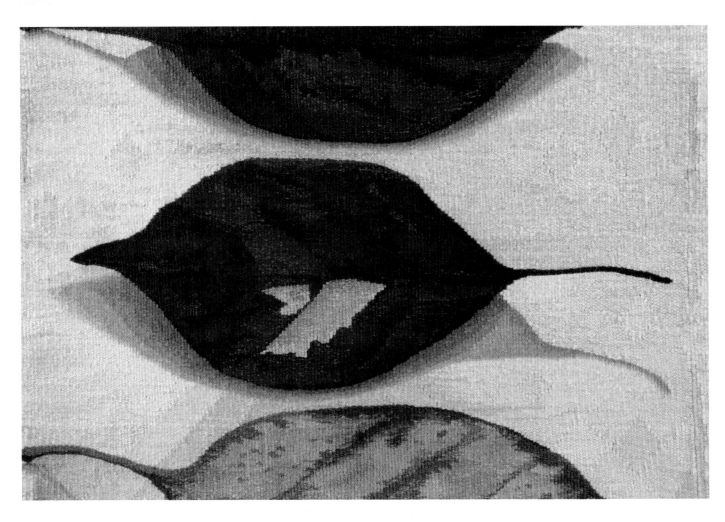

Here are a few of the many ways that artists use the element of shape in their tapestries. Jane Freear-Wyld's tapestry *Earth: Canadian Rockies at Dawn* has numerous organic shapes defined by small woven lines. Kathe Todd-Hooker frequently makes extensive use of soumak to outline edges of shapes within her complex tapestries like this one, *Requiem for the almost/always too late*. Rebecca Mezoff uses both organic and geometric shapes in *Emergence IV*. Elizabeth Buckley, in *Molten Beneath Strata*, combines subtle ways to show soft and hard edges to give suggestions of heat waves flowing upward from the core of the earth. In Erin M. Riley's tapestry *Undressing 3*, the organic shapes of a partially seen human form fill almost three-quarters of the composition. Geometric and organic shapes play important roles along with contrasts of light and dark in LaDonna Mayer's tapestry *Asheville NC*, one of her 51 Cities series.

Linda Wallace's tapestry *One Is for Sorrow* breaks out of the rectangle with the two side panels. Likewise, Sue Weil makes use of extending beyond the rectangular format with her tapestry *A Peek into Monet's Garden*. Connie Lippert's *Prairie* shows the shaped or scalloped edges that are created by the way the technique of wedge weave is done.

Nancy Crampton and her husband, Dan, have collaborated for a series of twelve tapestries in which he has designed and forged a wrought-iron frame in a style for each design she has woven. In *Streetscape*, you see one of these joint efforts.

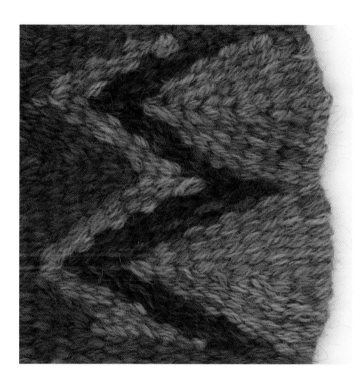

LEFT Detail of wedge weave sample by the author. The irregular edge of wedge weave is one of its characteristics.

RIGHT Jane Freear-Wyld. *Earth: Canadian Rockies at Dawn,* 2016. Tapestry: 9" × 6.5". *Courtesy of Jane Freear-Wyld; Chris Dant, photographer*

Susan Iverson has used methods to give three-dimensional effects to many of her tapestries, often by using a pulled-warp technique to shift the wefts after weaving. Her piece *Horizon: Dawn's Dance* and the multipart piece *Fleeting* both use these ways to give three-dimensional form to the images. Barbara Burns also used pulled warps for her *Little Devil Corset*.[3]

Susan Martin Maffei incorporated many techniques in addition to tapestry for her multipart work *Pandora Box-9 Spot Lady Bug-Disappearing*. She combined sculpture with weaving as she wove tiny three-dimensional bugs with stainless-steel warp and silk and wool weft. The oak leaves were shaped as they were woven by using multiselvedge warps. All components are held in handmade boxes.

Betty Hilton-Nash's *A, B, Cs of Tapestry* takes the idea of small children's blocks as an inspiration when creating the 9" square "blocks" of tapestry. Each side of the blocks shows a word or image beginning with the letter of the block.

Kathe Todd-Hooker. *Requiem for the almost/always too late*, 2018–19. Tapestry: 13.5" × 13.5". *Courtesy of Kathe Todd-Hooker*

Rebecca Mezoff. *Emergence IV*, 2011. Tapestry:
46" × 15". *Courtesy of Rebecca Mezoff*

Elizabeth J. Buckley. *Molten Beneath Strata*, 2017. Tapestry: 84" × 28".
Courtesy of Elizabeth J. Buckley, artist and photographer

TOP Erin M. Riley. *Undressing 3*, 2014.
Tapestry: 46" × 48". *Courtesy of Erin M. Riley
and PPOW Gallery*

BOTTOM LaDonna Mayer. *Asheville NC*—from the 51
American Cities series, 2011. Tapestry: 20.75" × 24.5".
Courtesy of LaDonna Mayer

Linda Wallace. *One Is for Sorrow*, 2017. Tapestry: 30" × 27".
Courtesy of Linda Wallace; photography by Terry Zlot

Connie Lippert. *Prairie,* 2015. Tapestry in wedge weave: 25" × 30".
Courtesy of Connie Lippert; photography by Eli Warren

LEFT Sue Weil. *A Peek into Monet's Garden*, 2019. Tapestry: 16" × 19" (framed size). *Courtesy of Sue Weil; photography by Jay Daniel / Black Cat Studio*

BELOW Nancy C. Crampton. *Streetscape*, 2018. Tapestry woven by Nancy C. Crampton, with iron frame for hanging forged and fabricated by Dan Crampton. Tapestry: 12.75" × 7.5", with total size (including frame) of 14" × 9.5". *Courtesy of Nancy C. Crampton; photography by Mark Bugnaski*

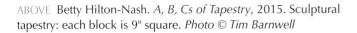

ABOVE Betty Hilton-Nash. *A, B, Cs of Tapestry*, 2015. Sculptural tapestry: each block is 9" square. *Photo © Tim Barnwell*

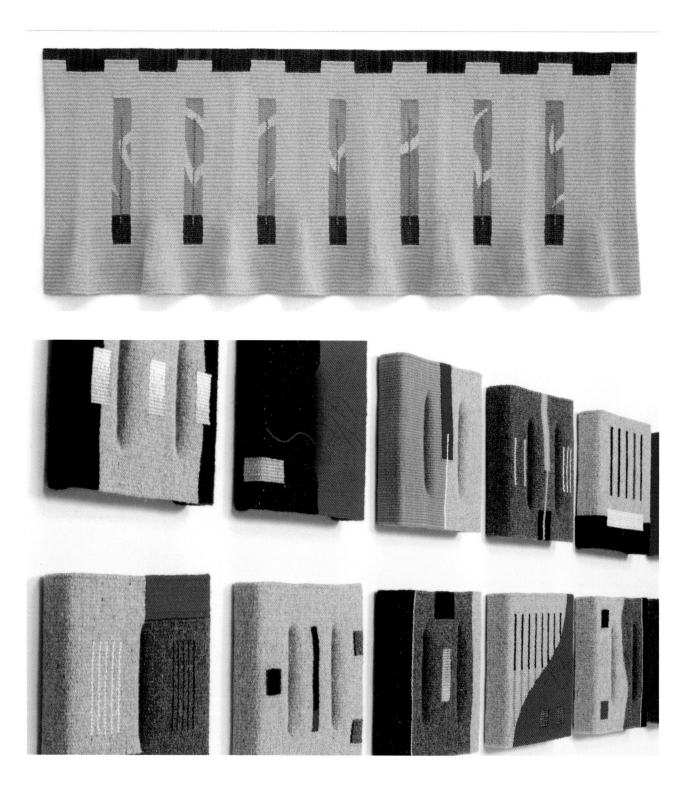

TOP Susan Iverson. *Horizon—Dawn's Dance*, 1998.
Tapestry: 25" × 63.5" × 3". *Courtesy of the artist;*
photography by Taylor Dabney

BOTTOM Susan Iverson. *Fleeting* (detail), 2015.
Tapestry: 24" × 7'10" × 2". *Courtesy of the artist;*
photography by Taylor Dabney

Susan Martin Maffei. *Pandora Box-9 Spot Lady Bug-Disappearing*, ca. 2018. Tapestry with woven and constructed components: when closed, 13" × 13" × 4"; opened, 13" × 17" × 13". *Courtesy of the artist*

Barbara Burns. *Little Devil Corset*, 2018. Tapestry: 9.25" × 9.75" × 8". *Courtesy of Barbara Burns, weaver and designer*

VALUE

Value refers to qualities of light and dark. You see difference of value both in colors of the spectrum and in the absence of color when white, a range of grays, and black are used. The term *notan* refers to simplifying or reducing value into basic areas of light and dark in a composition.

- Value allows one to create difference, or *contrast*, between areas.
- The quality of value in color is sometimes deceptive. High-intensity colors may be either very dark in value (clear violet, primary blue, or emerald green, for instance) or very light in value (yellow or yellow-orange, for instance).
- Using weft blends in gradual stages allows for value gradations from light to dark.
- Value gradation may also be created with a series of passes that increase and decrease in size as they move from one value to another.
- Extreme value contrast can be stark, dramatic, and graphic.
- Low-value contrast can create subtle harmony. It may also be detrimental if shapes intended to stand out well from each other are woven in close values.
- When combining yarns for tapestry, one may use either highly contrasting values or values that are close. The term *chiné* describes values that are highly different when combined into a weft bundle. *Mélange* is the term for placing close values (or hues) of colors together into the weft.
- Value "keys" are ways to describe overall effects of light or dark within an artwork. A tapestry woven in primarily light-value yarns would be a *high-key* composition. One woven so that there is an overall darkness to the work would be described as *low-key*.

Sampler of value gradation. Lower area with increasing and decreasing number of passes from dark gray through medium gray to light. Upper area combines six strands in weft, six values from dark gray to white, for gradual change, dropping one and adding one to maintain the six. *Chris Dant, photographer*

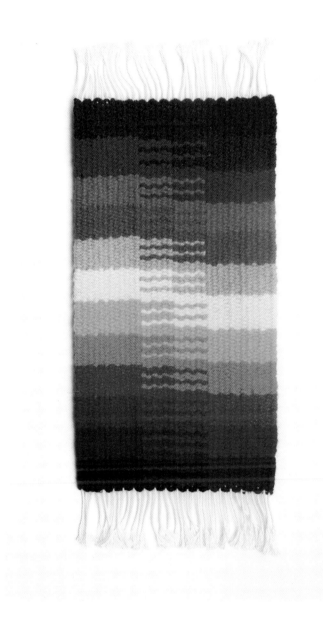

Sampler of colors in which the light and dark values of full-intensity hues may be clearly seen. Three versions of this were done, each using different setts and spectrum range of yarns from different sources. This one is 6 epi. *Chris Dant, photographer*

Another sampler of value gradation with changing sizes of passes. This uses three values to make a transition from darkest to lightest through a regular number of passes. *Chris Dant, photographer*

La Donna Mayer explored value extensively in a series of tapestries based on fifty-one cities in the United States—in *Santa Fe* she uses a variety of value differences in the simplified shapes of the southwestern architecture. With Don Burns's tapestry *Green Park*, the quality of similarity of value between extremely different intense hues may be seen: the green, dark pink, and orange that fill most of the composition are all very intense but also close to the same value. Kathy Spoering makes use of extreme value contrast in *January*, giving a stark, graphic view of winter light casting long shadows of tree trunks across snow. Another example of extreme value contrast is found in Pat Williams's tapestry *Failure to Communicate*, in which white

contrasts sharply with the black and red of hair and clothing. The background of low-key brown adds to the graphic quality.

Subtle changes in value from light to dark are seen both in the warm colors of the curving interior shapes and the cool colors of the background in Rebecca Mezoff's tapestry *The Space Before Knowing*.

Sarah Warren's tapestry *On the Move* makes use of low-value contrast throughout most of the tapestry, giving the small, curving yellow-orange line in the upper third even more impact as a main emphasis point.

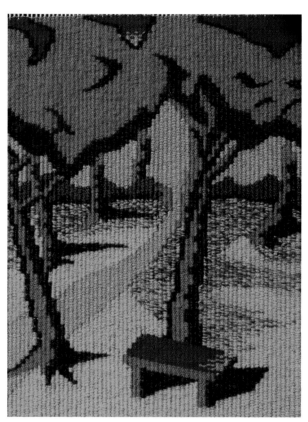

LaDonna Mayer. *Santa Fe NM*—from the 51 American Cities series, 2011. Tapestry: 24.75" × 24.75". *Courtesy of LaDonna Mayer*

Don Burns. *The Green Park*, 2009. Tapestry: 9.5" × 7.5". *Courtesy of Don Burns*

Kathy Spoering. *January*, 2010. Tapestry:
18" × 18". *Courtesy of Kathy Spoering*

Pat Williams. *Failure to Communicate*, 2013.
Tapestry: 44.5" × 59". *Courtesy of Pat Williams;*
photo © Tim Barnwell

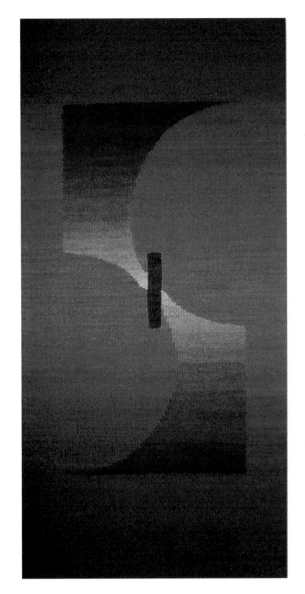

Rebecca Mezoff. *The Space Before Knowing*, 2008. Tapestry: 30" × 15". *Courtesy of Rebecca Mezoff*

Sarah Warren. *On the Move*, 2008. Tapestry: 32" × 23.5". *Courtesy of Sarah Warren*

TEXTURE

Texture is both tactile and visual. It refers to how something feels or how it appears to feel. In tapestry there are many opportunities to use texture in the selection of yarns. Several techniques also lend themselves to adding textural effects.

Texture is always a part of tapestry weaving, sometimes subtle and sometimes obvious. For instance, cutbacks, made of diagonal lines moving one direction and then back in the opposite, may add a subtle texture to the surface when done with the same color. Also, slits between shapes may be pulled open a bit to give a subtle shadow at edges.

- Texture contrast may be seen when different types of weft yarns are used: shiny yarns in contrast with matte surface yarns, for instance.
- Texture may be created with such techniques as soumak and rya.
- Texture may be suggested or simulated—for instance, consider how one could weave the bark of a tree or the roughness of stones.

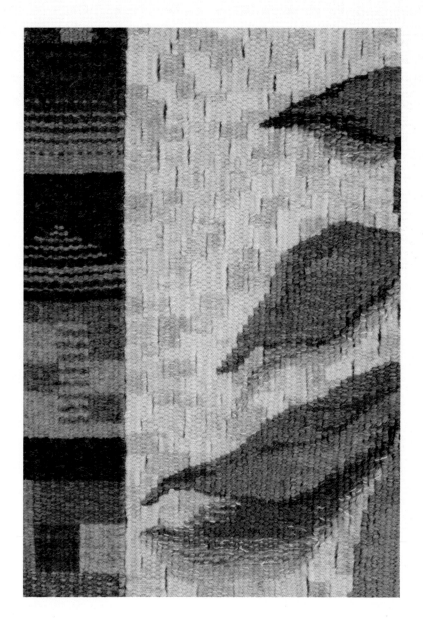

Detail of *Hickory*, a tapestry by the author (see page 37). This shows the texture effect of having many small vertical shapes woven without joining the slits between. *Photo © Tim Barnwell*

TOP Detail of David Johnson's tapestry *Transformation*, 2014 (see page 40). Johnson's use of soumak gave a rich texture to the surface. *Courtesy of David Johnson*

BOTTOM Rya sample by the author. This is one of many pile weaves that may be used with tapestry. *Chris Dant, photographer*

In one of my tapestries, *Hickory*, slits between many rectangular shapes of the background are slightly pulled to allow shadow between the shapes to be obvious and adding texture to the design. Pat Williams makes use of heavily textured yarns in portions of *Phoenix or Bust*. Both the volcano-like shape at the bottom and the hair of the figure are woven with yarns that are quite different than the rest of the surface, giving a strong textural contrast. Lyn Hart uses several setts to show texture differences in her small tapestry *indigo monsoon*. In another of Lyn's tapestries, *cielo sin alas*, she creates texture by having variety of yarn type, eccentric weft, and areas of wedge weave.

Tommye McClure Scanlin. *Hickory*, 2016. Tapestry: 26" × 19" (42" × 24" framed). *Photo © Tim Barnwell*

Pat Williams. *Phoenix or Bust*, 2013. Tapestry: 47.75" × 23.75". *Courtesy of Pat Williams; photo © Tim Barnwell*

Kathe Todd-Hooker's tapestry surfaces are alive with the texture of soumak. Kathe employs the method extensively in many of her works, as in this one, *Nasty Ladies unite! Do it now before it's too late!* David Johnson also often uses soumak in his tapestries; for instance, in *Transformation*, soumak is used throughout the piece and creates a highly textured surface.

Barbara Heller skillfully creates an illusion of texture in her tapestry Stonewall #21, *Stonewall Blues*, as she simulates the rough surface with subtle color changes as seen in real stones while maintaining a weaverly approach. Likewise, a feeling of implied texture plays over the surface of Elizabeth Buckley's tapestry *Fossil, Feather, and Light.*

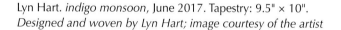

Lyn Hart. *indigo monsoon,* June 2017. Tapestry: 9.5" × 10". *Designed and woven by Lyn Hart; image courtesy of the artist*

Lyn Hart. *cielo sin alas,* May 2019. Tapestry: 24" × 25". *Designed and woven by Lyn Hart; image courtesy of the artist*

Kathe Todd-Hooker. *Nasty Ladies unite! Do it now before it's too late!*, 2019.
Tapestry: 14" × 14". *Courtesy of Kathe Todd-Hooker*

David Johnson. *Transformation,* 2014. Tapestry in soumak
weave: 45" × 48". *Courtesy of David Johnson*

TOP Barbara Heller. *Stonewall #21—Stonewall Blues*, 2012. Tapestry: 2.5' × 3'. *Courtesy of Barbara Heller; photography by Ted Clark, Image This Photographics Inc., Vancouver, BC, Canada*

BOTTOM Elizabeth J. Buckley. *Fossil, Feather, and Light*, 2013. Tapestry: 25" × 18". *Courtesy of Elizabeth J. Buckley, artist and photographer*

SPACE

Space, or an illusion of depth, may be created in several ways:

- Shapes may seem to overlap one another.
- Suggestion of horizon can gives the viewer a sense of depth. Simply weaving horizontal areas in colors similar to those seen in land or sea and sky can cause us to "see" depth in a tapestry because we are so accustomed to orienting ourselves to the horizon.
- Linear perspective is a traditional method of suggesting space on a flat surface. With this effect, parallel edges that move away from the viewer in the "picture plane" seem to converge at a vanishing point in the distance.
- Distance may be suggested with color changes: bright, clear colors can seem to be nearer, while dull or softer colors seem to recede. The reverse may also happen, when darker "heavier" colors are placed near the bottom while lighter-value colors are seen higher up in the composition. In landscape, *atmospheric* (also called *aerial*) *perspective* refers to this effect in creating a sense of distance.

Mary Cost beautifully suggests a close view of adobe buildings through overlapping of shapes in her tapestry *Purple Sky I*. Linear perspective is used by Don Burns in *The Yellow Park* as well by LaDonna Mayer in her tapestry *Indianapolis IN*. Janet Austin gives the viewer a definite horizon to relate to in her tapestry *Anticipation*.

In *Mountain Waves VII*, Sarah Warren uses low-key color values with dark near the bottom, suggestive of a foreground in her stylized landscape. The small amounts of lighter and brighter color she uses midway up have even more impact by contrast with the darker colors below and above, drawing the viewer's eye into the space.

TOP Linear perspective is seen in this photograph of a highway as it moves into the rural landscape. *Photograph by the author*

BOTTOM Atmospheric perspective (also called aerial perspective) is evident in this photograph of a northern Georgia landscape where the trees on the mountains take on a blue hue in the distance. *Photograph by the author*

TOP LEFT Mary Cost. *Purple Sky I*, 2009.
Tapestry: 34" × 22". *Courtesy of Mary Cost*

TOP RIGHT LaDonna Mayer. *Indianapolis IN—*
from the 51 American Cities series, 2012. Tapestry:
23" × 14.25". *Courtesy of LaDonna Mayer*

BOTTOM Don Burns. *The Yellow Park*, 2009.
Tapestry: 9.5" × 7.5". *Courtesy of Don Burns*

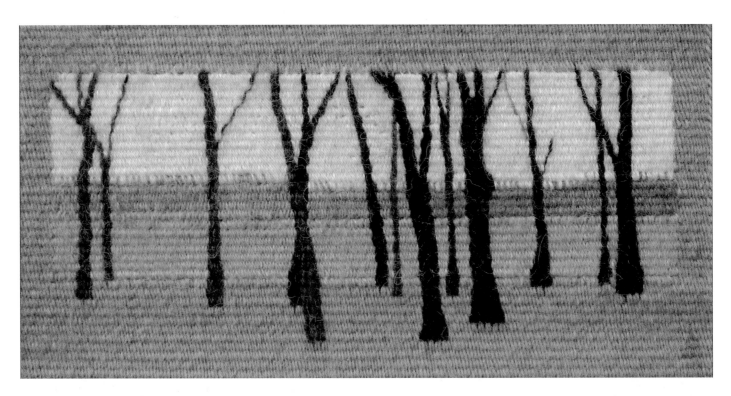

TOP Janet Austin. *Anticipation*, 2014. Tapestry: 6" × 9".
Courtesy of Janet Austin, artist and photographer

BOTTOM Sarah Warren. *Mountain Waves VII*, 2019.
Tapestry: 20" × 42.5". *Courtesy of Sarah Warren*

COLOR

Tapestry offers many approaches to follow—from images that represent reality to those that are more abstract. Indeed, the structure of weaving itself suggests design options to the weaver through the essential grid of warp and weft. Of all the basic elements and principles of art and design, color may be one of the most important for tapestry weavers.

In tapestry and other weft-faced weaves, the skeleton of the warp, critical to the structure but for the most part hidden, allows the weft to play the major visual role. The type and size of weft fiber, quality of spin, and whether the yarn is single or a multi-ply are all important to the color effect created.

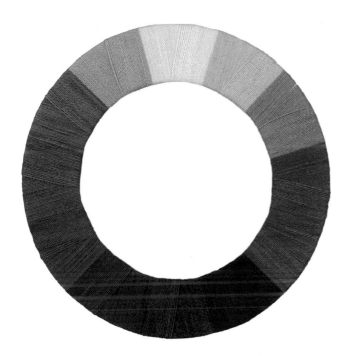

Artists and craftspeople, scientists, philosophers, and poets have studied, experimented with, and written about the art and science of color for hundreds of years. In the late 1600s, Sir Isaac Newton first proposed a circular form to arrange the colors he observed when he used a prism to break light into a band of colors—the spectrum. According to author Betty

Edwards, when Newton put the colors of the spectrum into a circle, it made two things happen: color relationships were more easily visualized and memorized, and both the similarity of adjacent colors *and* the contrast of opposite colors became clear.[4] Since Newton's time, many others have studied how humans observe and react to color phenomena and have proposed their own theories about systematic ways to look at color.

Artists and designers often use the theories presented by these studies as guides for color use. It is important to remember, however, that theories are only starting points. There are always exciting and inspiring ways to apply color in artworks that seem to break all the rules.

The best training . . .

Good painting, good coloring, is comparable to good cooking. Even a good cooking recipe demands tasting and repeated tasting while it is being followed. And the best training still depends on a cook with taste.[5]

—*Josef Albers*

A color wheel made with commercially available yarn

Fibers of various types show different characteristics. These cones are Alv two-ply worsted wool spun in Norway by a family-owned spinning mill founded in 1898. Currently available in the US through Between & Etc.
Chris Dant, photographer

Small samples of different kinds of yarns, made by the author. The hangtags let me know what yarn I've used for the sample. These are quick to do and give lots of information about how fiber types will look in weft-faced applications such as tapestry. *Chris Dant, photographer*

Color as it functions in tapestry and other weft-faced weaves has qualities that are not the quite the same as those seen in other media, such as painting or photography, because the fibers of the weft yarn affect how we experience the colors. Weft-faced weaves are also different from other weave types in which the warp and weft often both play significant roles in the visual effect of color. In weft-faced weaves such as tapestry, the surface will both absorb *and* reflect light, causing the color appearance to sometimes be different from what might be expected.

There are other factors that influence the visual effect in weft-faced weaves. In tapestry, for instance, the sett of the warp has an impact on the surface and thus on the way color is perceived. The same color of yarn used with a warp sett of 8 ends per inch (epi) may look slightly different when used at 6 epi. Yarn of another fiber type in the same hue could also vary in visual effect. For instance, think of the way light is absorbed into wool yarn and reflected from shiny yarns such as silk or mercerized cotton. Techniques other than flat-woven tapestry will show the quality of the color of yarns in other ways—soumak or rya, for instance. Rya particularly will give depth to the color because of the pile of the surface. Plus, the length of the pile and the direction that it's seen from will also affect the way the color appears.

Using color to your advantage begins with learning about the language of color. Basic colors from which other colors derive are called *primary*. There are two different systems for color mixing: one for light, called *additive* color mixtures, and another for pigment, called *subtractive* color mixtures. The primary colors for each system are different.

Additive color primaries are red, green, and blue. When additive primaries are mixed, in theory, white is created. This is as if the spectrum, the band of colors created when light rays pass through a prism, is projected through a second prism to reassemble into white light. Subtractive color primaries are red, yellow, and blue. In theory, when these are mixed together they yield black since they absorb all the colors of the white light spectrum. Detailed explanations of color primaries and how they are used in a medium, whether paint, dye, printing industry, internet, video, or photography, may be found in many places.[6]

For purposes of considering color in tapestry, we will be using subtractive color and the three primaries: red, yellow, and blue. We'll begin with the concept of the color wheel. Since Newton's color wheel in the seventeenth century, many ideas about systematic color arrangements have been advanced, including other types of color wheels and even color solids.

The twelve-color wheel, like that shown on page 45, is the one that's familiar to most people. This is made up of twelve equal sectors, with three colors identified as primary: yellow, red, and blue placed at equal distances apart around the wheel. Mixtures of the primary colors create the secondary hues: orange, violet, and green. Further mixing between the primary and secondary colors gives intermediate, or tertiary, colors.[7]

Samples of natural dyes in primary and secondary colors, by the author. These were done with Osage orange (yellow), madder with nearly exhausted bath (orange), madder (red), logwood chips (purple), indigo (blue), and Osage orange top dyed with indigo (green).

When beginning to study color, one often uses paints and attempts to mix the secondary colors by doing exactly what color theory says to do—for instance, mixing red and blue to make violet or purple. How many of you have made a murky, *sort of* purplish color with that mixture? I certainly did, before learning that a bit of bluish red, rather than one that had an orange undertone, would be needed to mix a clear purple. Also, the blue used in the mixture would work best if it didn't lean toward green. In other words, in the practice of color mixing with paint, several versions of "primary" will give the most successful secondary and tertiary colors.[8] The same is true for mixing colors of dyes.

A good working understanding of color theory will be helpful when choosing colors of yarns, especially when dyeing your own colors. While there is a wide range of colors of yarns readily available in almost every fiber type, you may want to dye your own. Perhaps you'll use a hit-and-miss method for dyeing, with a little of this and a bit of that to create color mixtures. While this can be enjoyable, you may soon find that dyeing with control of hue, intensity, and value, and with replicable results, is what you prefer. Both synthetic dyes and natural dyes may be used as you delve into creating your own yarn colors. Resources for dyeing information are listed at the end of this book.

BASIC DEFINITIONS ABOUT COLOR

Defining Color

HUE is the color.
VALUE is how dark or light.
INTENSITY is how bright or dull.

Describing color: First, color can be described in three basic ways: the *hue*, the *value*, and the *intensity*.

- *Hue* means the color and its position on a color wheel.
- *Value* of color refers to the quality of light and dark. In paint, white, gray, or black is usually added to a pure hue to make tints, tones, or shades. In dye, the amount of dye in the dye pot gives what's called the depth of shade or value range. Tints are light values, tones are grayed values, and shades are dark values. For the hue of red, for instance, pink is a tint; burgundy is a shade. It's interesting to note that each color, in full saturation around the color wheel, is of different value. Red, for instance, falls in the middle range of value if comparing full-intensity red to a gray scale.

- *Intensity* is the saturation of color. Hues at full intensity are as bright as the color can possibly be, with no dilution of visual effect. Intensity changes are made in paint by mixing a hue with its opposite or complement, with any other hue, or with white, black, or gray. With dye the same applies, except you wouldn't mix with white for a tint or pale version of the color. Instead, you would use less dye in the same amount of liquid in the dye pot to the weight of yarn being dyed.
- **Approaches:** Color choices may be *realistic, expressive, decorative,* or *symbolic.* The purpose of the idea and image/subject may help determine the approach to color that is chosen.

Kathy Spoering used a realistic approach to color in her tapestry *August: The Dog Days of Summer.* Kathy designed her cartoon from a photograph she'd taken of the family dog, Booker, as he retrieved a stick from the lake.

In one of my own tapestries, *Phoenix,* I chose to use colors in an expressive way to represent results of wildfires in the southeastern United States. The small bits of green included were symbolic of rebirth.

About *A House Divided*

The germination of the idea . . . started with the Black Lives Matter movement. The central motif of respect in black and white speaks to this. As the 2016 election season continued with its inflammatory rhetoric, it became necessary to add other motifs such as the LGBT flag colors, the Mexican flag colors, and the women's suffragette colors. Perhaps if we could just respect each other, we could begin to bridge the divide that is now reality in our country. . . .

The flowers have the following meanings. Chamomile represents energy in adversity. Dogwood is love, undiminished by adversity. Hawthorn is hope. Mullen means take courage. Olive leaves represent peace. The rose is love. Snowdrops offer consolation and hope. The aster is for patience.

The weaving of this piece has been a great solace to me during the last few months. My hope is that people viewing the piece will take away a positive feeling of hope and a more compassionate feeling toward their fellow human beings.

—Betty Hilton-Nash

LEFT Kathy Spoering. *August: The Dog Days of Summer,* 2011. Tapestry: 18" × 18". *Courtesy of Kathy Spoering*

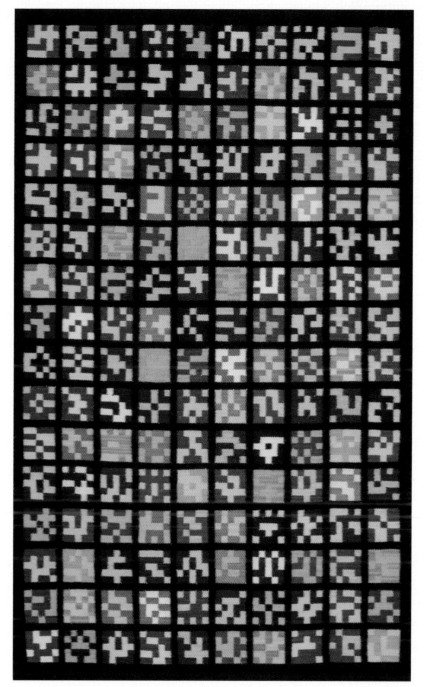

Tommye McClure Scanlin. *Phoenix*, 2017.
Tapestry: 60" × 31". *Photo © Tim Barnwell*

Michael F. Rohde. *Declarative*, 2018. Tapestry: 76" × 47" 0.5".
Courtesy of Michael F. Rohde; photography by W. Scott Miles,
www.TheScientificPhotographer.com

Betty Hilton-Nash combines what appears at first to be a decorative use of color and placement of floral forms in the border of *A House Divided*. However, for Betty the chosen objects and colors are full of symbolism and help her make a statement she is passionate about.

Michael F. Rohde's Language series explores symbolic color, each of the tapestries designed with selected colors to represent particular aspects of the "as yet un-deciphered language." *Declarative* is predominantly woven in red and black. Michael says that this color use "reflects bold statements, not always polite or even true." *Derogatory* (seen in progress on the loom) makes use of reds, white, and blue in the colors of some flags, according to Michael.

TOP RIGHT Betty Hilton-Nash. *A House Divided*, 2017. Tapestry: 18" × 56". *Photo © Tim Barnwell*

- **Relationships:** Colors may follow "rules" of *harmony* or *contrast*, as found in the color schemes or colorways proposed by master colorist Johannes Itten. Color harmonies, according to Itten, are created when colors are selected in systematic relationships to each other.[9] The color wheel is useful in seeing these relationships. Itten noted several harmonious color relationships found when certain geometrical configurations are superimposed over a color wheel and rotated to point out combinations of two, three, four, and six colors. Another master colorist, Josef Albers, described the "relativity" of color when he discussed contrasting effects such as warm/cold and how one color could appear differently on different background colors.

Michael F. Rohde. *Derogatory* (photographed in progress, 2019). Tapestry: approximately 78" × 49" × 0.5". *Courtesy of Michael F. Rohde; photography by Michael F. Rohde*

Refer to the color wheel with overlay diagrams on page 102 to see how the relationships in *a* through *c* were found.

a. **Complementary or two-color arrangements:** A complementary relationship exists between two colors located opposite each other on the color wheel. Complementary pairings are among the most vivid combinations of colors to be found. Complements intensify the visual effect of each other when placed side by side, but when mixed or woven together they result in dulling or neutralizing each other.

b. **Triads or three-color arrangements**: These are combinations of three colors found by placing an equilateral triangle or an isosceles triangle over the color wheel to locate colors at the points of the triangles.

The equilateral triangle points to three hues that are as far from each other as they could be on the color wheel. For instance, the three primary hues, red, yellow, and blue, would be a triad. So would the secondary hues, orange, green, and violet. Two more triads of this type are found in the tertiary hues. The isosceles triangle points to two hues on either side of the complement or opposite of any chosen hue. This is also called a *split complement*. For instance, yellow, red-violet, and blue-violet are a triad of this type (violet is the complement of yellow, with red-violet and blue-violet found at each side).

c. **Tetrads or four-color arrangements:** The four colors located at the corners of a square or of a rectangle superimposed over the color wheel are called tetrads.

d. **Hexads or six-color arrangements:** One of these includes the three primary and the three secondary colors, and the other possible hexad contains all of the tertiary colors.

- **Other harmonies:** In addition to those mentioned by Itten, other combinations of colors often described as *harmonious* include

a. **Monochromatic**—This color arrangement is seen when tints, tones, and shades of a single hue are used. A weaving in all blues, for instance, would be in a monochromatic color arrangement. A range of values of one hue can be easily achieved when dyeing one's own yarn.

LEFT Color study using Johannes Itten's ideas of color harmony. In this version, pick and pick with one color as constant and other colors selected to relate to the first color in several of the color harmony relationships. *Woven by the author; Chris Dant, photographer*

RIGHT More color harmony explorations. *From bottom to top*: analogous colors (warm), analogous colors (cool), monochromatic (values of red-violet), complementary (yellow-orange, blue-violet), triad of equidistant hues (orange, green, violet), colors selected by online palette generator, using a photo of flowers as source. *Woven by the author; Chris Dant, photographer*

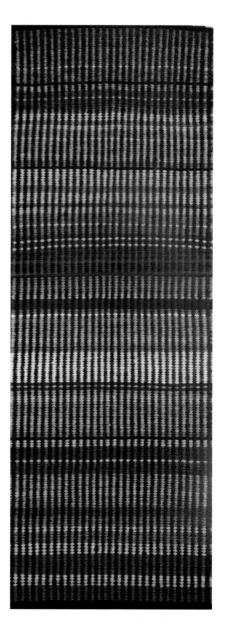

b. **Analogous colors**—related colors on the color wheel. Usually you would consider three side-by-side hues to be related—for instance, a primary, a tertiary, and a secondary (red, red-violet, violet, as one example). The analogous relationship may be extended slightly on either side, but keep in mind what colors are shared among the hues. Deb Menz gives a good description of analogous color choices in her book *Color Works*.[10]

- **Color contrasts**—seen in the difference among colors. Itten described seven types of color contrast:

    a. **Contrast of hue**: Simply difference in the hues used

    b. **Contrast of temperature**: Difference in the warm and cool effect of the color

    c. **Contrast of value**: Difference in the light and dark nature of the color

    d. **Contrast of intensity or saturation**: Difference in the quality of hue—the brightness or dullness of the color

    e. **Complementary contrast**: The contrast or difference of opposites as found on the color wheel

    f. **Simultaneous contrast**: This is a complex effect, since colors are almost never seen in isolation, as Albers notes in *Interaction of Color*. Colors are constantly interacting with each other when they are put together. For instance, light colors may appear lighter when surrounded by darker colors, and yet their quality of lightness may not be as noticed when surrounded by colors more near them in value. Warm colors may appear

Contrast of hue. 8 epi, ½" high rows using two color wheel adjacent hues in hachure. *Beginning at the bottom and moving up (around the color wheel)*: violet into red-violet; red-violet into red; red into red-orange; red-orange into orange, etc. *Woven by the author; Chris Dant, photographer*

Color temperature—warm-cool relativity comparison. Woven sample of blue-violet moving through violet into red-violet and then red in increasing and decreasing number of passes. Red-violet appears relatively warm compared to the violet and blue-violet. *Woven by the author; Chris Dant, photographer*

warmer when surrounded by cooler colors. Likewise, cool colors may seem to be even cooler when surrounded by warm colors.

g. **Contrast of extension**: Bright colors seem to visually expand more than duller or darker colors. For instance, a small amount of yellow will visually seem to balance larger areas of darker or duller colors.

• **Bezold effect:** Wilhelm von Bezold described this effect in the late 1800s. He was a rug designer and was seeking ways to make significant color changes with only one color adjustment. "He found . . . when intense colors or values such as black and white were evenly distributed throughout a design,

the color effect was changed."[11]

White used with other hues will make all colors seem more subdued; some will appear pastel and others will seem to be darker. Black, especially when used as outlining, will cause colors to appear lighter, brighter, or both.

Complementary contrast using opposite pairs around the color wheel. Six rows of six squares woven side by side. Weft: five strands of wool in transition from solid color, *at left*, through four steps of gradual weft color change, to solid opposite color (solid, 4-1, 3-2, 2-3, 1-4, solid, etc.). *Chris Dant, photographer*

Simultaneous contrast. Red-violet squares in the larger squares; red-orange and violet squares at the top appear to be different colors. The yellow-green on blue-green and yellow-orange at the bottom likewise appear different. *Chris Dant, photographer*

- **Dominant color or color key:** Itten calls this the "harmony of the dominant tint," and it is made up of colors influenced with a same overall quality—think of the appearance of colors in the landscape at dawn or sunset, for instance. Consider the idea of a dominant tint when thinking about how to weave transparency effects in tapestry.

Mary Stewart describes the effects of a dominant color as "color key" and says this type of color arrangement "can heighten psychological as well as compositional impact."[12] Consider a range of variations of one color in a monochromatic way in a tapestry. Would this lend itself to suggesting or enhancing an overall feeling or "mood" to the image?

Bezold effect in pick-and-pick sample: black and white in one pick, and twelve spectrum colors in the other pick. See how the hues appear to be either lighter or darker, brighter or less intense, when interacting with white or black lines of pick and pick. *Chris Dant, photographer*

Dominant color or color key in this sample is from the cool side of the color wheel. Notice the small areas where weft colors are blended to make a transition between green and blue. *Chris Dant, photographer*

Chromatic grays and earth colors:[13] Chromatic grays are neutrals that show a bias or lean toward a hue or color temperature. Think about warm or cool grays, for instance. These look quite lively in color when compared to achromatic grays made from black and white.

In paint, chromatic grays may be made from mixtures of any pair of complements or may be made when all three primaries are combined. Adding the mixture to white in various amounts gives a wide value range of chromatic grays.

In yarns, gray colors often lean toward a warm or a cool tone, and the effect can be heightened when used along with a warm or cool hue. Blending gray yarns of warm and cool leanings can create a more lively neutral than either alone.

In paint, earth colors are those made from earthen pigments processed by the artist, or commercially made to resemble earth tones. In yarns, one may see a range of cool and warm browns, dull oranges, and tans representing earth colors. For natural dyers, several sources yield beautiful earthen-colored hues, including black walnut and henna.

Detail of *Earth Echoes*, tapestry by the author. The overall color key of the tapestry is warm earth colors. The weft yarns were dyed with black walnut and with henna. The design was based on an earth pigment painting; the natural dye colors "echoed" those.
Photo © Tim Barnwell

APPLYING COLOR TO TAPESTRY

In many ways the tapestry weaver has both great advantages and interesting challenges when deciding how to use color theory ideas in designing and weaving. A distinct advantage, for instance, is the wonderful quality of the way yarn reacts to light. Much of that reaction relates to the type of fiber that makes it up. For instance, is it wool, and from what sheep breed? Is it spun as woolen or worsted? Is it a singles or a plied yarn? If plied, is it two-, three-, or more-ply yarn? Other fibers also have different appearances depending on type and way they have been processed. Whether wool, cotton, linen, silk, or synthetic fibers, each offers unique qualities that play a distinct role in the way color will appear in tapestry.

For the tapestry weaver, both the warp and weft are important in the visual effect of the work. Even though the warp is typically concealed in tapestry, just as with the weft, the fiber can play a significant role in the visual effect. For example, cotton seine twine will give a different quality to the finished tapestry from that of linen or wool used as warp. Even when hidden by the weft, each gives a distinct surface quality and "hand" or feel to the weaving. The size and ply of the warp, as well as the sett, are also factors in the appearance of color in the tapestry.

Both the warp sett and the weft choice also play a role in the "bead" of the tapestry, the term used to describe the individual coverage of a weft over a warp end.[14] Is the bead rounded? Is it flattened? Other aspects include how the weft is used. Will it be as a single strand in each pick, or will multiple strands be used to make up the weft? If multiple strands, are all the yarns of the same sort or is there a mixture of types within the weft bundle? Are you making a close blend of value within a mixture (called mélange), or will there be a contrast in the blend (called chiné)?

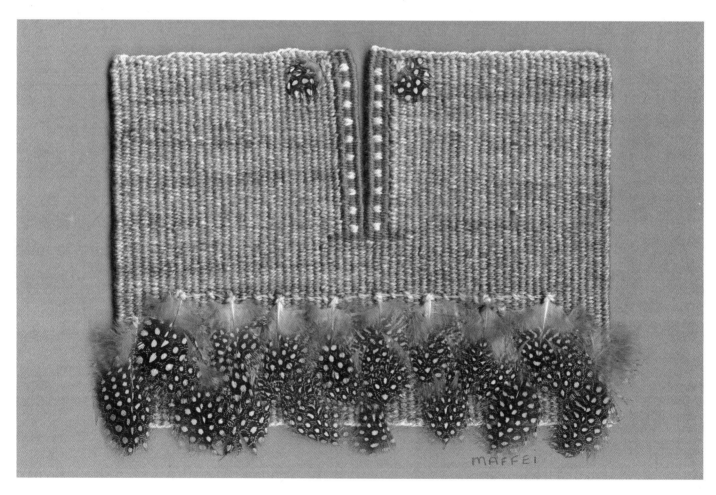

Susan Martin Maffei. *Feather Works—Guinea Fowl*, ca. 2014.
Tapestry with found feathers: 7" × 8". *Courtesy of the artist*

It is always inspiring to see how others who work in tapestry use color. For instance, start with a look at how Susan Martin Maffei uses a monochromatic palette for her small tapestry *Feather Works—Guinea Fowl*. The warm variety of yellow-orange is a perfect backdrop for the cool grays of the spotted guinea feathers.

In *Blue Notes, Phase VI*, Heather Gallegos-Rex uses monochromatic blues in different values for a complex study not only in color but also balance of dark and light areas.

Next, take a look at how Mary Cost has used a simple color palette in her tapestry *Piling Up*. Composed of mostly red-orange and bright blue, the work gives a sense of monumentality to a close view of an adobe structure.

In *Perseverance*, Mary Jane Lord uses warm and cool colors to impart a sense of vibrancy to the slow progress of the turtles across the tapestry.

Archie Brennan's *Vacationing Wrestler—Drawing Series XLV* uses warm orange and yellow-orange hues to frame the figure. In stark contrast are the cool blue and bright white of the shirt, and the neutral tones of face and hair.

In *Fauvist Woods* by Don Burns, intense color contrasts are created through his use of vivid warm and cool colors.

Heather Gallegos-Rex. *Blue Notes Phase VI*, 2018. Tapestry: 31.5" × 23.5" × 1.5". *Courtesy of Heather Gallegos-Rex; James Hart Photography, Santa Fe, NM*

Mary Cost. *Piling Up*, 2012. Tapestry: 30" × 38". *Courtesy of Mary Cost*

Robbie LaFleur has also used warm and cool contrasts in her tapestry *Great-Grandmother with Chickens*. The small areas of yellow and yellow-orange colors are intense but are well balanced within the larger area of blue-green and deep-red background and border.

Many more examples of tapestries showing inspired use of color are to be found at the American Tapestry Alliance (ATA) website in the artist pages.[15] Additionally, there are other color resources at the ATA website in the "Educational Articles" section. Find those in "Choosing Colors," essays by nine tapestry artists, edited by Linda Rees,[16] and in Kathe Todd-Hooker's article "The Simple, Short Version of Colour Movement in Tapestry (or Ways to Achieve Optical Blending with Yarn)."[17]

TOP Don Burns. *Fauvist Woods*, 2004. Tapestry: 31" × 28". *Courtesy of Don Burns*

BOTTOM LEFT Mary Jane Lord. *Perseverance*, 2011. Tapestry: 17" × 14". *Courtesy of Mary Jane Lord*

BOTTOM RIGHT Archie Brennan. *Vacationing Wrestler*—Drawing series XLV, 2007. Tapestry: 39" × 26.5". *Courtesy of Archie Brennan; photography by Chris Dant*

Robbie LaFleur. *Great-Grandmother with Chickens*, 2000. Billdevev, Norwegian tapestry: 23" × 20.5". *Courtesy of Robbie LaFleur; photography by Peter Lee*

Great-Grandmother with Chickens

I wove this tapestry in the millennium year of 2000, based on a photograph from approximately 100 years before. My great-grandmother Gunvalde, who emigrated from Norway in the 1880s, is standing in the front yard of my childhood home, which wouldn't be built for another 50 years . . . .

In my study of billdevev, Norwegian tapestry, I came to love the abstracted medieval style. But rather than copy an old piece, I wanted to adapt the style to my own story. On the edges I used a typical Norwegian wavelike border of overlapping curves but added stalks of wheat as a nod to the important crop on the family Minnesota farm founded by Norwegian immigrants.

—Robbie LaFleur

THE PRINCIPLES OF VISUAL DESIGN

Now, let's turn to the ways we may use the elements we just discussed. One goal is to organize the elements to be interesting and pleasing to the viewer. Something to keep in mind, however, is that we are designing within our own culture and place in time.

Evolution of design principles

[T]he so-called principles of design are the result of long-term experimentation. The history of art can be regarded as a history of the types of formal organization which have been found effective in various times and places.[18]

—Edmund Burke Feldman

Let's look with open-mindedness at the organizational methods we commonly called principles as we acknowledge that someone from another culture may be designing in ways that are different, yet equally interesting. You may find that the suggested explorations coming up next give you new insight into how a design can be effectively planned. Try things with paper and on the loom to see what you think. Ask someone else to take a look at your work and give you feedback. In the end you may find that your own design instincts may be the most valid way for you. There's nothing wrong with that! After all, a main goal of these studies is for you to gain confidence in your ability to go to the loom with images you feel good about and weave tapestries.

For the purpose of looking at how designs can be organized for tapestry work, we'll consider these fundamental principles: balance, emphasis, repetition and rhythm, proportion, and variety. You may want to make studies on paper and in small tapestries to explore these ideas. Several suggestions for things to try will be given in Part Two.

Barbara Heller. Cover Up series—*The Surgeon*, 2002–03. Tapestry: 35" × 25". *Courtesy of Barbara Heller; photography by Ted Clark, Image This Photographics, Inc., Vancouver, BC, Canada*

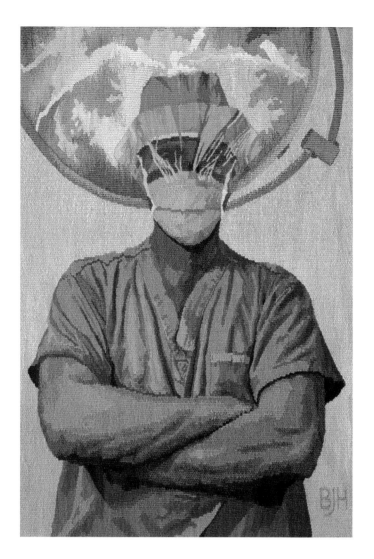

BALANCE

Balance refers to the appearance of "rightness" of placement and may be used to create specific effects.

- Balance may be formal or symmetrical. Balance of this type lends itself to dignified, calm, stable design. Think of a human face and equal parts arranged on either side of a midline of the nose. A version of formal balance is radial, with everything placed around a central point.
- Balance may be seen in a modified symmetry. Sometimes this may be more visually interesting than pure formal balance but still carry some of the calm, stable features of symmetry.
- Balance may be informal. Informal or asymmetrical balance is more casual, unusual, and often more exciting. Asymmetrical balance often lends a dynamic effect to a design.

Robbie LaFleur. *The Farmer's Daughter's Yggdrasil (Tree of Life)*, 2019.
Tapestry transparency in the style of the 19th-century Norwegian artist Frida Hansen:
43" × 22". *Courtesy of Robbie LaFleur; photography by Peter Lee*

Barbara Heller has created a nearly symmetrical composition in her tapestry *The Surgeon*, where only a few differences of shapes are to be seen from one side to the other.

In *The Farmer's Daughter's Yggdrasil (Tree of Life)*, Robbie LaFleur has used formal balance with subtle variations of size and placement of shapes within the composition.[19]

Triple Dog Joy, by Mary Jane Lord, makes use of a modified symmetry by placing the figure of the dog central in the composition, surrounded by background colors in blues and yellow-greens that lead your eye around in a more casual way.

Asymmetrical balance is shown in Joan Griffin's tapestry *Forest Edge*. In the composition, Joan places a group of large tree trunks at the left side, near the viewer. Branches of the trees reach across toward the right, where lighter and seemingly more distant trees are to be found.

Pat Williams shows a figure dressed in a black-and-white-striped blouse in her tapestry *The Refugee*. The composition is balanced informally by the band of colorful rectangles, as well as the several smaller shapes at the left that serve as a visual counterweight to the bold figure that leans into the design from the right.

Barbara Heller has used an asymmetrical balance in her tapestry *Moira*. The large headless figure at the left of the composition suggests a sculpture of one of the Moirai, or Fates. Although turned to the left, a wing of the figure extends to the right, where it lines up with the three squares below. Each of those holds one of the three implements important to the mythology: a distaff with fiber, a spindle, and scissors to cut the thread.

EMPHASIS

Emphasis may cause the viewer to look more carefully at one or more areas. These may be thought of as *focal points*.

- Emphasis may be achieved by using a strongly contrasting element in a small amount; for instance, a bright green among larger areas of duller greens and browns.
- Emphasis may be created in several areas or focal points. Too many focal points may be confusing to the design, however, with each competing for the viewer's attention.
- Directional lines or edges of shapes that lead the eye to an area may create emphasis.

Joan Griffin. *Forest Edge*, 2012. Tapestry: 24" × 50".
Courtesy of Joan Griffin

- Isolating a shape within a design may also create emphasis. Remember that putting the focal point in the center will create a "bull's-eye" effect. Likewise, placing emphasis too near the edge may lead the eye off the side of the design. Neither effect may be wanted.
- Emphasis may be *radial*, moving out from or into a center, enhancing the "bull's-eye" effect intentionally. Radial balance would be a component in this manner of creating emphasis.

RIGHT Mary Jane Lord. *Triple Dog Joy*, 2016. Tapestry: 20" × 20". *Courtesy of Mary Jane Lord; photography by Randy Swing*

BOTTOM Pat Williams. *The Refugee*, 2018. Tapestry: 38" × 37". *Courtesy of Pat Williams; photo © Tim Barnwell*

Barbara Heller. *Moira*, 2018. Tapestry: 5′ × 3′. *Courtesy of Barbara Heller; photography by Ted Clark, Image This Photographics Inc., Vancouver, BC, Canada*

Sue Weil gives emphasis to the brightly colored areas within the tapestry *New Growth Rising from the Ashes*, with the contrasts shown between the two color-filled areas and three shapes of mostly white yarns, in which thin lines of dark are seen.

Janet Austin creates several focal points in the tapestry *Another Forest Through the Trees* by making several small shapes strongly contrast in value to the dark colors surrounding them.

Rebecca Mezoff leads the viewer's eye through the tapestry *Halcyon Days II* by using a thin line that travels up from the bottom right to turn into a geometric labyrinth-like shape in which the color of the line shifts from dark to bright. Moving out, the line continues upward and across the composition to the left, where it reverses direction to direct the eye out at the upper left.

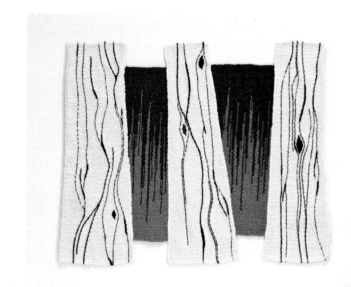

TOP Sue Weil. *New Growth Rising from the Ashes*, 2018. Tapestry: 23" × 29" (framed size). *Courtesy of Sue Weil; photography by Jay Daniel / Black Cat Studio*

BOTTOM Janet Austin. *Another Forest Through the Trees*, 2016. Tapestry: 8" × 9". *Courtesy of Janet Austin, artist and photographer*

In *The Aqua Park*, Don Burns directs one to look from the lower left, as a path enters the composition, to the horizon near the upper third of the tapestry.

Mary Cost has isolated a small shape within the tapestry *Morning Patio*. The small dark cruciform becomes a focal point because of the contrast of size and color. That small shape helps balance the doorway, the shape of which extends out of the right side of the design.

Betty Hilton-Nash uses an almost radial balance with her tapestry *A Butterfly Garden, an Homage to Dom Robert*, in which caterpillars, butterflies, and flowers all surround the central thistle shape.

REPETITION AND RHYTHM

Repetition of shapes can become patterns that our eye expects and can set up powerful visual rhythms. Feldman says that there are four types of rhythm: *repetitive, alternative, progressive,* and *flowing*.[20]

- Repetitive or regular rhythm, for instance, is seen when shapes of the same or similar sizes are repeated in a sequence. In tapestry, using repeats of bands or weft-way stripes, pick and pick vertical, or warp-way stripes can set up a regular pattern. Too much regularity may be boring; a series of stripes of the same size could be enlivened by slightly changing something—the color, size, or placement, for instance.

- Rhythm may *alternate* or be *irregular* when shapes of contrasting colors or textures are used at various and not-measured intervals. A good example of irregular pattern in nature may be seen in the intervals among many trees in a forest. The shapes of the trunks may all be mostly similar in size and placement, but most of the time there will be interesting variations within the similarity. Likewise, buildings can show distinctive alternating or irregular rhythm in the overall pattern of windows. Some may have blinds closed, while perhaps others have curtains. Houseplants or other objects might be seen in some of them.

- The rhythm within a design may have a *progressive* development in which the shapes, colors, and textures may be perceived to change in predictable ways. By adding a slight variation, this rhythm can stay engaging to the viewer. Think about a figure used in the background, perhaps a diamond shape that's made with a series of cutbacks that reverse in direction in a regular way to create the pattern. What if changing the color slightly, or making the sizes of the diamonds larger or smaller, interrupts the pattern?

- The rhythm may be *flowing* and lead the eye in curvilinear movements. Think of waves or the edges of clouds. Eccentric weft lends itself to flowing rhythm as it moves over the edges of shapes.

Rebecca Mezoff. *Halcyon Days II*, 2006. Tapestry: 40" × 26". *Courtesy of Rebecca Mezoff*

TOP LEFT Don Burns. *The Aqua Park*, 2009.
Tapestry: 9.5" × 7.5". *Courtesy of Don Burns*

TOP RIGHT Mary Cost. *Morning Patio*, 2011.
Tapestry: 55" × 33". *Courtesy of Mary Cost*

BOTTOM Betty Hilton-Nash. *A Butterfly Garden, an
Homage to Dom Robert*, 2014. Tapestry: 40" × 40".
Courtesy of Betty Hilton-Nash; photo © Tim Barnwell

Sicilian Defense

Scrolls have played an important part historically in the use of fiber in narrative arts and this has influenced much of my work in tapestry. Working always on a grid of warp and weft the geometrics of letters and numbers fit so well into the subtle background patterns of the work that uses American chess notations and traces of an important chess game between Fischer and Petrosian that established the moves of Sicilian Defense.

—Susan Martin Maffei

In *Sicilian Defense*, Susan Martin Maffei repeats the black and white of a chess board in a regular way. But the composition is much more complex than that. Her tapestry takes inspiration from several cultural traditions, as well as being a record of a famous chess match. More about the tapestry may be found at her website.[21] This is one of her many tapestries that are inspired by games.

Heather Gallegos-Rex uses progressive rhythm in her two tapestries, *Umbral Notes* and *Umbral Notes II*. In these two tapestries, Heather progressively decreases and then increases the size of the horizontal bands. She also beautifully shows the way that dark and light can reverse in placement to present quite a different overall effect.

In *Fleeting*, composed of fourteen individual tapestries by Susan Iverson, one can see the use of an irregular rhythm. The fourteen tapestries are presented in two rows of seven each, setting up a repetition that is orderly and regular. There are a few simple shapes within each tapestry, but each has been done in different ways, using a limited palette of black, two grays, and white with bright pink, yellow, and light blue. In this way, Susan has created a visually intriguing composition.

With *So Many Plover Birds*, Nicki Bair used rhythm that flows through the shapes of the birds as they fit together almost perfectly as if in a tessellation. Joan Griffin has created a flowing visual rhythm in her tapestry *Swept Away*, as well as setting up movements of color across the width of the tapestry to lead the eye along the waves from one side to the other.

TOP Susan Martin Maffei. *Sicilian Defense*, ca. 2007–10. Scroll and bag combining tapestry weaving, silk lace, rayon lining, plexi rods: 65" × 12" for scroll and 20" × 9" for bag, closed.

BOTTOM Susan Martin Maffei. Detail: *Sicilian Defense*.

TOP LEFT Heather Gallegos-Rex. *Umbral Notes*, 2014. Tapestry: 38" × 35" × 1.5". *Courtesy of Heather Gallegos-Rex; James Hart Photography, Santa Fe, NM*

TOP RIGHT Heather Gallegos-Rex. *Umbral Notes II*, 2018. Tapestry: 39" × 34.5" × 1.5". *Courtesy of Heather Gallegos-Rex; James Hart Photography, Santa Fe, NM*

BOTTOM Joan Griffin. *Swept Away*, 2019. Tapestry: 30" × 48". *Courtesy of Joan Griffin*

The Journey Back

When *The Journey Back* was begun, the bottom section was intended to be a hem for a future piece. In 2012 Linda Wallace experienced significant brain injury from surgery, radiation, and infection. When she recovered physically, she had lost her ability to weave the tapestries that had been her medium for many years. "Over one / under one" made no sense.

Without expectations, she began to play at the loom, using simple, rectilinear shapes and strong color to explore and rehabilitate. As the tapestry slowly grew, it took on a life and was no longer something to be turned to the back. Rectangles became squares; patterns became regular.

And then came the day when Wallace decided to return to curvilinear, organic shapes: she drew how she felt, how she saw, and, as she wove the increasingly challenging swirls, the central swirling legs. She used lashing to connect the squares woven in the background. The lashings are fragile, as is Wallace's hold on health.

—*written by Linda Wallace*

Linda Wallace made extensive use of repetition and rhythm in her tapestry *The Journey Back*. After an almost incapacitating injury and extended recovery time, Linda began weaving again. She started simply at first as her mind and body "relearned" how to weave. The repetitive actions gradually made sense, and by the end, she had a remarkable tapestry that celebrates the repetition of the simple process of weaving as well as a determined spirit.

Linda Wallace. *The Journey Back*, 2015. Tapestry: 44″ × 33″. *Courtesy of Linda Wallace; photography by Terry Zlot*

PROPORTION

Proportion deals with relationship of parts, particularly relative sizes of parts to each other.

- Proportion may be achieved intuitively or innately. One often senses a "right" proportion among shapes within a composition.
- Proportion may be planned for, using approaches such as the golden section or the Fibonacci series. More about these ideas will be mentioned later.
- Proportion is used when determining the size of the finished object and the relationship of width to length.

- Proportion can also relate to the accuracy of the size relationship of parts of the objects in a design. For instance, is the head in proportion to the rest of the figure in a way that is realistic, or does it seem to be exaggerated either intentionally or accidentally?
- Proportion and scale are similar but are not the same. Scale can refer to size; for instance, is the tapestry large, medium, or small? Are the shapes within the tapestry of a scale that allows the warp sett to work successfully?
- Scale also refers to how objects within the composition compare to each other—is something in the design large or small relative to other things? We often understand the scale of things by how they compare to us, in our human size relationships. Changing the "normal" scale among things in a composition may be a way of emphasizing the importance of something.

TOP Susan Iverson. *Fleeting*, 2015.
Tapestry: 24" × 7'10" × 2". *Courtesy of the artist; photography by Taylor Dabney*

BOTTOM Nicki Bair. *So Many Plover Birds*, 2012.
Tapestry: 12" × 9". *Courtesy of Nicki Bair*

Barbara Burns uses a realistic proportion for the figure in her tapestry *Ingrid—Dancer in Repose*. Although the whole figure isn't completely shown, the viewer can understand the position of the figure by what is included.

In my tapestries, I often use Fibonacci numbers to choose the number of things to include, as well as the overall proportion of the design. For instance, with the tapestry *Five Leaves for Miss Lillian*, there are five leaves included (five is one of the numbers of the Fibonacci sequence), and the proportion of the rectangle used for the composition is approximately the ratio of the golden rectangle, 1:1.618.

LEFT Barbara Burns. *Ingrid: Dancer in Repose*, 2016. Tapestry: 40" × 26". *Courtesy of Barbara Burns, weaver and designer*

RIGHT Tommye McClure Scanlin. *Five Leaves for Miss Lillian*, 2018. Tapestry: 50.5" × 31". *Photo © Tim Barnwell*

BOTTOM Pat Williams. *The Beginning*, 2002. Tapestry: 28″ × 30″. *Courtesy of Pat Williams; photography by Randy Crump*

Pat Williams uses an exaggerated sense of scale and proportion in her tapestry *The Beginning*. In it, the figure fills the space of the room to the extent that she has to crouch on the floor and bend her head. By being "out of proportion" to the room, the figure seems to be trapped in the smaller-scale space.

In *The Voices*, a large-scale tapestry by Erin M. Riley that measures 72" high by 100", the tapestry makes a bold visual statement. Erin says this about the tapestry: "That piece is 100% about #MeToo. They are screenshots from the testimonies of Aly Raisman in the Larry Nassar case [*shown*] on all of the news stations. She says, 'We are here. We have our voices, and we are not going anywhere.' It was kind of about how overwhelming it was to be bombarded with such horrible details, but also that it's a strong and empowering show of strength and solidarity."

By making such a large tapestry in which the figures are shown as massive in scale, the impact is intensified.

In Sarah Swett's work *Rough Copy 6: Postage Due*, she overturns one's expectations of scale by creating a tapestry "postcard," complete with stamps and writing, that's 60" high and 42" wide. This was one of thirteen tapestries in which Sarah contrasted the speed of the quickly written words on small scraps of paper with the years of time it took to weave the series of large tapestry versions.

VARIETY

Variety is difference and contributes interest to a composition.

- Diversifying the elements used in the design may create variety, but at the same time too much variation can be confusing.
- Variety may be achieved by using one color, but in several ways—for instance, red / red-orange, red / red-violet, and a "spectrum" red all together to give an all-over "red" effect may create a more interesting effect than only one version of the color.
- Yarn selected for both the warp and for the weft can add textural difference and give variety.

Becky Stevens creates an intricate variety of angular shapes in her tapestry *Calico*. In the play of positive and negative, one's eye is treated to multiple dark and light changes leading up to the stylized cat shape perched high in the composition. The overall angularity of the design is relieved by the curves of the back and tail of the reclining cat.

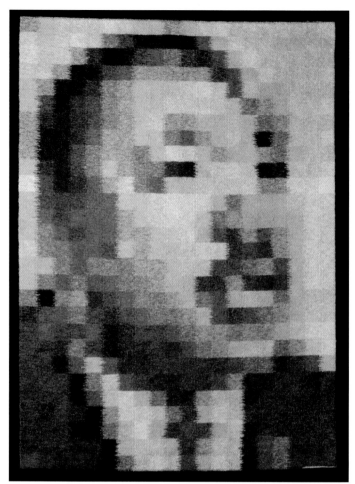

Michael Rohde achieves a rich variety of warm grays by the use of undyed alpaca yarn in his tapestry *The Dream*. Michael has woven a number of portraits inspired by photographs blown up to a large scale, using low-resolution images to yield large pixels as his design idea.

Sue Weil creates variety in her tapestry *Climate Change in 35 mm*, as she repeats three squares in a vertical strip that echoes a strip of 35 mm film. Within each square she has variations of white, black, and red shapes. Although the design of each square is different, the components are similar, as well as the colors.

Becky Stevens. *Calico*, 2017. Tapestry: 15" × 15". *Courtesy of Becky Stevens*

ABOVE Michael F. Rohde. *The Dream*, 2009. Tapestry: 43.5" × 31.5" × 0.5". *Courtesy of Michael F. Rohde; photography by Andrew Neuhart*

Michael Rohde has this to say about his technique of working with photographic images:

"I have used photos of faces, some recognizable, some not, and reduced the image to 20 pixels wide. This produces the weaving plan, from which I again approximate the colors for each pixel and weave, row by row a set of squares, to generate an abstracted face, some from the art canon, but many of remarkable people who should be role models for all of us."[22]

Nicki Bair creates variety both of color and form, within a limited palette of greens, red, and a small amount of yellow, in *My Spiral Tapestry*. The sculptural form is over 13 yards long and woven in a pulled-tapestry technique. She says that "the shape is a helicoid; a remarkable form which packs great densities into small spaces." When hanging, the helicoidal spiral is alive with an organic energy.

Next, let's look at bringing these ideas from the elements and principles together into a unified composition where all parts work in concert to achieve the design and expression you intend.

ABOVE Nicki Bair. *My Spiral Tapestry*, 2009. Three-dimensional pulled warp tapestry: as woven, over 13 yards long × 9" wide; tapestry flattens into a cylinder shape 3" high and less than 9" wide for transport. *Courtesy of Nicki Bair*

RIGHT Sue Weil. *Climate Change in 35 mm*, 2018. Tapestry: 44" × 15". *Courtesy of Sue Weil; photography by Jay Daniel / Black Cat Studio*

TYING IT ALL TOGETHER INTO A UNIFIED COMPOSITION

One objective when creating a composition in any medium is to make a pleasing arrangement of shapes within the design space. This is true whether working in a realistic, expressive, or nonobjective way. When designing for tapestry, one considers the overall composition and must also think of how it will be most successfully woven. Delving into design studies, both on paper and in woven samples, will give you a wealth of information on which to base decisions when you're planning tapestries. I encourage you to explore, keep notes about what you're doing and what the results were, and use the discoveries to your advantage to make the best tapestries you can.

What are some strategies for creating a unified composition that will capture a viewer's attention and lead them through the visual space you have created? Examples of those mentioned here may be found in many artworks. Elaborations on a few tried-and-true approaches can lead in many directions. In fact, you could stay with essentially the same overall design format—say, a rectangle of certain proportions—for years and never run out of ways to continue to develop it.

First, let's look at the design space itself and how the shape, size, and proportion of the space sets the stage for whatever images you put within it.

THE DESIGN FORMAT

The design space or format plays a big role in how the principles and elements work together. Will the format be square, rectangular, or another shape? If it's a rectangle, in what direction will it be used—in a horizontal or a vertical orientation? Is the width greater than height, or the other way around? We've been accustomed to using the terms "landscape" for horizontal and "portrait" for the vertical orientations in word processing and desktop publishing.

A traditional proportion for rectangular format is one based on what's called the golden ratio: 1 to 1.618. The terms "golden rectangle," "golden section," "divine proportion," and "phi" are all names by which this concept is known. The ancient Greeks used the proportion in many ways, and it has been widely adapted by artists since.[23]

The Fibonacci sequence of numbers has also been used to determine the proportions of rectangles. The sequence begins with 0 and is followed by 1. The next number in the sequence is determined by adding the preceding number: 0, 1, 1, 2, 3, 5, 8, 13 . . .

The golden rectangle and Fibonacci numbers are interesting ways to determine the proportions of rectangles for design formats. When using Fibonacci numbers, for instance, you might try selecting the height and width of the rectangle from a combination of two of the numbers. Let's say, if you want a long and narrow rectangle, perhaps you'll use a 3:8 ratio for the shape. The overall size would then be determined by using one or the other as the starting point: 3 = 12" wide, which would make 8 = 32" (3/8 ÷ 12/X = 32").

The position of elements within the format may also depend somewhat on whether the image is representational, expressive, or nonobjective. How will the choice of format enhance your design concept or subject matter?

The format that you choose may also be determined by factors such as size desired for the finished tapestry and the loom available for the weaving.

Another basic aspect to consider is how the images are oriented within the format of the design space: bottom, top, left, right. How and where things are placed can give an amazing difference of impact to the image. Simple cut-paper shapes may be used to try different versions in small studies and can be very informative. Several suggestions for explorations of design space or format will be given later in Part Two.

THE RULE OF THIRDS

Also known as division of thirds, this idea relates to placing important areas of the design at or near the intersecting points of horizontals and verticals that divide the format into thirds.

Photographers often consider this when planning a composition. In fact, when using a camera, maybe you've noticed that the viewfinder may feature a grid that shows this division of the image area. Placing key features in areas other than the

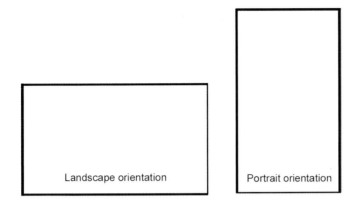

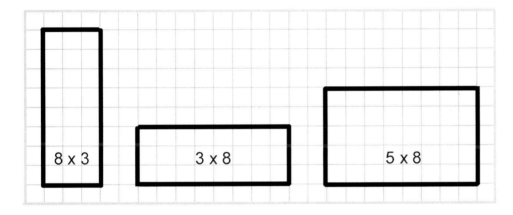

Landscape orientation

Portrait orientation

8 x 3

3 x 8

5 x 8

LEFT Rectangular design formats showing orientation of horizontal (landscape) or vertical (portrait) and Fibonacci numbers used as proportions for a few rectangles.

BOTTOM Rule of thirds used in quick sketch of flowers to find interesting placement.

center can cause the viewer to become more engaged in the design space.

Putting important parts of the design in alignment with or adjacent to the lines implied by the rule of thirds can provide points of emphasis or *focal points*.

Awareness of the rule of thirds idea may encourage you to avoid splitting the composition in half, either horizontally or vertically. For example, in a landscape tapestry, placing a horizon at either the lower or upper third of the composition might give a more interesting use of positive/negative space in the design than putting it in the center. Consider, for instance, how the view of the landscape would change if you were viewing it from a "worm's-eye" view rather than from a human vantage point. Would the horizon then be in the upper third of the design space? Or how about from the viewpoint of very high—as if you were on a mountaintop looking down—would that put the horizon into the lower third of the design?

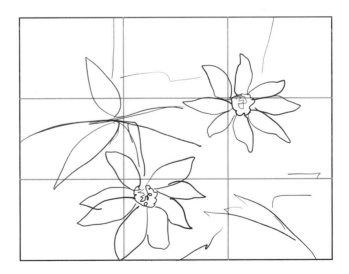

Look at several of your photographs, designs you're developing for weaving, or finished tapestries to see if you've used this unifying concept of rule of thirds, either instinctively or with deliberate planning. If the image is small enough to place a transparency sheet over it, measure and mark lines at one-third of the height and width. Do you find that you've organized the composition with significant focal areas at or very near the intersection of these lines?

CONTRAST

In Linda Wallace's tapestry on page 25, see how the small dark crow in the larger lighter area draws our eye? The role of contrast is important in almost every aspect of how the elements function within the principles of design. Contrast is simply difference—yet it is quite complex. For instance, it can be seen in size, shape, color, and texture of the design. Perhaps you want a dramatic contrast to bring the viewer's eye to a certain place. An extreme

value contrast at the spot you want to emphasize will make that happen.

If you use yarns of mostly one texture but have an area woven in quite a different texture, that part of the tapestry will attract notice because of the contrast of surface.

Within a composition of mostly cool colors, any small areas of warm color will instantly bring the viewer's eye to it. Take a look at Silvia Heyden's tapestry on page 9 and notice the way the small areas of warm red amid the blue pull our attention. Likewise, if there's an overall warm color key to the design, small areas of cool color will become emphasis points.

Sometimes it's useful to see the whole composition in terms of the overall distribution of dark and light values. The Japanese concept of *notan* is one that you may wish to make use of in this instance. According to artist and author Dianne Mize, notan means "dark/light" and is a way to reduce the observed into "an underlying simplified pattern" of only dark and light area. Joann Wilson's notan studies on page 136 will illustrate this idea and will be discussed more fully later.

 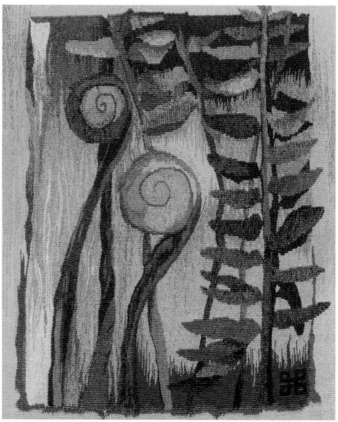

Checking the values of a tapestry by converting to black and white. Notice how in the black-and-white version the lighter values in the background and the large fiddlehead are nearly the same even though the yellow-green seems so much lighter in the full color version because of its intensity.

If you're working representationally, you might try a notan study by reducing the image to two values only: black and white. Does the placement of the dark and light areas help direct your eye through the composition? Do the light and dark areas seem to be balanced in the design?[24] Sometimes squinting your eyes as you look at the reference will help you eliminate middle values as well as details, making the darks and lights more evident.

One of the quick ways to judge the contrast in your tapestry is to photograph it and convert to black and white. You might be surprised at the lack of contrast you'll see! Because intensity of color often attracts our attention so strongly, we often overlook the quality of the value contrast. Sometimes that's just fine, especially if we want a low-key effect to the composition. Becoming sensitive to the differences and similarities in intensity and value of color will help in making choices that effect contrast.

DOMINANCE AND SUBORDINATION

What is most important in the design? What do you want to be seen first in a composition? How will you set up the conditions so that the viewer's eye is drawn to it? Will you then give the viewer other things to experience within the design? Steven Aimone speaks of "visual hierarchy" as a way to organize and prioritize among the elements and principles.[25]

The size of a composition element is often the first thing noticed if it's different from the others, either larger or smaller. Extreme difference of color can also be a factor in setting up a dominant area or areas. Contrast of any kind will play an important role as well. An example of how even small differences are noticed first is seen in Susan Iverson's tapestry shown on page 28.

Location of main focal point is yet another way to achieve a hierarchy of elements in a tapestry. The center of an area is often where one wants to look first, for instance. Directional movements set up by emphasis areas, or linear connections among shapes, can also lead one to a place of importance in the composition.

Supporting roles are played by the subordinate components in the design, providing the difference or contrast necessary to emphasize the dominant point(s). Maybe more-neutral colors surround the brightest, most dominant area, or perhaps the majority of the rest of the space is calmer to allow an active element to seem even more important. The neutral background and border of the author's tapestry shown on page 37 serve to highlight the dominance of the central, more colorful shape.

OPEN OR CLOSED COMPOSITION—BREAKING OUT OF THE DESIGN SPACE

When the shapes all exist within the boundaries of the design format or space, you may think of it as a closed composition. If the shapes are cut off in some way by the edge, it's considered to be an open composition. As an example of a closed composition, imagine a photo of flowers where all the blossoms are contained within the format and you see their entire shapes.

Now, imagine that the photographer shifted the vantage point so that not all the same flowers are visible. Some of the petals are out of the framework, and more of the surrounding foliage is in view. The photographer could also zoom into the image to enlarge and create an interesting interplay of positive and negative shapes within the design. An open composition is the result, one in which your eye can be led into the design from the outside, and it may also be directed out of the format.

Another way that the design space can be broken is if shapes do indeed break out of the composition. Look back at Robbie LaFleur's tapestry on page 61 to see how she has woven shapes out into the border that frames her central image. One way this could be done is by having a border as a framework around the design and extending the image into that space in some places. Yet another option is to literally extend shapes beyond the edges of the main composition. With tapestry this could give an interesting technical challenge of shaped weaving or adding supplemental warps to the tapestry. Sue Weil often extends the edges of shapes within her tapestries as seen in the example on page 65.

Cropping the flower creates a more dynamic composition with interesting positive and negative shapes.

Part Two

Design Explorations

THINGS TO TRY | EXAMINE THE DESIGN SPACE
DELVE INTO THE ELEMENTS | EXPERIMENT WITH THE PRINCIPLES
A TAPESTRY STUDY GROUP'S DISCOVERIES

Horizon

You can use the brush of a Japanese monk
or a pencil stub from a race track.

As long as you draw the line a third
the way up from the bottom of the page,

the effect is the same: the world suddenly
divided into its elemental realms.

A moment ago there was only a piece of paper.
Now there is earth and sky, sky and sea.

You were sitting alone in a small room.
Now you are walking into the heat of a vast desert

or standing on the ledge of a winter beach
watching the light on the water, light in the air.

—Billy Collins, from *The Art of Drowning*[26]

Billy Collins eloquently expresses with a few words how we can almost "see" depth in space by the placement of a simple horizontal line on a page. In the same way, whether a page of paper or a tapestry, the area in which we plan our designs by using the elements and principles is one for which there are many solutions.

Coming up next will be several things to try as studies or as a way of exploring various visual ideas. Delve into these ideas in any way, or any order you wish, keeping a sense of play in your experimentations. There is not a right or wrong way to plunge into these suggestions. After all, as we all know, *doing* something, *trying* something is the key to wrapping your head around ideas. Now, many of the design ideas presented in the last chapter will be put into practice. Even though you may feel you understand what value means, or how color contrast works, if you physically experiment with the ideas and train your eye to see them, that will lead to a deeper understanding of how the elements and principles can enhance your tapestry-making experience.

The words—"study" and "exploration"—have pretty much the same meaning, but in a way, exploration implies heading off on a journey when you're not sure what you might find. A study seems to suggest there's a definitive answer to be discovered. With any creative process of design and art making—is there a right answer? Maybe or maybe not; it depends on the circumstances of the making and the desire of the maker.

Read over these suggestions. If you are experienced with design, just a quick look might be all you want to do. A few of the explorations might prompt you to consider ways of approaching designing that you haven't tried before. Maybe one or more will cause you to think about old ideas in new ways.

If you're new to designing—and especially if you're feeling uncertain or insecure in your own abilities—I believe that once you begin trying things, seeing and comparing results, you'll start to grow in your confidence. I truly feel each of us has our own unique visual voice and that finding our own is significant.

You should feel free to move around in these suggestions, doing some while skipping others. There is not a particular sequential plan to these ideas. You might also want to devote only a few minutes to some of the explorations and spend lots of time on others. After all, the more you're working on paper exercises, the less time you're spending at your loom or in other parts of your life! Still, the effort you put into honing your visual skills will ultimately pay off in the tapestries you'll design and make.

THINGS TO TRY

In the suggestions ahead, you can work with visual ideas by using paper and an assortment of art supplies, or by doing small tapestry samplers. An advantage of working small is that you'll be spending less time with the making of each. The small size also quickly gives you an overview of the impact of the whole composition. Any design that seems worthwhile might then be done in a larger and more elaborated version. You might want to keep any of the explorations you try out in file folders or a portfolio for future reference—maybe to be added to as new ideas come to you about something you tried earlier.

Prepare a workspace where you can be messy with materials. You may want to cover the table with plastic or with sheets of newsprint you can change when needed. You will want to have a good light available and an assortment of tools and supplies, as suggested below. Most of these can be found at art or hobby supply stores or ordered online.

I'll mention several things to try with each element and principle that can be done on paper. Ways in which you might take those to woven versions will be suggested for several of the concepts, and I'm sure many more will occur to you.

Please keep in mind that there is not a right or wrong way to do any of these things! As you work with them, other ideas will probably come to you—take those new thoughts where they might lead you. Explore, examine, contemplate, and—most of all—play.

The following are only suggestions of the types of supplies you might want to use for the upcoming exercises. You certainly can explore the ideas with just a few tools and materials. Take stock of what you might have on hand, and improvise if you wish. (If you have children around, see what art materials they might have, and ask if you can borrow some of them for a while!) If you do want to purchase supplies, I'd suggest looking for the student- or school-grade options for many of the items—they will do the job we need just as well as more expensive materials.

- **Paper:** Papers of a variety of types—drawing paper, regular copy paper, cardstock papers in white, a few grays, and black—will be good to use for several exercises. Scrapbook papers are excellent sources for an assortment of colors and patterns. "Found papers" from magazines, junk mail, and other print sources offer a variety of color, pattern, and texture. Newsprint paper, grid paper, graphite transfer paper, and tracing paper can be helpful.

An assortment of tools and supplies will be useful for trying out the design explorations. These are just a few of the options you might want to have on hand.

- **Tools & Supplies:** Media and tools for working with paper exercises include pencil, colored pencils or markers, vine charcoal, Sharpie™ or other permanent marker, crayons, watercolor pencils, watercolors or acrylic paint, black permanent ink, brushes of small and wide sizes, Magic Rub®, or art gum eraser. Other tools and supplies include scissors, glue stick or double-sided tape, and metal-edge ruler. Repositionable adhesive is also handy. A cutting mat and X-Acto® knife are useful as well. Add a palette for paint (this can be a foam picnic plate), a couple of containers for water (empty yogurt tubs are good for this), and paper towels. A viewfinder or cropping tool made from two L shapes cut from white cardstock can be used to place over images and shifted around to select areas or show different formats (a template for making one of these is provided in appendix C). Transparency sheets will be suggested for a few of the explorations, and transparent notebook dividers are an inexpensive option. You'll need dry- or wet-erase markers to use with the transparency sheets.
- **Loom & Supplies:** For woven studies, you might set up about a 6"–8" wide warp, with a sett of eight to ten ends per inch. Length will be your choice, depending on your loom. You could use the full width or portions of the warp for sampling various ideas. Add to that a variety of yarn types and colors as weft. Any of your commonly used weaving tools will be helpful: scissors, bobbins, etc.

- **Technology:** Digital camera or smartphone camera, computer with image-editing software, a digital tablet, and all-in-one printer all are useful. You'll notice that there will be suggestions for photographing stages of the explorations to record ideas and changes as you work. This is not a necessity, of course! But it offers an option for those who have access and are comfortable with working this way. Some of the explorations can be done with a digital tablet or on computer and then printed out, for instance.

Exploring design effects on paper may suggest many ideas for woven studies. Perhaps you'll want to devote a separate small tapestry to each element or maybe do a larger piece that holds several of the elements. If your exploration is about how sett affects an image, perhaps you'll weave several versions of the same cartoon with different warps and ends per inch.

You might want to attach a hang tag to record the purpose or even stitch a label with a few notes on the back of any woven samplers you do. Additionally, a written record that includes comments about the intent of the studies and the conclusions you've drawn from the results could be helpful later. If your woven pieces are small enough, you might want to collect them in a notebook in plastic sheet protectors along with the documentation.

As you work through these explorations, other ideas will probably occur to you. Try them out, if you have time, or make notes to follow up on the thoughts later. You may find that some of these explorations are sparking ideas for "real" tapestries. Designing with emphasis on the elements and principles is certainly a valid approach, and many artists have used purely formal design concepts as their desired way of working.

If your inclination is to use representational or pictorial imagery, or if you want to express feelings through the tapestry, having a strong underlying design structure for your composition will enhance the ideas you are presenting. Likewise, your increased sensitivity to how the elements and principles play significant roles in compositions will give you confidence that you can execute your ideas to create a strong visual statement in your tapestry work.

We'll begin the explorations by first looking at the design space or format and then move on to several suggestions for exploring the elements and principles.

EXAMINE THE DESIGN SPACE

The edges of the format—bottom, the sides, and the top—make up the boundary within which the images exist. How shapes interact with those edges can be key points in planning for interesting designs. Before looking at individual elements and principles, we'll begin with a few examples of ways that simple shapes can have diverse visual impact within the same format. These will use just a few cut-paper shapes placed onto a white background. Cardstock in white, gray, and black is suggested for these explorations, as well as a glue stick or double-stick tape to hold the shapes in place. Grid paper can be helpful also. Other supplies and tools needed are scissors, ruler, and black marker.

TAKE A LOOK AT SQUARE FORMATS

1. Mark out several small, medium, and large squares on a white sheet of paper, using a marker.
2. Use black or gray paper and cut out either a square or a rectangle, somewhat smaller than the smallest of your marked squares. Do one of the same size and color for each of your different sizes of marked squares.
3. Place the smaller shape within each of the larger squares, in the same relative position. Notice the visual effect of the same size of shape within each of the different sizes of design formats.
4. Glue these into place or use double-sided tape to adhere them.
5. An interesting woven version of this might be done based on the paper study. How you arrange the examples in the tapestry version will also become a designing exercise. You might put the several different sizes of the squares side by side, within a background of a contrasting value (or perhaps color). Or maybe weave a long vertical composition with the different sizes of background squares existing within a contrasting color background.

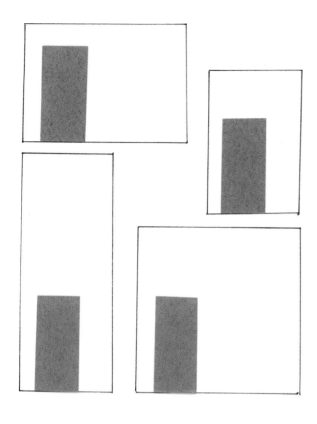

Three rectangles of different format proportions and one square are outlined. Each has the same-sized rectangle placed in approximately the same location within the space. See how the rectangle interacts with the edges of its format in each instance.

Consider the way a simple shape of the same size can have different visual effects depending on the design space in which it exists—how could this awareness be turned to your advantage when planning for a future tapestry? Will you possibly consider the scale of an object within your composition and how it relates to the edges of the design space? Will a flower, for instance, be designed in such a way to almost fill the space, leaving little background area? Or do you want to make it small and insignificant, surrounded in a larger background? These are the kinds of questions I hope you'll begin to ask yourself as you look at the ways the elements and principles will be tools for your design planning in the future.

EXPLORE RECTANGULAR FORMATS

1. Mark out several rectangles on a sheet or sheets of white paper with a marker. Make a variety of width-to-height examples. Turn some in a vertical direction and others in horizontal orientation. Possibly make one of these in the golden-rectangle proportion of 1 to 1.618 (for instance, if one side is 2" the other would be approximately 3.25"). Also try one with an extreme width-to-height ratio, perhaps choosing the ratio from two Fibonacci numbers, perhaps 2" by 8". Grid paper is useful for marking these out quickly.
2. As with the previous square format, cut a simple shape somewhat smaller than the smallest of the rectangles, using black or gray paper. Place one within each of the rectangles in approximately the same place. Consider how the same shape appears in the different sizes and ratios of the rectangles.
3. These studies might also suggest to you many ideas for woven versions.

Squares within larger squares placed lower or higher in the design space to see if the lower appears to have more visual weight. Does the upper square seem visually lighter?

Squares within larger squares placed at extreme left or extreme right. Which seems to enter and which seems to leave the space?

LOOK AT PLACEMENT WITHIN YOUR FORMAT

Placement of shapes within the format can have different effects. Try each of the following with both square and rectangular formats. Notice the visual effect of the smaller shape within each format.

1. Place a shape at or near the bottom edge. When shapes are located near or on the bottom edge, they usually appear to be heavier or "grounded."

2. Next, put the shape near the top edge. Does the shape seem to be more expansive in the higher location? Does it seem to "float" in the design space?

3. Try the same shape placed at the left side and contrast with another identical format in which the shape is on the right side. In Western culture there is a tendency to "read" the design from left to right, as we're accustomed to reading text. Do you find this to be the case in the design? Does your eye go to the shape at the left more readily?

4. Placement at the left can draw your attention, but right-side placement can draw your attention as well, especially if the shape is placed low. In this case it will act as a visual stop, almost like a period at the end of a sentence.

5. Center a shape within the format. This will have an almost bull's-eye effect. This may be very static in a composition. In your future design planning, is this an effect you'll want? If not, consider other placements for main objects/images to help avoid this. If you do indeed want attention pulled to the center by placing the main focus there, that's what you'll get.

Tommye McClure Scanlin. *Try This*, 2019. Tapestry design format exploration of effects of simple shape placement differences within series of square backgrounds. 39" × 14". *Chris Dant, photographer*

DELVE INTO THE ELEMENTS

Line

Let's begin exploration of line by using paper and a few mediums such as soft pencil, vine charcoal, ink, watercolor, or thinned acrylic paint. Suggested papers are regular copy paper, drawing paper, or sheets of cardstock in white, black, and gray. Grid paper with ¼" squares will also be helpful (a template for grid paper is included in appendix C for you to copy, if desired). An adhesive, such as glue stick or double-sided tape, will be needed. A few tools, including a brush or two, scissors, ruler, a utility knife, and self-healing cutting mat will be useful. The L-shaped cropping tool (template on page 178) makes it quick and easy to look at variations of a design. A digital camera will be handy to record versions of the studies, if you wish. A small container for water and paper towels and a roll of masking tape round out the supplies. Cover your workspace with plastic or newsprint and tape it down to keep it stationary as you work.

Work freely with these explorations as you begin so you'll have a feel for what to expect with the variety of tools and mediums. In this way, you might find the ones you prefer to work with for upcoming ideas with other elements.

EXAMINE THE DYNAMICS OF PARALLEL LINES

1. On white paper, make lines of different weights by using any of the mediums you have on hand. Vary the pressure of your tool as you work. Make these marks as mostly parallel lines from one side of a page to the other, but don't worry about whether the lines are exactly parallel. There's no need to use a ruler, for instance. Simply take a line from one side to the other and accept any wobbles or wiggles that may happen on the way. Fill a page with various weights and consistencies of marks. *Note:* You might want to tape the corners of the paper down so it won't shift as you make the lines.
2. Use the L-shaped cropping tool to select a closer view of some of the marks. Notice the texture and value differences seen in smaller selection? Think about how those textures and values could be interpreted in tapestry. Maybe even try it out in a small tapestry sample.

3. Consider photographing your selected view. Move the cropping tool to other locations and record several smaller parts of the larger sheet of lines with photographs that might be printed out later.
4. Next, cut the page of lines into several squares or rectangles. An alternative to cutting up this sheet is to make a photocopy of it to be used for cutting.
5. On a background sheet, rearrange the cutout square or rectangles in different ways. Don't try to reassemble them in their original position. For instance, turn some 90° to the way they were drawn when you arrange them. Notice the variety of linear patterning that will be created as you shift the pieces around.
6. Find an arrangement you like and attach them to the background sheet with glue stick or double-sided tape. Alternatively, photograph several versions of arrangements before deciding on the one to glue into place.
7. You might once again use the L-shaped cropping tool to select portions to enlarge. Photographing those different cropped versions is a good way to record each variation. Consider how a selected portion might be done in tapestry. What linear tapestry methods would lend themselves to the quality of the lines you've made and still remain "weaverly"?

Line exploration being done by a few participants in the author's tapestry class, Penland School of Craft, August 2019.
Chris Dant, photographer

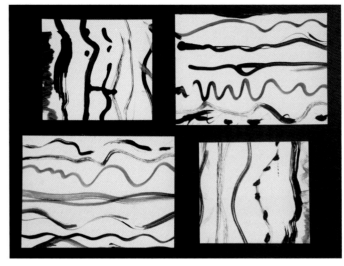

TOP LEFT Working with line exploration by using a variety of tools and black paint. Student at Penland School of Craft, August 2019. *Chris Dant, photographer*

BOTTOM Trying different placements for smaller squares and rectangles cut from the line exploration sheets. Student at Penland School of Craft, August 2019. *Chris Dant, photographer*

TOP RIGHT One variation created from line explorations. Student at Penland School of Craft, August 2019. *Chris Dant, photographer*

COMPARE EFFECTS OF ANGULAR AND FLOWING LINES

1. Make a series of angular lines, using a straight edge. Try different tools for doing the lines to give a variety of weights, textures, and values. Keep the lines from crossing over or overlapping each other, but vary the angles and the spacing. Put this sheet aside to use later.
2. Make a series of organic, flowing lines that cross the page without overlapping themselves. Again, use several types of tools. Let the lines loop and undulate but not cross over each other.
3. You might want to photograph or scan to copy both sheets before going to the next step.
4. Flip both sheets over and measure out strips of several widths across the paper. Cut these strips apart.
5. Arrange the strips side by side, alternating ones from the angular sheet with the organic group. Try variations of the arrangements to see different effects. Photograph or scan the versions. Glue a selected one onto a background sheet, if desired.
6. Once more, use the L-shaped cropping tool to isolate a smaller portion of the design. Consider how this would look blown up to larger scale. Could this image be interpreted in tapestry? Consider the ways certain tapestry techniques might lend themselves to weaving angular edges contrasting with flowing edges.

EXPLORE SIZES AND SPACING OF LINES

1. For this next series of line explorations, you'll use cut paper strips and ¼" grid paper (available in appendix C). Start by cutting several 2" to 3" long strips of black paper in ¼", ½", and 1" widths. Think of these black strips as the positive shapes/lines you'll be placing onto negative space of background paper.

2. Mark off a rectangle on the grid paper approximately 2" or 3" high by 8" wide. Place the strips parallel to each other in various spacing within the designated rectangle, following the measured lines of the grid paper. Try for an interesting arrangement as you place the positive (black strips) on the negative space of the paper.

3. Either adhere the strips in place or photograph the arrangement and then try others. Make a photo record of each design, if desired.

4. Next, use a similar setup with ¼" grid paper as background, with approximately 2"–3" by 8" as the design space. Have another assortment of black paper strips, this time all cut to ¼" wide by 2"–3" long.

5. Begin at either the left or the right side of your background rectangle as you flip a coin to determine whether a black strip will be placed over a grid space or if a space will be left empty. For instance, if you decide that heads means you'll place a black strip, then when the coin lands heads up, put down a strip to cover one of the grid spaces. In this case, tails up would mean an empty grid space.

TOP Creating two sheets filled with a variety of straight-edge lines drawn with varying angles, and flowing, organic lines in preparation for cutting up and recombining

BOTTOM One variation of arranging strips from both sheets to explore the combination of geometric and organic lines

RIGHT Two examples of a variety of widths of cut paper strips arranged to make an interesting combination of positive (dark) and negative (light) space

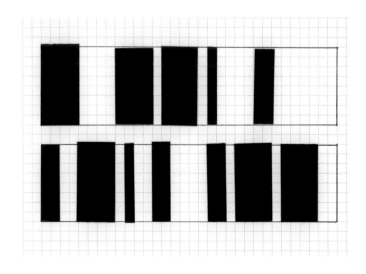

6. Make a series of coin tosses until the grid lines of the marked-off rectangle are used. You now have a pattern of dark lines and empty spaces that were randomly selected by the coin. Compare those to the designs that you made in the previous exploration.

7. You can take both these explorations to yet another step by reversing the placement of dark and light so that the positive becomes negative and vice versa. Use more dark strips for this, or fill in the dark areas with a drawing tool.

8. Take a look at both these examples both in horizontal and vertical directions. Imagine the horizontal orientation being interpreted in separate vertical color changes where you might use interlocking methods, or as slits that are either sewn on the loom or afterward. Notice that the vertical orientation might suggest patterns of weft-way bands of different colors.

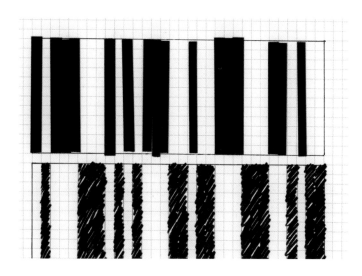

TOP *Top example*: ¼" strips arranged on a ¼" grid background sheet, following the toss of a coin for dark (strip) or light (background). Heads indicated use a strip; tails meant leave a space. *Lower example*: the reverse of the dark-light effect was filled in with a marker.

RIGHT A few shapes arranged on four colors of backgrounds, all without touching each other or the edges of the background

Shape

Exploring shape on paper can be done with many of the same tools and mediums used for line. Refer to those and add these: colored pencils or markers, watercolors, watercolor pencils, black and white acrylic paint, and a variety of colored papers, such as scrapbooking paper.

You may also find that taking digital photographs is a quick way to try different arrangements and to record your design decisions as you work.

LOOKING AT SHAPE WITHIN THE BACKGROUND

In the next exploration you'll see the effects of using the same shapes arranged in a different ways on four varied background colors. You could record your results for each of these by photographing the placements, or by lightly attaching the shapes with a bit of tape at the back and then scanning, or by making different examples for each (for a total of twelve design variations).

1. Prepare your backgrounds using papers of white, gray, black, and a color of your choice. Make these sheets about 5" by 7" in size.

2. Choose colors of paper from which to cut your shapes. Suggestion: make simple, bold shapes that you can duplicate easily because you'll be cutting out several of these.

3. For the first arrangement, place shapes on each of the background sheets in the same position so that the shapes don't

touch or overlap. Move them around until you feel there's an interesting placement of the shapes and the background. Think of these as positive shapes placed within the negative space of the background.

4. Next, make a second arrangement on each of the four background sheets, using the same shapes as in the first, and putting them in the same position on all four sheets. This time let one or more *touch* the edges of others, but still don't overlap any of the shapes.

5. Do a third arrangement of the same shapes onto all the backgrounds, this time making use of overlapping for some or with all of them.

6. Compare the variations of the same overall design made up of a few simple shapes on white, gray, black, and colorful backgrounds. Although the emphasis for this exploration was on seeing how the same shapes can be affected in different configurations, you may notice that color of the shapes on each particular background plays a strong role in the design effect.

7. As you do the exploration, you'll notice that the shapes engage with the background space either to lead your eye around easily, or maybe not. See how far you can continue to explore ways in which the overall design is modified by a few simple changes among the same shapes.

8. You might want to weave a small tapestry based on one or more of these simple studies. This would be an interesting way to sample both technique as well as design effect. For instance, if you have mostly straight vertical lines in the cut shapes, you might try different methods of joining slits as you weave, either by stitching as you go or by using a dovetail or an interlock method.

EXPLORING POSITIVE-NEGATIVE RELATIONSHIPS (FIGURE AND GROUND)

As mentioned earlier, the shapes and the background on which they appear can be described as positive (the shapes) and negative (the background). Another way to state this relationship is as figure (the shapes) and ground (the background). Positive-negative or figure-ground relationships are constantly at play in all visual representations, whether those are realistic, expressive, or nonobjective in style. In tapestry weaving, positive-negative relationships happen in a real way because you have to actually weave the background space within which the positive shapes appear! If you want a shape near the top edge, you can't simply weave it there without having the supporting area woven

The shapes arranged on those same four colors of background, with some touching of edges among the shapes

The same shapes now arranged on the four colors of background, with each overlapping in some places

first. Let's look at the interaction of positive and negative within a design space by doing a simple exercise. For this you'll use sheets of papers in white, black, gray, and a selected hue.

1. Stack together two of the same-sized rectangular sheets of paper, one black and one white. Make a single cut through both sheets, from one edge to the opposite edge, with a path that moves at an angle or a curve, or a bit of both.
2. Separate the two sheets and then use one from each color, from the opposite side of the cut, to place on a background of gray paper. This will put the rectangle back together, but now one side is white and the other is black.
3. Shift the two shapes around so that space is opened between them. When placed on the gray paper, a third shape will be created as the two original black and white shapes are separated. Try several ways for creating space between the black and white, allowing the gray background to become an important shape between the two. You might want to record each arrangement with a quick digital photo.
4. Try as many placement changes as you can think of, making a photo record as you go.

Now, use the other two parts of the original sheets and do as many variations as come to mind. This will flip the value—what was white will be black; the black will be white in this combination.

5. How important does the gray shape created between the two contrasting parts become to the design? Is it now the negative space, while the black and white both seems to be positive shapes? Or does it seem to be the positive shape between two contrasting background colors?
6. How will the design be affected if the black and white shapes are placed on a background color other than gray? What would be the visual impact of bright red, for instance? How about if the background paper between were to be a patterned or textured paper? Does this varied surface cause any difference in the way it visual "reads" as either positive or negative?
7. Possibly you discovered several interesting placements of positive and negative shapes among the many things you tried with this simple activity of cutting a black and a white sheet into two parts. Consider making a few small weavings based on the most appealing of the designs created.

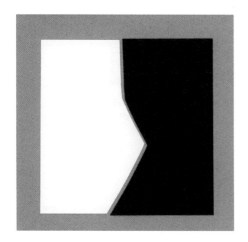

Positive-negative relationship exploration. First cut the same simple line across two sheets of paper stacked together, one white and one black. Separate the two and recombine with white at one side, black at the other, onto a third background color (gray, in this instance).

Try different ways of separating the two shapes to allow more of the background color to show. See how the background now becomes an important shape as well.

See how the same two white and black shapes look with a different color of background.

ANOTHER WAY TO LOOK AT POSITIVE AND NEGATIVE: COUNTERCHANGE

Counterchange is seen in a design in which a dark motif on a light ground alternates with the same motif in reverse order. Think of a checkerboard as an extreme example of counterchange. Once again, you will have a positive and negative relationship of shapes, but this time the balance of areas remains equal.

1. Begin with two sheets, one black and one white, placed side by side vertically or horizontally. Think of the dividing line between the two as the axis or centerline. All the other shapes to be cut will relate to this centerline, since together these black and white sheets become the background for what comes next.
2. Stack two smaller sheets of paper together, one black and one white. Make a simple shape by cutting both sheets at the same time.
3. Place the white shape on the black side of the background and the black shape on the white part, putting them exactly opposite each other like a mirror image.
4. Add another simple shape, placed along the axis of the black-and-white background, with opposite values paired.
5. Continue working with paired shapes in this way with the positive-negative contrast until you've tried several things and the composition seems pleasing. You can cut more shapes or open up spaces in the ones previously made—just continue to balance what you do in one with its "twin."
6. Glue in place or photograph. In fact, you might photograph each change you make as you develop the design, and then print those out as a record of your exploration.
7. How could you use counterchange ideas with tapestry? Are there any subjects that lend themselves to counterchange?

TOP Counterchange exploration. Begin by placing a white and a black sheet side by side, either vertically or horizontally.

CENTER Stack together black and white sheets of paper. Cut a few simple shapes while the sheets are together so that you have duplicates. Place the black shape on the white side of the background, and the matching white shape on the black background. The positions will be in a mirror image of each other.

BOTTOM Tommye McClure Scanlin. *Positive-Negative Feathers*, 2012. Tapestry: approximately 10" × 8". In this tapestry the same cartoon was flipped to weave the mirror image, with dark and light shifting places. *Collection of Micala Sidore; photo © Tim Barnwell*

CREATING SHAPE WITH A VARIETY OF MEDIA

For the next few explorations you will use crayon or colored pencils, watercolor pencils, and watercolors. Brushes of a couple of sizes, paint and palette, water container, and paper towels will be needed. Goals here are to create shapes that have textures and also to see the effects that a fluid medium has on the appearance of shapes, both within the interior of the shapes and at the edges.

MAKE SHAPES WITH RUBBINGS OF TEXTURES

Most people have done rubbings of coins or leaves some time in their past. This simple activity can be a good way to combine textures and shapes for potential design.

1. For this exploration, use thin paper such as tracing paper or regular copy paper. Select something for the rubbing that is slightly raised but not more than about the thickness of cardstock. In fact, you can cut a shape or shapes from cardstock to use for the rubbings. Put the shape onto the work surface and place the sheet of paper on top.
2. Stroke the edge of the tip of a crayon or colored pencil back and forth across the paper, paying most attention to the edges of the shape. Hold the paper firmly as you make the rubbing so it stays in place. Then, shift the paper so that there will be an overlap, and continue with more rubbings until you feel you have an interesting grouping of shapes.
3. An alternative to using colored pencils for the rubbings is to use watercolor pencils. Do the process as before, but afterward stroke a dampened brush across the rubbing. Depending on the quality of the watercolor pencils, there will be more or less paint contained in the pencil marks. You may want to test the pencils ahead of time to see how hard or lightly to do the rubbings to get the color intensity you want when adding water.
4. Explore the shapes created by the rubbings further by using the L-shaped cropping tool to select areas. Could any of these be developed into woven versions? Would the textures created by the rubbings suggest ways you might blend the weft in chiné or mélange ways?

TOP Rubbing of leaves made with colored pencils

BOTTOM Rubbing of leaves made with watercolor pencils, brushed with water

EXPLORING SHAPES WITH WATERCOLORS

When exploring shapes, the fluid, transparent quality of watercolor is a good medium for easily creating crisp, firm edges to contrast with softer, blurred ones. Additionally, because watercolor is transparent medium, once a layer of paint is dry it may be overlapped with another wash of a different color to give a color blend. Use watercolor paint to make a few simple shapes. See if you can create a crisp edge at one side and a softer, blurred one at the other.

1. First, fill the brush with color and stroke it onto the paper. Dip the brush in water and go back into one side of the stroke to thin the paint and make a lighter value. Make the paint stroke with one motion and move on—try not to brush back and forth into the same area, because this will cause the paint to lose some of its transparent quality.
2. Next, use just clear water only to brush a shape onto paper. While the paper is wet, load the brush with color and bring it into the dampened part, starting slightly to the outside of the wet area. This will give a crisp edge at the side where the paper was dry, and varying degrees of blur within the wet part.
3. Let the shapes dry and then lightly brush over some of them with more paint. See how much transparency you achieve as you do this. How could this transparent color effect be translated into tapestry? This may give you ideas for small samples to weave.

These suggested explorations will most likely give you many more thoughts about how shapes may be created with paper, pencil, and paint. Notice you weren't asked to "draw" the shapes, since you were creating them in different ways. Many of the effects gotten with these simple means can lend themselves to being incorporated into tapestries in which planned imagery is your goal. Approaches to creating edge differences, for instance, may be just what you're looking for with shapes within a tapestry you have in mind. Possibly figure-ground or counterchange explorations gave you some ideas for designing. Likewise, watercolor explorations to show soft or blurred edges may suggest transparency effects to use in application with tapestry ideas.

Shapes made with a few watercolor strokes. Some have overlapping strokes made to show the effect of transparency of the medium.

Value

Value is an important element within any artwork. It refers to degrees of light or dark and all nuances between those extremes. These explorations will be looking at effects of value with white, grays, and black only. However, value is an important aspect of color that will be discussed in the color explorations. Mediums to use will be the same as for our line explorations (see page 85) and will be done on a variety of papers in white, several grays, and black. Add a Magic Rub or art gum eraser to the tools for one of the explorations.

TRY VALUE GRADATIONS

1. Start by making a value gradation from light to dark, using a pencil to gradually increase the darkness. Do a strip about an inch wide as you fill in with the pencil, going back and forth until you build up the value as dark as possible with the tool. Use the pencil very lightly at first and add more pressure and overlapping strokes as you gradually build up

the value to as dark as you can make it. Alternatively, you may find it will be easier to move from dark to light rather than from light to dark—try both ways to see what works best for you and the pencil you're using. If you have several different pencils with graphite of varying softness, try all of them. Notice the quality of the darkest area—have you been able to make a "true" black or does your tool give you only a very dark gray?

2. Do the same process by using the watercolor pencils, moving either from light to dark or from dark to light. Brush over the strip with water to blend the color gradation further.

3. Make a similar value gradation with watercolor, ink, or thinned acrylic paint by gradually increasing the amount of paint or ink until the gradation is as dark as it can be. *Note:* you might find working from dark to light will work out best, gradually adding more water to make transitions to lighter values. Try both ways to see which you find most successful for making a gradual value change.

EXPLORE COMBINATIONS OF VALUES

1. In this exploration you will create several different values on assorted papers to use in making small collages. Use several of the mediums and two or three 8½" by 11" white sheets of cardstock or drawing paper. On the papers, outline a few areas about 3" square. Fill those areas with several different values, using any of the mediums you wish. Be sure to include a range of value from dark to light. Most likely you'll notice a texture inherent to the tool or medium you're using, and that's perfect. What you'll look for mostly at the next step is value relationships in the small designs to be created. However, the textural differences coming naturally from the medium used for the values made will add to the visual interest.

2. Cut a variety of shapes from the prepared group of values. Arrange them on white, gray, or black paper, leaving some bit of the background paper showing. Glue the pieces down once you've decided on the background color. You may want to photograph the results of the shapes on each background

A variety of value gradations made with different drawing and painting mediums

Collage made with simple shapes cut from a variety of values, created with different mediums and arranging them on a white background, allowing some of the white to show

before you decide on one to use. If you have remaining bits of the created value papers, try another design, possibly on a different background.

3. As alternatives, prepare several large sheets with value ranges, as described. You will be able to cut duplicate shapes from each value to place on backgrounds of different values, arranging them at the same time to keep the placement alike. Possibly you'll want to make duplicates of the value sheets with a photocopier or an all-in-one printer before cutting them up to have several to work with.

4. Notice if the compositions you've created fall into a high-key (overall light) or low-key (overall dark) value group. Or instead have you created an overall balance of the dark, medium, and light values? Once again, as with other explorations, think about ways one or more of these designs might turn into tapestry ideas.

TRY BACKGROUNDS MADE OF VARIOUS TEXTURES AND VALUES

1. Next, in a new collage exploration, rather than using a solid value of background like for the previous designs, try either or both of the following ideas for a background sheet.

2. For one, use pencil with soft graphite to scribble all over the surface of the paper intended for the background. Collage with an assortment of shapes as before, allowing some of the background to remain visible.

3. For a second version, mix a midtone gray with white and black acrylic paint. Brush this over a background paper, using a wide foam brush. Try to make texture differences with the brushstrokes as you fill the paper with the value. You might also try blotting some areas of the paint with paper towel while it's still damp, to give additional textures. Allow this sheet to dry and then use it as a background for collage as before, once again letting some of the background show. This time any textures of the papers you're using for the collage will be additional to any texture of the background sheet.

4. Try a negative process for creating values. To do this, first use soft vine charcoal to completely cover a sheet of white paper until you have an even tone of gray. You might even want to lightly rub over the charcoal with your fingers or a tissue to smoothly coat the paper. Next, use a Magic Rub or art gum eraser to lift out areas to give changes in value. This will work best by using a corner of the eraser. Don't try to erase back to pure white—that will be almost impossible. Do try to achieve a variety of light to medium gray values as you use the eraser as a drawing tool. Note of warning here! This will be messy, so prepare your workspace accordingly. You may even want to wear gloves while you do this.

TOP Collage made with the same shapes as in the previous collage, but with gray background

BOTTOM Collage made with same shapes as in the previous two collages, but with black background

Texture

Texture engages the sense of touch, whether in reality, when you can feel the surface of something, or visually, when a surface is treated in such a way that our eye "reads" and imagines the way it would feel. This tactile element is one that is intrinsic in every material you might use for weaving.

Texture can be beautifully featured in tapestries through the choices of yarns. It can be especially apparent when highly contrasting textures of yarns are used. It may also be important when weaving a subject in which you'll want texture to be represented—the bark of a tree, or maybe the grainy surface of a sandy beach.

Texture is also created when the weaver manipulates the weaving method in some way so that the tapestry moves out

5. The charcoal is very easily disturbed with your fingers and will transfer off onto anything it touches. You may want to keep this design exploration in a plastic sheet protector or between two pieces of paper. You can also spray it with art-medium fixative or even hair spray—either of those will help prevent the charcoal from rubbing off. For the least messy way to keep a record of this exploration, either photograph and print the image or slide the design into a plastic sheet protector to scan and then print.

6. Imagine a tapestry design being developed from this approach, one in which you use many values of gray yarns and sparingly have black and white as emphasis.

Negative process to create values. Vine charcoal covered the page first. Next, a drawing was made into the overall gray by using an eraser. A few charcoal lines were added afterward to increase the value contrasts.

Several small rectangles outlined and filled with textures made by an assortment of tools: steel wool, paper towel, permanent marker, sponge, watercolor brush, and ebony pencil used in three ways

texture—a visual replication of something from nature, for instance. Can you make marks with the tools to simulate hair, the bark of a tree, or the roughness of a stone, for instance? To do this, try any of the mediums and tools. You might place the object at your workspace as reference or use a photograph with a detail of a textural surface as you try to replicate the effects you see.

4. Make a visual texture by doing rubbings of actual textural things. You can use the side of a crayon or a colored pencil for the medium, and sheets of white copy paper for the surface.

5. This is similar to the rubbing explorations earlier, when looking at the element of shape. This time the idea will be to see how the surface of the rubbing records the texture, rather than simply finding the overall outlines of the shapes.

6. Look around your house to discover anything you can place the paper on top of to make a rubbing. Even a cone of yarn might lend itself to having its side subjected to rubbing. Do you have a loom reed around? What texture would result

of a flat plane. Pulled warps, wedge weave, and eccentric weft all can cause the surface to shift, dip, or bulge, adding not only to the shape and form, but also to the actual texture of the tapestry.

Explore texture with paper and various methods and mediums. Possibly these will lead you to ideas that might be developed into small tapestry samplers in which texture of materials, process, or both become the focus. As you become more aware of the effects of texture, your options for using this element in interesting ways for tapestry increase.

1. Create a variety of textural effects on paper, using as many of the tools and supplies as you have on hand. Do this by drawing out a number of small rectangles on a white paper background, into which you apply the medium in several variations.

2. Notice the quality of textural effects made with each medium.

3. Next, within a few small rectangles marked out on a new white background sheet, try to create an effect of *simulated*

Textures made to simulate feather, hair, and tree bark

Textures created by making rubbings from objects in the studio, including a couple of baskets from rubbing over it? Baskets? Give it a try! As you begin, many things with a textured surface that can be used will come to mind.

7. Try watercolor pencils for the rubbings, as suggested in the shape explorations. Brush on water to change the effect of the texture as the colors become more fluid.

8. You might want to make a photocopy or scan of all the texture rubbings you've done, and print one or more copies that you can use for collage in which you combine the textures. You might also want to try textures used in combination with solid sheets of other papers.

9. As you look at the collection of textural explorations, can you imagine ways these could be interpreted in tapestry?

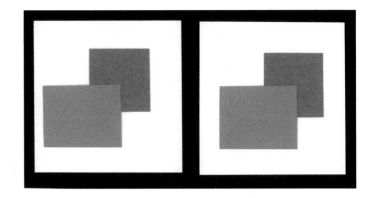

Space

The element of space may be thought of in two ways. In one, we identify space associated with three-dimensional objects, where we can see the areas around and, sometimes, into or through the forms. This emptiness or volume is the negative space associated with the positive form. Differently, on a flat, two-dimensional surface, one may experience space as the emptiness between shapes, as a shallow space created when shapes overlap, by movements set up with other elements to lead our eyes in directions, and by the use of methods such as linear perspective and atmospheric or aerial perspective.

Use any medium to try these explorations. You may also like to have on hand several landscape photographs that distinctly show three areas: foreground, middle ground, and background. A landscape that shows distance will be especially useful for this purpose. Additionally, collect photos of sidewalks, streets, or roadways taken with a viewpoint from the center or near the center of the pathway. Also find examples either online or in books of artworks from any era in which landscape is the dominant feature.

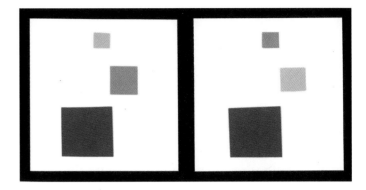

2. From cardstock, cut three or four smaller rectangles or squares of different sizes and enough to use the same sizes of shapes in each of the formats you've made.

3. First arrange the shapes without touching each other, although one or more may touch edges of the format, if you wish.

4. Next, arrange the same type of shapes within another matching format, but this time let one or more overlap each other.

5. Finally, put the largest of the shapes at the bottom, followed by the next in size placed slightly higher up, arranging one after the other until the smallest is near the top of the format.

EXPLORING SPACE WITH SHAPES

1. Outline two or three small rectangles or squares of the same size on an 8½" by 11" sheet of white cardstock. For instance, these could be 3" by 3" or 5" by 4" or 3" by 5" or any other size combination that will fit. These will be the formats into which you'll try the next steps. For rectangles, think about the way they are oriented—horizontally or vertically.

TOP Design space with a couple of shapes placed so they will overlap. In the left-side example, the shapes are placed slightly off-center. In the right-side example, the same overlapping arrangement of the two shapes are centered in the design space. Which seems more stable in the space?

BOTTOM Comparison of effect of size, placement, and value of shapes. *At the left,* the values of the shapes are similar to what we usually observe when we see objects in depth: dark values near and lightest values farthest away. *At the right,* the two upper shapes reverse values.

6. In each of these, you've shown an example of three ways that shapes may create space within a design space: first, by simply existing in the design area without any particular relationship to other shapes; second, in a shallow use of space where shapes may be seen in front of and behind others as they overlap; and third, when you've used the concept that shapes seem to become smaller when in more distant space.

7. You can enhance the sense of space by also incorporating color with these relationships. As you'll see in color explorations, the quality of color, whether light, dark, bright, or dull, can enhance visual effects in many ways, and one of those is how shapes seem closer or more distant. Look again at the example on page 98, where the largest shape is at the bottom and the smallest near the top, with a medium size between. If you change not only the size and placement but also the color, value, or intensity of the shapes, the effect of spatial distance can become more pronounced than if all the shapes are the same color, value, and intensity.

8. Try the same exploration, this time consciously changing the color, or value and intensity, of the shapes to give as much depth as possible with only a few simple means. Dark colors can appear to have visual weight; lighter value and also less intense colors can seem to be more distant.

EXPLORING SPACE WITH HORIZON LINES

Next, let's consider how the design space or format may be turned into a representation of the world simply by placing a horizontal line across the width of the design format. This idea was beautifully presented in Billy Collins's poem "Horizon," which began these explorations. Collins says that when we put a line *one-third* of the way up from the bottom of the page, the world of earth/sea and sky is there. Yes, that will indeed bring us a feeling of space in depth we are familiar with from our experience of the world. But what if you look at the horizon from different viewpoints?

- What if your view of the land fills more than one-third of the design area?
- What if your view of the sky and land is about equal?
- How about if the sky fills the space and is expansive, with the horizon being very low in the design area?

1. To explore these differences of horizon placement, draw outlines for several rectangles, making each of the same size and proportions. Next, draw a horizontal line across the width of each, at different levels. This line will now represent the horizon that we observe in the world when the sky and the land appear to meet in the distance. Notice the difference of effect with the horizon placement. As you do this, think about the orientation of the design format—are they in horizontal or vertical position? We often associate a horizontal direction with landscape—after all, on a document format on a printer, horizontal orientation is often called "landscape." However, we can also experience landscapes in vertical orientation. Think about the impact that dramatic cumulus clouds would have if the sky were dominant in a vertical composition.

2. Next use the rectangles containing your horizon lines, and from the bottom corner of each rectangle, draw a diagonal line to meet or nearly meet along the horizontal line. Can you now imagine that you're standing in the center of a roadway or sidewalk, looking toward the horizon? The illusion of space in depth is now pretty convincing—yet, all you have are three lines on a rectangle! By drawing the diagonals to meet or nearly meet at the horizon line, you've created a vanishing point.

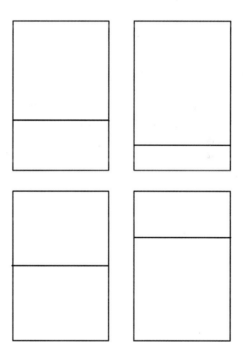

Four simple horizon line placements. The first one, *at the top left*, is drawn one-third of the way up from the bottom, as in the Billy Collins poem. Notice that all these formats are drawn in a vertical orientation. How would the effect change if the format were horizontal?

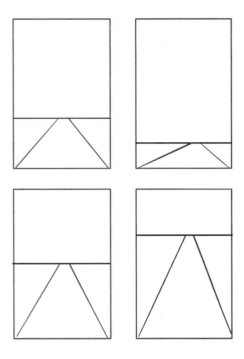

3. Next, refer to the photographs of sidewalks, paths, or roadways you've collected. Use a method for tracing the major movements seen within the photo (see next page). Take a look at the tracing to notice the way that lines drawn along edges of paths will move in diagonal directions, starting near or at the bottom of the page and ending where there is a stopping point, perhaps a direction change for the road or a building in the distance. If the photograph was made of a flat stretch of land with a road traveling away from the viewer in a straight line, you'll see that the angles of each side of the road will seem to come together to converge at the horizon in a vanishing point, much the same way the diagonals did in the simple exercise first mentioned. We rarely actually see this vanishing point unless we have a view of a flat expanse ahead of us all the way to the horizon.

Simple road or pathways sketched into the previous horizon line placements. Do you feel a different sense of space in depth with each example?

SEE HOW COLOR PLAYS A ROLE IN CREATING SPACE

For the next explorations of space, please refer again to your collection of photographs of landscape scenes. For the first exercise, select one that shows a distinct difference of color value and intensity in these three areas: foreground, middle ground, and background. For instance, a mountain landscape may give a good representation of these differences.

1. Draw a rectangle onto white cardstock that replicates the format of the photograph, either horizontal or vertical and in the same proportions (the same aspect ratio of height to width). See page 149 for a way to calculate aspect ratio for changing the size of the area.

2. First, locate the horizon line position within the photograph's format—is it low, middle of the page, or high? On your drawn rectangle, approximate the location of the horizon line by making a pencil line across.

3. Notice the difference of colors as the landforms move back toward the horizon. If you have a photograph with lots of grasses and foliage, you will probably notice that the foreground area colors are brighter and are located near the bottom edge of the picture. As you move up from the edge, you're seeing farther back into the space. You'll notice that the colors are less intense and details are less distinct. This area is generally called the middle ground. Higher still on the page, you find the background, and there the colors are usually lighter and the least intense. Interestingly, the sky's color (with exceptions of sunrise and sunset) will be similarly be lighter and less intense at the greatest distance, the horizon. As you look at the sky directly above you, notice how much more intense the blue happens to be.

4. Using either colored pencils or watercolor pencils in colors similar to what's seen in your reference, fill in the rectangle that you've divided into basic land areas and sky. Don't try to make details; simply fill the areas with colors. If you see bright greens or yellow-greens in the foreground, those will be at the bottom of the page—quickly scribble those in with the pencils or watercolor pencils. Do the same as you look at the different areas of the overall space. As mentioned, notice the quality of the color you see in the sky—would you use lighter strokes of the pencil near the horizon and bear down more heavily to make brighter blue as you near the top of the page?

5. Think about how this quick rendering of space in depth could turn into a tapestry. You might have a simple design in which horizontal bands of woven color could be reminiscent of landscape. See how Nancy Nordquist used a version of this effect in her tapestry *Loss*, shown on page 135.

EXPLORING SPACE THROUGH DIRECTIONAL MOVEMENTS

Another way to use a photograph as reference for study of spatial effects is by placing tracing paper or a transparency sheet over it and drawing the outlines of the basic movements as seen. These will record the edges of major masses of land and the directions those take. (If using a transparency sheet, use either a wet- or dry-erase marker so that the sheet can be used again later, if desired.) An alternative way to trace the major outlines seen in the image would be to use a graphics tablet and pen along with a photo editing app. The following suggestions offer other simple ways to study the effects of space in depth.

1. Locate the basic movements seen in your photograph, and trace the outline of those. Notice in your source image the color quality found in each area. You may want to duplicate these movements onto a sheet of white paper and use a color medium to indicate the changes of color intensity within the space, once again not making detailed drawings but instead suggesting the quality of the color (bright, dull; light, dark).

2. Find an artwork online or in a book to use in a similar way as described above. Trace the major movements the artist has used to create space in depth. Also notice how color changes may also be seen to indicate the spatial quality of an artist's version of landscape.

3. Use cut paper on a background sheet to suggest the concept of space in depth through converging lines. On the background, decide on a horizon line at any point you want, and draw a pencil line across from edge to edge of the paper to indicate it. Next, imagine you are standing in a road that starts directly in front of you. How would the angles of each edge of the road be shown?

   Cut paper shapes into the diagonals suggestive of the angles you would see from that position, and place those relating to the horizon line.

   Next, imagine that you are not standing in the center but are at one side of the road, so that you're "seeing" it from a different position. How, then, would the angles be shown differently?

Color

There are many ways in which you might examine the element of color by doing studies on paper, as well as by using yarn. Having colored papers in many hues, as well as tints and shades, will be handy. Scrapbook papers may be found in a wide range of colors at many hobby stores. An extensive assortment of hues in multiple tints, tones, and shades is available in the more expensive option, called Color-aid Paper. Collections of found papers in a variety of colors are also helpful. These can be from old magazines, posters, and mailing flyers.

Watercolor or acrylic paints, watercolor pencils, and regular colored pencils are useful. You'll want brushes of several sizes and containers for water. Other suggested tools and supplies are several transparency sheets, a permanent marker, a glue stick or double-stick tape, scissors, a metal edge ruler, and possibly a self-healing mat and utility knife.

A good way to begin explorations of the element of color is with a color wheel. A twelve-color wheel is one that's most familiar to use. You may want to make a version of your own, using any color medium you have. A template of a color wheel is included in appendix C, which you might want to copy onto cardstock to fill in with paint or paper. You might also want to adhere a copy of the template to a sturdy piece of cardboard to use for making a yarn color wheel.

EXPLORING THE COLOR WHEEL

Let's take a look at a few of the several color relationships that may be found on the color wheel. These systematic arrangements are often called color schemes or color chords.[27]

1. Make a color wheel with any medium. Select colors that are as close to what you judge to be "true" versions of primary (red, yellow, blue), secondary (orange, green, violet), and tertiary hues (yellow-orange, red-orange, red-violet, blue-violet, blue-green, yellow-green). Fill these in on the segments where they belong on the wheel. Yellow is often placed at the top, and the other two primary colors, blue and red, at equal distance points around the circle. Between each primary, put the appropriate secondary hue that the two adjacent primaries would create, if you were mixing those in paint: yellow + blue = green; yellow + red = orange; blue + red = violet. Then, between primary and secondary, the tertiary colors will be located: yellow + green = yellow-green; yellow + orange = yellow-orange; blue + green = blue-green; blue + violet = blue-violet; red + orange = red-orange; red + violet = red-violet.

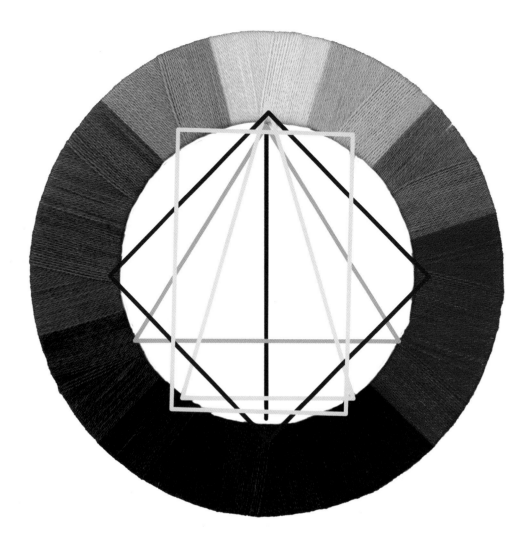

2. You can make five transparency sheets to use for overlays on the color wheel to point out several of the systematic arrangements or color chords, as described by Johannes Itten. These diagrams are shown overlaid on this color wheel. Templates for making your own diagrams are given in appendix C, page 181. Use a permanent marker to make the diagrams on separate overlays.

   a. On one transparent sheet, draw a straight line pointing from one primary to a secondary color exactly across from it; for instance, from yellow to violet. These are complementary or opposite colors. As you rotate this transparency, you'll see the line will point to complementary pairs all around the color wheel. Complements are seen to be vivid combinations when they're used together. Conversely, when mixed in mediums such as paint and dye, they will neutralize the vividness or intensity of each other.

   b. On a second transparency, draw an equilateral triangle with corners at yellow, red, and blue. This is a primary triad. When you rotate the transparency sheet one way or the other by one color, the triangle will point to a new group of three colors—tertiary hues. One more rotation will put the triangle pointing to the three secondary colors.

Color wheel with several color arrangements (called color "chords" by Johannes Itten).
Single line (complements); triads—equilateral triangle and isosceles triangle
(split-complement); two tetrads or four-color combinations (square and rectangle).

At the last rotation, you'll see the other three tertiary colors in the combination. This makes four combinations, of three colors each, possible with the equilateral triad.

c. For the third transparency, make another triangle. This one will be an isosceles triangle with the apex pointing to yellow, and the other two points located on either side of violet (the complement of yellow). This triangle shows another triad color arrangement that is a bit less intense in color effect than the first. This is often called a split-complement group of colors. Rotate the triangle around the color wheel to find other combinations of this triadic grouping. There will be twelve color combinations, of three colors each, to be found with this triad.

d. For the fourth transparency sheet, draw a square with the corners or vertices arranged at yellow, blue-green, violet, and red-orange. As you rotate the square around the color wheel, each time it will show a combination of four colors that include a primary and its complementary secondary, and two tertiary colors that are opposite or complements. As you turn the square in rotation, you will find three different combinations of four colors.

e. On the fifth transparency, draw a rectangle with the vertices pointing at yellow-green, yellow-orange, red-violet, and blue-violet. You see four tertiary colors combined with this grouping. Turn the rectangle to shift it over by one color in either direction, and you'll find a group of four that has two primaries and two secondaries included. Shift once more and find a new group of four made up of only tertiaries. As you turn the transparency around the wheel, this will continue to be the case—either all tertiary colors in the group, or two primaries and two secondaries. Notice that in all instances, each color is paired with its opposite or complement. There will be a total of six color combinations found by using the rectangular form for the tetrad.

3. When you look at the color combinations you can find by using the transparency diagrams on the color wheel, remember that they can be even more varied when not only the pure hues, but also tints, tones, and shades of the colors, are used. After all, any one of these color combinations can be used not only in the pure hues but also with tints, tones, and shades of some or all of the colors. It's amazing just how quickly the complexity and richness of color effect can be increased! You might consider making variations of the color wheel in which you use tints, tones, or shades (or a combination of these) to add to your pure-hue one.

EXPLORE
COLOR ARRANGEMENTS

1. Try out several of the color arrangements as described in the previous section by making small nonobjective designs either with cut or torn paper collage or by using paint, colored pencils, or markers.

2. Yarn wrappings of selected color arrangements are also great ways to explore these color ideas. An alternative to making wrappings with an assortment of colors on one strip would be to use the small cardboard holders available for embroidery floss. Fill several of those with as many colors as you have available. Group the yarns into color wheel arrangements and select from those for the color groupings.

3. Look back at the color wheel to see the hues that are near each other, usually three or four, in which there is some common shared hue. For instance, with red, red-orange, and orange, you have similarity because all have red as a component. You would also see a similarity found with red-violet, red, and red-orange. Here again, red is the common color among those. As you move around the color wheel, you'll find more of these groupings of related colors; these are called *analogous colors*.

a. Make several small designs in which analogous color schemes are used. You might want to try the same three or four colors, but in different values or intensities for each.

b. Look for examples of analogous colors in nature. You'll find many examples in flowers or in fall leaves, for instance. Select a photograph to work from that has a strong example of analogous colors, and design a small nonobjective composition, matching the color as closely as possible with your available medium. Try to also match the amount or the ratio of each of the colors observed.

4. Monochromatic color schemes are those that are made up of one color and many variations of the hue. Different values of tints and shades can be used, as well as variation of tone made by changing the intensity or brightness/dullness of the color.

a. Make a small nonobjective design with a monochromatic color scheme, using any available medium.

b. You might want to design a small tapestry that is based on this design. Perhaps you'll want to use not only a variety of the tints, shades, and tones of the hue, but also different textures of yarn.

5. Color can be used subjectively on the basis of feelings or preferences. Try some of the color ideas from above, but use a particular color as a starting point for exploration. For instance, start with a favorite color you may have.

   a. From among the available colors of papers or from the other art mediums, select a color you like. Notice the quality of the color—is it bright and intense, or light and pastel? Or is it dark? Dull? Earthy? Try to describe the color in words, perhaps relating it to other senses—how would the color feel, sound, or smell, for instance?

   b. Locate where the hue would be found on the color wheel—if it is a pure color, that will be easy. For a mixed or a muted tone, you may have to look carefully to identify its location on the color wheel. For instance, a brownish earthy color might actually be a red-orange or orange in hue that has a dark or neutral effect.

   c. Once you've decided the color location on the color wheel, find other colors that will work with it in any of the systematic arrangements explored in the transparency exercise above. Make a small nonobjective design in which the original favorite color is used in combination with other colors from a chosen color scheme.

   d. The amount of each color may also be changed for different visual effects. For instance, use more of the initial color in the design, making it the dominant color, with the other colors playing subordinate roles.

   e. Flip the dominant/subordinate roles, with the initial color being used only in a few places as an accent color.

   f. NOW, think about this: What if you selected your absolute least favorite color to use in a small amount in this composition? You might be surprised at the results. It could very well be just what the design needs to give it more interest.

6. Make a color arrangement based on something from nature. Select a photograph that shows colors that interest you. Don't think too much about what color scheme is there—just respond to the colors.

   a. Determine the quality of the colors. Do you see very intense color as well as duller or darker colors?

   b. Decide on the amount or ratio of the colors that you see. Are there more greens and small amounts of reds and pinks in a photograph of flowers, for instance? With paint, colored pencils, or paper collage, create a small nonobjective design based on the colors from the photograph. Place the colors in approximately the same location in the design as you see them in the original source, and use the same ratio or amount of the colors.

   c. Design a small tapestry that is based on the colors found in the design source. Rather than making a realistic representation, create an abstracted design in which the colors are featured.

7. Use an online color palette selector with the same photo to see the color choices that will be created.[28]

   a. How does the color selection differ, if at all, from those you originally chose when looking at the photo?

   b. Use cut or torn paper to make a small composition based on the computer-generated palette.

   c. You might design a small tapestry based on this image. Look again at the color explorations by the author, shown on page 51, to see a few ways that color studies can be interpreted in tapestry.

EXPERIMENT WITH THE PRINCIPLES

One of the goals for designing is to bring the elements together through the use of various principles to give the impact you want for the tapestry. As you begin designing, it soon becomes evident that the elements and principles can be combined in countless ways. Often one or two of the elements play the most important role in a composition, and selecting which to emphasize will be one aspect of the design process. Color may be dominant, for instance, or texture may come to the forefront. It's possible that the intent for the image will help clarify your decisions about which elements to emphasize.

Now is a good time to take a look back at the tapestries shown in Part One. With your deeper understanding of the effect the elements play on the overall design space or composition, consider the many ways in which the artists made use of those in subtle or bold ways to create impact for their tapestries. Consider how they were able to merge the elements into such principles as balance, emphasis, repetition and rhythm, proportion, and variety to successfully tie together their compositions.

In whatever ways you choose to plan your own designs, the elements and principles will always be there, working together as the composition is created. Keep in mind that there is no "right" way to do this. No secret formula. At times, that may be frustrating and daunting.

Sometimes, jumping in and trying many things is the best way to start a search for ways to interpret an idea. At other times the expression you want to make with the composition gives the initial ideas and leads the way into the final design.

View the designing stages as necessary and valuable steps toward planning the tapestry and beginning to weave. The time you spend with these initial efforts is not time wasted. It is a central part of developing the design into one you feel strongly about and will be willing and happy to spend hours weaving.

Let's consider a few ideas about the principles of balance, emphasis, rhythm and repetition, proportion, and variety, using some of the mediums and methods as used in the element explorations. Photographs or artwork references will be helpful for a few of these. You may also want to think about specific ways that these ideas can be interpreted into tapestry, and go about weaving a few samples.

Balance

Balance is an important principle of design. It can be obvious in some instances. In others, it may be subtle. We may not immediately notice how the balance is achieved, but if it isn't there, we spot it right off. In two-dimensional works the effects of balance are caused by how elements and other principles are used. In three-dimensional pieces, balance is often necessary to keep the forms in place. For these explorations, let's look at ways that you can set up a balanced visual effect in two-dimensional space.

SYMMETRICAL OR FORMAL BALANCE

This type of balance is seen when shapes and movements relate equally from side to side or top to bottom, or radiating around the center.

1. A simple cut-paper exercise can show perfect symmetry if you fold a sheet in half and cut at the edge opposite the fold. Open the page up and see the balance of the two sides. You can elaborate on this by cutting openings within the shape while it's folded. This is very much like making snowflakes by folding paper into quarters and making cuts, something that many of us did as children.
2. In artworks, often a perfect symmetry is modified somewhat to make the design more dynamic. Consider how you could arrange shapes within a space so that they are almost symmetrical but show some variety.
3. Find a photograph of something in nature that shows symmetrical balance. See if shapes are truly balanced on each side or all the way around in a radial way. Or is there something that gives a bit of difference? Good examples to look for are found in flowers and leaves.
4. Next, find examples in nature of almost or approximate symmetrical balance. Look at trees, for instance. Notice the arrangement of limbs extending outward. On some trees, the placement is closer to a sense of symmetry than others.

5. Either online or in books or magazines, find examples of symmetrical or nearly symmetrical balance in artworks. Online collections from major museums are a good source for this.[29]

6. Place a transparency sheet on top of the selected image and use a wet- or dry-erase marker to draw the major outlines of the shapes. Does the work show exact symmetry or, instead, is there some bit of variation so that you might call it almost symmetrical? If you want to save the image, make a scan or a digital photograph of it before cleaning off the marker lines from the transparency sheet.

Emphasis

This is one of the aspects of a design we will see right away. Something in the composition will draw our attention, and our view will go there. When used well, emphasis can lead the viewer to important areas of the composition. On the other hand, unintended emphasis will be a factor in causing a design to be less successful.

We often use the term "focal point" when discussing the main area(s) of emphasis. To help us with our exploration of the impact of emphasis, let's begin by looking at the work of others.

1. Assemble several photographs. In each one, decide if the photographer has shown a clear area of emphasis. Can you describe how the focal point(s) were set up in the photographs? Does it seem that the photographer has used the rule of thirds mentioned on page 76 when composing the image?

2. Find images of artwork either online or in books. Select examples both of realistic and nonobjective artworks, and in those, consider the various ways the artists have created emphasis. Choose one of the photographs or artworks to overlay with a sheet of transparency film. Use wet- or dry-erase marker to draw the major outlines of the larger shapes you see. Notice the placement of the emphasis areas as you do this. Have directional movements or placement of shapes (or both) caused the focal points you see? Or has the emphasis been made in other ways—and, if so, how do you think this has been accomplished?

3. Emphasis can be created by difference or contrast as well as by direction. Look for examples in the photographs or artworks where this is the case. Describe for yourself if the effects are made by color or value contrast. Are sizes or

texture contrasts causing emphasis? You might like to have a notebook or journal in which you make small thumbnail sketches of compositions that particularly appeal to you. Maybe make written notes about how the effects are created in the examples you've selected.

4. You might try a cut-and-torn-paper collage to design a composition in which emphasis has been created by one of the methods you've seen in the photographs or artworks of others. With the collage, simplify the shapes to make bold visual effects. To do this, possibly use extreme value, color intensity, or textural contrasts in emphasis area(s), or make large shapes that will move the eye around in angular or flowing kinds of ways.

5. You may wish to plan a small tapestry based on the collage. In what ways can you adapt from the source to interpret into woven form? For instance, does the collage have torn edges, and could those be suggested by a woven method such as pick and pick, or by using eccentric weft?

Emphasis might also show no clear focal point(s). In fact, if the composition is made up of elements that are equally or almost equally distributed, you usually see an overall pattern. Patterning is found in many weave structures and in printed textiles. This takes us now to an exploration of the overall distribution of images or motifs and how these may set up repetition and rhythm with the elements.

Rhythm and Repetition

Repetition is easy to understand. Repetition is easy to understand. Repetition is easy to understand. You get the point! We find repetition in the patterning of textiles, in the brick courses of buildings, in books stacked on shelves, in cans and boxes of groceries in stores, and on our loom in the warp threads we weave into. With the idea of repetition there can also be variety, because in visual work, some difference set up within repetition helps keep the design lively. As variety begins to enter the repetition, different kinds of rhythms are set up.

Visual rhythms somewhat relate to acoustical rhythm. Think about the rhythm set up with the beat of a drum and how the percussion can be varied in speed and loudness. Also consider the flowing rhythm of a waltz. How would each of those types of auditory rhythms be interpreted in visual ways? The term "motif" can be used to describe a visual component that repeats. Let's explore how repetitive motifs can set up different kinds of rhythms.

1. Use a piece of cardstock for background. Choose a simple shape (square, triangle, or rectangle) and cut out a number of the shapes from another color of paper. Make these shapes all of the same size, and place them in a repetitive pattern to fill the background sheet: square, square, square, square, etc. First, space them equally apart and take a digital photo to record the arrangement. Alternatively, temporarily tack them down with a bit of repositionable adhesive[30] and scan or photocopy them.

2. Use the same group of shapes on the background, this time changing the placement somewhat. Keep them in alignment along rows or columns but vary the spacing. That might look like this: square, square, (space), square, (space), (space), square. Again, record the effect with a photo or by otherwise copying the page.

3. For the third exploration of the idea, this time add a second type of shape among the first, possibly using the second type only in a few places. For instance, square, square, square, triangle, square, triangle, etc. Once more, record the effect.

4. Next, cut equal amounts of the second type of shape and place in an alternation with the original type of shape: square, triangle, square, triangle, etc. The rhythm is similar to the first one you created, but has the shape variation with the alternation. What if one or two of these shapes were different colors among the sameness of repetition? Do these now become areas of emphasis or focal points within the overall pattern?

5. Another way to explore repetitive patterning is by making a simple relief print motif from either a potato or a firm school supply eraser[31] to use as if it were a rubber stamp. Several folded sheets of paper towel in a foam picnic plate can be used as a temporary printing pad. For the printing medium, saturate the towel layer with acrylic paint thinned to the consistency of cream.

6. If you're using a potato as the relief stamp, cut it in half with a knife and then carve into the cut side to open up spaces and leave flat raised areas. The raised parts will pick up the paint for the printing. Remember, with a relief printing the image will show in reverse. Blot the potato with a dry paper towel after you make the cuts and before dipping it into the paint, to absorb some of the moisture. This will make a clearer print. You might want to redip in the printing pad each time so the motif print stays the same consistence, for the most part. Or you might want to try stamping with it a few times until it totally runs out of paint. That would also give variation within the similarity.

7. As an alternative printing material, use a firm school supply eraser (not a soft, kneaded type). This will cut easily with an X-Acto knife and can be reused many times over.

8. Use either of the printing tools you've made to stamp the motif on the background, first using a regular repetition without variation.

9. On another sheet, stamp the design in a random pattern when the motif possibly overlaps in some spots.

10. The pattern may be varied by using different stamps in alternation and also by changing the colors as the repeats are done.

11. Finally, create a flowing rhythm by making a repeating series of lines on a background page, using any of the mediums and tools. An interesting version could be made by using different sizes of brushes and a fluid medium such as ink or thinned acrylic paint as you make the repeating lines. Let the lines curve and undulate from one edge of the paper in somewhat parallel arrangements. Some variation between the spacing of the lines will happen naturally.

Repetition and rhythm may be used in many ways with tapestry. After all, the process of weaving itself is an almost endless series of repetitive movements of weft interweaving with warp! Consider the following as possible starting points for ideas to try.

1. Patterns of horizontal lines of varying width can be done from edge to edge by making different numbers of passes. Horizontal linear patterns might also be done in selected areas. For instance, consider weaving a group of squares or rectangles, with some of them having solid colors and others being filled with thin lines.

2. Repeating vertical lines can be made by using pick and pick. Pick and pick woven in such a way as to make aligned or alternating dots also is an interesting use of repetition done in a weaverly way. Shapes within the tapestry can be given repetitive patterning through either of those methods.

3. Flowing rhythms can be set up in linear ways with the use of contrasting colors to give outlines of shapes through eccentric weave, soumak, or twining.

4. Backgrounds in tapestries can be broken into repeating patterns of squares, rectangles, triangles, and diamonds. These not only add subtle repetition and rhythm but also have a technical advantage of breaking up large background areas into smaller weft bundles, lessening the likelihood of drawing in of edges.

Proportion

The shape of the design format and the relationship of things within it all play roles in the principle of proportion. Like balance, this principle is one that we often sense when it is "off." Even so, there are ways to plan proportion so that we don't have to depend on hit-and-miss methods when designing.

The first consideration is the scale and proportion of the overall design space or format. It may be rectangular or square or even irregular in shape. We also take into account the relationships among shapes within the design. Is it important to the idea that the proportions are "correct" to successfully represent the subject you'll weave? Or will an exaggeration of proportion be what's needed to enhance the expression of a feeling or concept?

WORKING WITH A VARIETY OF FORMATS

Let's start by looking at format and the impact that proportion can have on a design.

1. A way to quickly measure and mark out formats is to use grid paper. Paper with ¼" grid is usually easy to find, and a template for a ¼" scale grid is included in appendix C. You might also like to make grid sheets of different widths and color of lines by using an online grid maker like those found at Kevin MacLeod's website, Incompetech.[32] Use a black marker on two or three sheets of grid paper to draw several squares and also several rectangles of various sizes and proportions.
2. Make at least one rectangle that conforms to golden-ratio proportions of 1 to 1.618 in size. For instance, a rectangle that is 4" by approximately 6½" in dimension would be of that proportion.
3. Draw several of the rectangles based on combinations of Fibonacci numbers. Remember from the discussion of Fibonacci numbers on page 76 that the numbers are derived by adding each in the sequence to the preceding number, beginning with 1; thus the sequence begins 1 + 1 = 2, 1 + 2 = 3, 2 + 3 = 5, and so on. The size of the unit chosen to represent term 1 can be anything you wish. For instance, you want the unit to represent 1"; selecting the Fibonacci numbers of 3 and 5 would give you a 3" by 5" rectangle. If other choices were made by keeping the numbers in sequence, you could have 5" by 8" or 8" by 13", etc., as the dimensions. You could also take the numbers out of sequence, perhaps using 5 by 13, 3 by 8, or 5 by 21.

4. Next, use a few simple cutout shapes of squares or rectangles, each of the same size, placing them within each of the formats. How does the overall shape and proportion of the design space affect the shapes within it?

WORKING WITH SCALE AND PROPORTION

Next, experiment with scale and proportion by finding images in photographs that are of similar things (people, animals, or plants, for instance) and are of different sizes.

1. Cut out several of these and combine into a composite photo or photomontage made up of images in size relationships that are out of scale to our usual way of seeing them. For instance, maybe a person is as tall as a skyscraper or a grasshopper is as large as a dog.
2. If you feel comfortable with image-editing software, an alternative would be to select, size, and reposition images digitally into a composite design.
3. How does the change of scale of the familiar objects affect the overall idea of the composition?

Variety

Variety gives liveliness to a composition. Yet, too much can cause confusion. As with most things, moderation of effect is often best. In tapestry you might find that using a weft bundle of two or three strands of the same hue in slight variations will add visual complexity to the color within the composition. At other times, it may be that different sizes of shapes used within the design will give the desired variety. For instance, if the image contains the shapes of leaves, showing several sizes of those not only will give more variety to the design but will echo what nature creates. Tapestry has an advantage over many other art media in being able to use several types of yarns within a design to accentuate variety by size and texture differences.

To explore this principle, you might want to try these ideas with small tapestry samples.

1. Set up a warp for a sett of around eight to twelve ends per inch.
2. Seek out a variety of textures of yarn and weave simple shapes of squares or rectangles, placing different surface textures side by side. For instance, maybe use wool next to mercerized cotton in a few of the shapes. Or try linen next to silk. What about weaving a bouclé yarn beside unmercerized cotton? See if you can explore as many types of yarn as possible.

3. With setts of eight or twelve ends per inch, you can group warps two by two, either across the width or in selected places to give variations of density of the woven surface. If you double up the warps at eight ends per inch, you'll have a sett of 4 epi. With 12 epi, doubling up would give six warps per inch. A light color of weft will best show the surface difference when the setts are doubled. For the double sett, also try increasing the size of the weft in areas and also use it singly in places. See how much variety of surface texture you can make by simply changing the sett and using the same color of weft yarn. Light values will show the effect most dramatically since the texture or bead of the weave will be more clearly evident. You might want to look once again at Lyn Hart's *indigo monsoon* tapestry on page 38 to see how she's used difference of sett to create a visual impact.

4. Vary the sett by using different warp sizes within in the same warp on the loom. Perhaps combine 12/6 cotton seine twine set at 10 or 12 epi with 12/12 set at 8 epi; you might make the sett change across the width even more dramatic by closer spacing, larger warps, or both. This difference of sett will make beating the weft into place more challenging but will give variety of the surface in interesting ways. As before, these surface variations will be most evident with lighter colors of weft because of the way that light will interact with the yarns.

These explorations can be expanded in many ways, and, as you work your way through them, other ideas will occur to you. Sometimes you may want to do woven samples, and other times you might want to move ahead with planning a tapestry using some of these ideas. In my work, over the years I frequently make small tapestry samples, especially whenever I've been planning for a workshop. At this point, however, it seems that I'm doing more idea explorations on paper before turning to the actual tapestry. Many pages are filled with images and journal notes until I finally arrive at the point of feeling comfortable with a design idea.

The bottom line is that you find the best way *for you* to move ahead as you grow both in tapestry weaving and designing abilities. As my friend and mentor Edwina Bringle told me many years ago: "Take what you can use and throw the rest away!"

A TAPESTRY STUDY GROUP'S DISCOVERIES

In early 2019 I visited a meeting of the Atlanta-area (Georgia) tapestry study group to ask if they'd be willing to carry out sample weavings to explore design. Several individuals said they'd like to take part in the proposed activity and took off in different directions over the next six months to try ways that line, shape, texture, color, and value could be interpreted in "weaverly" ways in tapestry techniques. We met in person a couple of times at my studio, had email exchanges, and used a private blog I set up so they could show progress, ask questions, and share resource information of interest. Although I'd served as a mentor in the American Tapestry Alliance distance-learning program in the past, this experience with the tapestry study group was a venture into a method of semidistance teaching that I hadn't tried before. I'm grateful to each of the participants for their diligence to their own studies and for their patience, and generosity to me and to each other as we all navigated our way through an unfamiliar method of sharing.

These were among the suggestions I gave to the study group members:

What will you want to do in your study? This is up to you, but my suggestion would be to pick an element or principle and decide how you'd like to explore it. You have the copy of my handout "Design Concepts—Tapestry Thoughts," and it mentions several ways the elements and principles may be interpreted through tapestry.

For instance, if you chose line, you might want to try different ways that line could be created in tapestry. Color investigations could go in other directions.

You might find it helpful to document your studies in some way for future reference. In fact, anything that comes to mind about your results could be useful information to keep on hand!

Here are the results of the woven explorations by Terri Bryson, Mary Alice Donceel, Nancy Dugger, Deb Gottlieb, Mary Jane Lea, Dinah Rose, and Sarah Thomsen, along with selected comments from each person's notes about their approaches and results. In addition to the woven samples, several of the group, including Izumi Hubbard, tried out several of the paper exercises.

Terri Bryson decided to work with small samples to explore the subtle changes that come about when color differences are used with a few simple shapes and lines. The finished sizes for the samples were approximately 5" by 4¾", woven on a small frame loom by using a cotton warp and wool weft. She used primary colors in the first one. She worked without a predetermined plan other than the chosen colors, saying, "The woven image popped into my head just before weaving."

Terri wove two more samples in which she used secondary colors in a similar design configuration, but with the colors arranged differently in each.

She continued her color explorations by weaving a long, narrow strip, using hatching and hachure to see varieties of color interactions. At the top of the warp she explored texture in several ways, using neutral colors.

TOP LEFT Terri Bryson. Tapestry study group participant. Exploration to see how primary colors interacted in a small sample. *Courtesy of Terri Bryson; Kenneth J. Bryson, photographer*

CENTER Terri Bryson. Tapestry study group participant. Exploration of secondary colors in similar design arrangements as with primary hues. *Courtesy of Terri Bryson; Kenneth J. Bryson, photographer*

CENTER BOTTOM Terri Bryson. Tapestry study group participant. Another version of combining secondary colors in a simple arrangement of shapes and lines. *Courtesy of Terri Bryson; Kenneth J. Bryson, photographer*

RIGHT Terri Bryson. Tapestry study group participant. In this sample, Terri explored various color interactions, using hatching and hachure. In the upper portion she tried several methods of creating texture, including soumak and different weights of wefts. *Courtesy of Terri Bryson; Kenneth J. Bryson, photographer*

Mary Alice Donceel explored potential of line in tapestry methods for two samplers. "My first sample looks at the woven horizontal line, and what can be done to smooth it out, with variations on line thickness." It was woven at 8 epi with four strands of Fårö yarn in weft bundles. Her other sample for line explored various ways to create vertical lines, including leaving the slit between vertical shapes so that the shadow created line, vertical soumak, vertical twining, and wrapping up one warp while stitching to adjacent edge.

Mary Alice also explored color in several samples, all woven with five strands of 8/2 cotton with a warp sett of 6 epi. For one, she did a gradation between the two colors, changing out one strand at a time from the weft bundles: 5:0, 4:1, 3:2, 2:3, 1:4, and 0:5 of colors A:B. In this example, there was simply a change of the color from top to bottom, with no individual shapes within the overall design area. In another, she also worked with color gradation but with a different design effect: the two colors used for the gradation (yellow and orange) were used at the left, with a separating band of black between them in the lower area. A small column of black was placed between the left side, and the gradation blends of weft on the right of the tapestry. In her more extensive study of color transition effects, she first dyed a color series from yellow to cyan, with 20% increments of mixture. The resulting yarns were woven as small shapes up a vertical column, seen on the right in her sample. The next two columns were woven with wefts holding five strands in each bundle, "changing out one more strand each time, so getting a 20% change there also." In the second of the blended columns, she also used hatching as the new color was added to the bundle. On the left side she used a progression of passes to see the gradation of color.

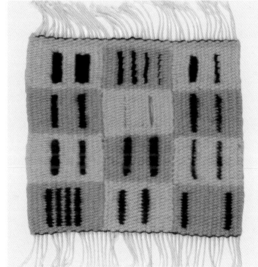

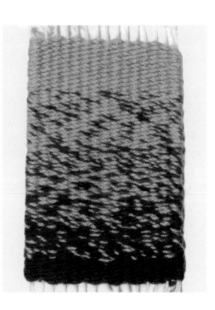

M. Donceel. Tapestry study group participant. Several ways of weaving horizontal lines of different thicknesses, attempting to create as smooth an edge as possible, were explored. *Courtesy of M. Donceel; Kenneth J. Bryson, photographer*

M. Donceel. Tapestry study group participant. Several vertical line-making options were explored. *Courtesy of M. Donceel; Kenneth J. Bryson, photographer*

M. Donceel. Tapestry study group participant. Color transition by weft blending, moving from a red-violet to yellow-green in several steps. *Courtesy of M. Donceel; Kenneth J. Bryson, photographer*

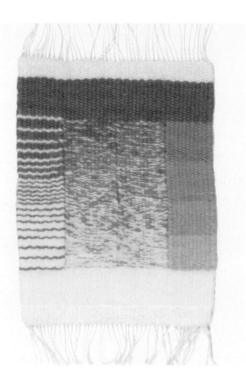

Nancy Dugger teaches tapestry weaving and for her studies she explored several techniques not only for her own work but also for possible use in future classes.

First, she explored texture and used many of the techniques she was introduced to during Maximo Laura's workshop held at an American Tapestry Alliance retreat in 2018. To those methods she added several other techniques found in Peter Collingwood's book *The Techniques of Rug Weaving*. She described her methodical exploration:

To begin, I decided to do the same techniques on three different setts, using a variety of weft yarns to compare textures. I kept notes for each technique and the weft yarns used, knowing I would not remember what I did a week later.

Sample 1 is set at 6 epi, using 12/12 seine twine for warp with four strands of most yarns for the weft. The weaving is bulky. It was very difficult to control the selvedges, and the warp is well covered. Some effects are practical at this sett, but others don't seem to have a practical application (like the uppermost blocks). The exercise was informative, allowing me to have a good reference for future work.

Sample 2 is set at 8 epi, using 12/9 seine twine for warp. When I began the second sample, I thought it would make a better comparison to use the same yarns and colors. Weaving soon proved difficult, and I quickly reduced the number of threads in the weft bundle to make the weft cover the warp. It worked well in some techniques and not so well in others.

There was not a whole lot of difference in appearance between sample 1 and sample 2. The selvedges were still difficult to control, and there are lice (areas where the warp shows) in some techniques. The weft did not cover as completely. Some techniques are neater or more controlled in their appearance. I was expecting a greater difference.

Nancy continued to explore, taking on a design to be used with varied warp setts and with different wefts. She selected 12/9 cotton seine twine to be set at 6 epi and 8 epi and woven with single-ply carpet wool for two of the samples. Next she set up a warp at 10 epi with 12/6 seine twine and used the weft as in the previous samples, the single-ply carpet wool. Another warp of the same sett was woven with two-ply wool. She says: "The major difference is the stairstep curves at the lower setts. The carpet wool . . . appears to have smoother curves than the two-ply wool weft at the same sett."

She observed that the one woven with single-ply carpet wool yielded a smoother surface. Since she's used this particular yarn quite a lot, she thinks her experience working with it contributed to that. Nancy said: "Altogether, these exercises were very informative, and I will have the samples to refer to when I need to figure out solutions or solve problems, and to draw inspiration from."

LEFT Nancy Dugger. Tapestry study group participant. Texture sample 1, to explore techniques. Warp of 12/12 cotton seine twine, sett for this sample of 6 epi, with four strands of yarn used as weft. *Courtesy of Nancy J. Dugger; Kenneth J. Bryson, photographer*

RIGHT Nancy Dugger. Tapestry study group participant. Texture sample 2, to explore techniques. Warp of 12/9 cotton seine twine, sett at 8 epi. Fewer strands of yarn were combined for this closer sett than in sample 1. *Courtesy of Nancy J. Dugger; Kenneth J. Bryson, photographer.*

LEFT Nancy Dugger. Tapestry study group participant. Sample A: warp was 12/9 cotton seine twine, sett at 6 epi. Weft: single-ply carpet wool. One of a series of four samples with the same design woven with different size of warp and sett. *Courtesy of Nancy J. Dugger; Kenneth J. Bryson, photographer*

RIGHT Nancy Dugger. Tapestry study group participant. Sample B: warp was 12/9 cotton seine twine, sett at 8 epi. Weft: single-ply carpet wool. *Courtesy of Nancy J. Dugger; Kenneth J. Bryson, photographer*

Deb Gottlieb used 8 epi of 12/9 cotton seine twine with a variety of wool and cotton wefts for her sample. Her intention was to study shape and create a feeling of roundness of a form by the way the values were used to show shadow and light reflection. In addition to the study of shape, she also used soumak to help round the curves of the upper and lower edges of the cylinder.

Deb described her exploration as follows:

I chose shapes and started with taking a photo of a can of baby peas without the label, and with a light shining on it for reflection. After starting and stopping multiple times, I decided I didn't have all the colors and experience to properly show the reflection and the lines on the side of the can. I changed the design to a simple clip art cylinder with a reflection and chose different colors of purple. The hatching on the front of the cylinder with the dark purple, light purple, and reflection was to create a curved effect.

The most difficult part was the reflection, and to do it over I would make it much simpler and narrower and eliminate the off-white. I changed the black border of the sides and top of the cylinder to 8/2 cotton from Harrisville Highland single strand on the bottom because the 8/2 cotton gave a smoother finish. I was pleased with the curves at the very top, top side, and bottom. To enhance this, a light shadow could have been added.

Deb Gottlieb. Tapestry study group participant. Warp was 12/9 cotton seine twine, sett at 8 epi. Various yarns for weft, including wool and cotton. *Courtesy of Deb Gottlieb; Kenneth J. Bryson, photographer*

Mary Jane Lea wove a sample in which she explored several ways that line may be made through weaverly means, including hatching, horizontal bands of varying widths, using Fibonacci series as choices for the number of passes to use, and pick and pick. In the same sample she included a section of diagonals woven as a small band of different values. She used various values of green for the sample.

Mary Jane also worked with a sketch she had made of sea, shore, and grasses to explore various ways that line and texture could be suggestive of place. See her sketch and tapestry on the loom on page 9. She found this quote attributed to Pablo Picasso to be a meaningful one for her explorations: "I begin with an idea and then it becomes something else."

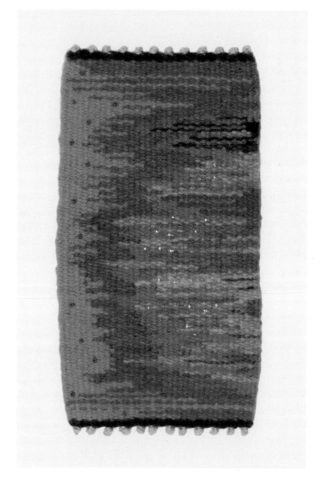

Mary Jane Lea. Tapestry study group participant. Value study in green. Warp was 12/6 cotton seine twine, sett at 12 epi. Weft was two-ply crewel wool, used one strand. *Courtesy of Mary Jane Lea; Kenneth J. Bryson, photographer*

Mary Jane Lea. Tapestry study group participant. *The Water Is Wide*, 2019. Tapestry: 8" × 4.5". The initial image and idea came first. Next were value explorations, and finally this tapestry was woven. *Courtesy of Mary Jane Lea; Kenneth J. Bryson, photographer*

Dinah Rose explored color extensively in her samplers. Her warp was 12/6 cotton seine twine sett at 8 epi. Dinah used many hues of two different small wool yarns to get as close to color wheel versions as possible. In one sample she began by using hatching and hachure to combine primary and secondary complementary colors.

Next, she used several of the color harmony combinations from Johannes Itten, which he calls "color chords." She listed those in the order they were woven in small bands across the width, with each color interconnected with the previous with a small area of hatching:

(1) complementary colors using primary and secondary
(2) four three-color chords from color wheel
(3) three four-color chords from color wheel
(4) twelve five-color chords from color wheel
(6) two six-color chords from color wheel

In another color sampler, Dinah explored split complements in light, medium, and dark values. At the left side of the sampler, she showed the three values of the color used for the right side. A small band of black separated each group of different hues.

At the right side, and making up the major area of the sampler, Dinah used wedge weave technique. The three values of the adjacent hue were used in the diagonal bands of wedge weave along with three values of the split complements of the hue. She separated the wedge weave sections with a small band of white and black. This turned out to be a visually complex exploration, giving Dinah lots of information about the ways in which colors interact. She said, "I found I liked some combinations better than others."

LEFT Dinah Rose. Tapestry study group participant. Exploration of harmonious color chords. Warp: 12/6 cotton seine twine, sett at 8 epi. Weft: four strands of crewel wool. *Bottom to top*: complementary, four three-color chords, three four-color chords, twelve five-color chords, two six-color chords. *Courtesy of Dinah Rose; Kenneth J. Bryson, photographer*

RIGHT Dinah Rose. Tapestry study group participant. Exploration of split complements, using three values of each. Warp: 12/6 cotton seine twine, sett 8 epi. Weft: two-ply crewel and another small wool. Weft colors she used are shown in small strip (*at left*); *at right*, the split-complementary colors used are wedge weave technique. *Courtesy of Dinah Rose; Kenneth J. Bryson, photographer*

Sarah Thomsen decided to first explore lines. She used two different setts of 12/6 cotton seine twine (12 epi and 8 epi), with both placed side by side on the same loom. She worked on each one simultaneously, using warm and cool colors of weft (yellow-orange and dark blue for one, and orange and violet for the other). After weaving a small area of the darker weft at the bottom of each one, she noted using the following sequence of color change:
(1) one pick on each one
(2) seven passes on each one in the dark color
(3) one pass on each one in the orange
(4) six passes on each one in the dark color
(5) two passes on each in the orange
(6) five passes on each in the dark
(7) three passes on each with orange . . . and so on

Sarah also worked with several explorations of diagonals at the top of both the warps as separate samples. She also tried a shape with a few curving edges at the top of one.

LEFT Sarah Thomsen. Tapestry study group participant. Exploration of lines through different number of passes, and pick and pick. Diagonals of different slopes ended this sample.
Warp: 12/6 cotton seine twine, sett 12 epi. Weft: one strand, Appleton tapestry wool. *Courtesy of Sarah Thomsen; Kenneth J. Bryson, photographer*

RIGHT Sarah Thomsen. Tapestry study group participant. Exploration of lines through different number of passes, and pick and pick. Diagonals of different slopes and curving shapes ended the sample. Warp: 12/6 cotton seine twine, sett 8 epi. Weft: one strand, Harrisville Highlands wool. *Courtesy of Sarah Thomsen; Kenneth J. Bryson, photographer*

Endings Are Only Beginnings

Fear. Fear of creating an initial design. Fear of translating a design from any medium into tapestry. Fear of taking a tapestry off the loom and executing finishing techniques. Fear is paralyzing. . . . Friends and weaving groups can help you over the hump. . . . Overcoming Fear is the most important lesson I learned from the journey of unraveling tapestry, be it fear of design or execution. . . . So instead of Fear, I must get to work. Who knows what I might discover? Maybe I will find I have the makings of a tapestry weaver after all.

—Mary Jane Lea, August 2019

Part Three

Discover Your Ideas and Expand Them

IDEAS—WHERE DO THEY COME FROM? | IDEA STARTERS—SETTING THE STAGE | DESIGN APPROACHES—A FEW EXAMPLES

Why create a design? What function can it serve? What can it express or reveal? The purposes of design fall roughly into five categories: descriptive (to document the visible world), narrative (to tell a story or send a message), emotive (to evoke a mood), utilitarian (to perform a practical function), and decorative (to creatively arrange design elements, such as color and shape). Keep in mind that most designs serve more than one of these purposes. In fact, overlap is almost inevitable. Usually, however, one design purpose is primary, and the success of any design can be judged by how well it achieves its purpose.

—Steven Aimone[33]

Steven Aimone succinctly describes what everyone who makes images will confront—in one way or another. Why? What? And to those, I'll add this question: How? Those three points were ones that I "discovered" for myself once upon a time, and I'll investigate them in more depth as this chapter unfolds.

I wanted to share the discovery because it isn't earth shaking in the big picture of things—but it was earth shaking to me at the time I realized it. The empty loom calls for a warp; the empty warp calls for something to be woven. But what?

In this section I'll share a few thoughts about the search for what to weave, make some suggestions that you might consider as idea starters or design prompts, and also show examples by former students of mine who have explored different ways to fill the empty warps with engaging tapestries.

IDEAS—WHERE DO THEY COME FROM?

Often we find ourselves eager to begin a new tapestry, but maybe there isn't anything that calls out to be woven. In this situation, what are some ways to move ahead?

An ongoing practice of using sketchbooks or journals can provide you with a wealth of potential ideas to develop into tapestries. These are places to quickly jot down ideas with a few sketched lines, or in brief words as reminders of something appealing about a place, an artwork you've seen in a museum, an article you've just read, or something that popped up in your social media. Maybe you'll keep a digital journal or have a sketchbook app on a mobile device, instead of, or in addition to, a paper journal. The point is to build a habit of recording ideas and images in whatever way you like.

Many people are familiar with Julia Cameron's book *The Artist's Way*. One suggestion from the book is to write "morning pages"—three pages in longhand, and, preferably, done first thing in the morning. These pages are a place to pour out anything that wanders into your mind. Cameron encourages you not to edit or even reread what you've written. I've been doing morning pages since 2009 and have found them to be very helpful in lots of ways. Not only have they given me a place to vent frustrations or fret over anxieties, but I've also made plans for upcoming classes or written about design ideas I may be struggling with. The thirty to forty-five minutes spent with this daily practice helps focus my thoughts for the day.

Even if only in morning pages done for yourself alone, or words you may choose to share with others, writing can be part of your design practice. It can help you clarify ideas and discuss with yourself important aspects of images to focus on. It can also be a way to feel comfortable with composing statements about your work. Whether you make tapestries only for your personal gratification or do so to exhibit and sell them, most likely there will be times when you're called on to have an artist statement. Getting into a habit of using writing as part of the process of making tapestries (or any artwork) can deepen your experience by enriching your thoughts and concepts for the work.

Now . . . on to the images you hope to make in tapestry. A few years ago, when floundering with directions in my tapestry life, I realized that there are three basic questions to ask and to answer that can help when making design decisions. Those questions are simple: What? Why? How?

Let's start by thinking about *what* you might want to weave. Tapestry gives you the ability to create images in a way that's different from other weaving methods. Yes, there are other ways to create woven images within the broader world of weaving, such as various inlay and pick-up techniques, not to mention more complex means that may include multishaft and computer-assisted looms. That said, the unique qualities of tapestry demand a different mindset from other weaving methods. You haven't necessarily made complicated color and texture choices for the warp or decided on threading, tie-up, and treadling sequence for the design effect as you would for other types of weaving. Manipulation of the warp as needed for pick-up weaves is nonexistent with tapestry.

With tapestry there is nothing except the skeleton of the warp until you, the artist/weaver, put weft into it.

Before you begin, there are several decisions to make within the narrow bounds of weft-faced, plain-weave tapestry. Those include the type and sett of the warp and the choices for weft yarns. An important decision, of course, is the image to be woven. This is the question of "What am I going to weave?" that each of us answers before starting a tapestry.

The direction you might take for what to weave runs the gamut of styles for images created in any art form. As mentioned before, those may range from representational or pictorial, expressive or abstract, to a nonobjective use of the elements of design. All of those are valid approaches to designing. The first decision might be to choose your approach or intent for the tapestry image. What is the subject that you want to weave?

If selecting a pictorial style, for instance, do you want to represent a landscape, seascape, cityscape, or cloudscape? Maybe flowers from your garden will be your choice of subject. Possibly your ideas turn to using human or animal forms as subjects. If your preference is toward representation, you may want to use your own photographs as reference, or you may choose to draw or paint directly from the scene, objects, or people to develop your design ideas.

Perhaps you'd like to abstract from nature to emphasize the feelings evoked by the colors of the season, but without specific representation of objects. Maybe you're inspired by other artworks—for instance, you might be motivated to adapt or interpret a design based on the colors and the flat use of space in a Japanese woodblock print. Maybe Georgia O'Keeffe's paintings of flowers will give you a new way to look at what's growing in your garden, with tapestry thoughts in mind—or perhaps you'd like to contrast organic shapes reminiscent of nature with the geometry of man-made things in an abstract way.

It could be that using the elements and principles of art and design in a nonobjective way is most appealing to you. Stripes or bands of colors may offer an intellectual and visual challenge that can be carefully planned out or developed intuitively as you weave, responding to the positive and negative shapes and spaces that develop between the stripes. There are numerous ways that nonobjective designing may be used in tapestry.

All of these and many other strategies to assist you in deciding on the *what* aspect of tapestry design are open to you.

What? Why? How? Words the author scrawled across a charcoal drawing one morning while she was at West Dean College for six weeks of tapestry study. The words echoed her frustration at the time about how to proceed with tapestry. *Photo by the author*

No matter whether the tapestry is to be representational or pictorial, abstract or expressive, or nonobjective, any imaginable idea may provide the seed for the design idea to grow.

Let's consider some ways in which you might tackle a representational or pictorial approach. Working in this way, you are echoing the shapes, colors, size relationships, and perhaps textures of something from the world around you. How you go about creating the design on which the tapestry will be based is wide open. For instance, you may want to work with photographs. If that's the case, consider using your own photographs whenever possible. Not only would this be original imagery, but also it's more likely to hold special meaning for you.

You certainly don't have to be a professional photographer to capture images that can spark your imagination for a tapestry design. Almost everyone now makes use of digital photography, and most of us have a camera readily at hand with our mobile phones.

If you're drawn to details, many things may catch your eye as you walk around your neighborhood. Instead of the close, intimate view, maybe the overall landscape may appeal to you. Likewise, a spectacular display of colors at sunset may be the beginning point of your ideas. Could your pet become the subject of a tapestry? All those examples and countless others are sources for images you could collect as beginnings for tapestry design.

An advantage of taking digital photos is the ease of doing image editing on a computer. This offers many ways to take photos to the next stage of adapting into designs for tapestry, and you don't have to be a skilled graphic designer to use basic image-editing programs. Sometimes simply cropping the composition to eliminate extraneous details gives a stronger image. Manipulating with a software filter to simplify or modify the design is also a useful strategy.

Other ways to originate images include drawing, painting, collage, and mixed media. Indeed, any method for creating and refining images can be a starting point for tapestry. If at first you feel uncomfortable or unsure of your ability with these media, take heart. Anyone can find ways to use these methods to produce results from which to work for tapestry design. Two good references to guidance for exploring image making are *Drawing on the Artist Within* by Betty Edwards and *Expressive Drawing: A Practical Guide to Freeing the Artist Within* by Steven Aimone. Both offer many visual exercises that encourage creativity. Numerous other resources abound, both in print and on the internet; a quick online search for creative process will uncover a multitude of sources.

Once ideas are in place about *what* to weave, other decisions will follow. Although all three key points—*what, why, how*—are important in the initial stages of planning a tapestry, you don't necessarily move in a linear way from one to the next. Your starting point could be any one of these. Some of the possibilities for finding the *what* have been discussed. Now, let's move to *why*.

Why weave it? Wondering about *why* depends on many things, including the subject itself and its meaning for you. You may find that answering this question is more ambiguous than *what* you want to weave. Think of *why* as the concept, the reason for the making, the emotion or idea that you want to express through the design. Even though this may be an emotionally charged motivation, it certainly doesn't have to be. There are plenty of reasons to make tapestry without having deep meaning attached. Celebrating the beauty of colors and textures of the world around you is enough justification for a lifetime of tapestry making.

If you do want to express an idea or emotion, you may want to consider how the design of the composition lends itself to that expression. For instance, dark and dull colors may suggest a somber mood, while pastel or bright colors often lend themselves to happier, joyful emotions. Jarring, discordant colors and extremes of contrast would make a strong visual impact to go along with disconcerting ideas being expressed.

Horizontal movements in the design may be more grounded and peaceful, while diagonals can evoke more action. Tall vertical compositions lend themselves to monumentality. In *Drawing on the Artist Within*, Betty Edwards presents fascinating examples of how emotions can relate to types of lines, their directions, and placements in what she calls analog drawings.[34]

You may find yourself doing research about the topic you want to depict in tapestry. What you discover can give you insight into ways to select imagery and help you decide the manner in which design fundamentals can enhance the thoughts. Perhaps you've also written about the idea to help clarify your feelings. Could some portion of text become part of the design to add one more layer of meaning to the image?

Ultimately, before getting underway with the tapestry you have to consider the question of *how*. In many ways, this is the "workhorse" of creative making. When you engage in the *how* you are involved both in the design decisions and the technical aspects of the tapestry weaving process. Dianne Mize's book *Finding Freedom to Create* describes practical ways into aspects of design, based upon her years of teaching both novice and experienced artists.

Once you've determined the subject or approach you want to explore, there are many ways your design may begin to develop. For instance, as mentioned in the design explorations, you might make a crop tool by cutting two large L shapes from paper that you can then shift around, at right angles to each other, over a potential image to see design variations. You might scan or photograph the cropped version(s) and use a computer software program to do other changes, using tools such as further cropping, filter effects, and layers. You might also cut or tear from several copies of the image to rearrange into a collage.

You may want to work from your own sketches, drawings, or paintings to develop your images, either working to the scale you wish to weave or enlarging or reducing in size through such means as photocopying, scanning, or having it commercially printed.

Although making the design on grid paper isn't as useful for tapestry as when doing pick-up weaves, the grid may still be helpful. Putting the design into a grid is a way to see scale and proportion, especially when relating the size of the shapes to the number of warp ends that would be needed to weave them.

Tapestry techniques and methods also play important roles in the *how* deliberations. Are you going to be working from the front or from the back of the tapestry? How will you orient the design—will you weave the image in the warp direction or turned 90° to it? Will you use meet and separate? If so, will slits be attended to as you weave, in a "sew as you go" way, or will they be stitched when off the loom? Will you use an interlock or dovetail technique? What about hatching or hachure for color blending or for graphic effect? Will you choose pick and pick? How about surface texture—maybe soumak or rya will

have a role, for instance. Would you want to create a shaped tapestry, and, if so, what would be the technical challenges involved with that?

For the cartoon, you might draw it on paper that will be placed behind the warp as you weave, or maybe you'll choose to ink the design onto the warp. Have you drawn the design onto a grid that you can follow by measuring the parts and counting warps as you go? Do you want to weave without the cartoon as reference, instead following the ideas from your mind as you weave and the tapestry grows?

There are so many options to consider when planning for tapestry weaving. It's always a challenge for any tapestry weaver to make these decisions, yet exploring your options may give you an even more rewarding weaving experience and result in a more successfully designed tapestry.

Here's an example of how I used the questions of *what, why, and how* when planning the design for the small tapestry *Oak Leaf in Winter*. For the subject, I chose a drawing I'd made of a single fallen leaf. With that decision I answered the *what* question.

As I considered that image and *why* to weave it, I felt that the simple leaf drawing showed qualities of the brittleness of fallen leaves in early winter. In the drawing, the tension of the stem and the contrast with the shadow it cast on the white background suggested that sense of brittleness.

The *how* began to come together as the image was developed into the cartoon. To make the stem and the shadows as smooth as possible with the larger 6 epi sett I planned to use, I knew it

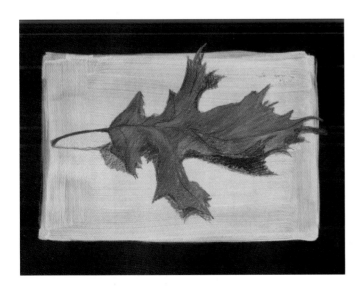

Tommye McClure Scanlin. *Oak Leaf.* Drawing in colored pencil and acrylic paint on black paper. 9" × 12" (approximate size).

Tommye McClure Scanlin. *Oak Leaf,* 2009. Tapestry: 12" × 18" (approximate size). *Collection of David Fore and Peggy McBride*

would be best to weave in the direction that the drawing was done rather than turned 90° on the warp. That way the slightly horizontal movement of the stem could be woven more smoothly in the weft direction, rather than up the warp.

In preparation for the cartoon, I scanned the drawing and used a filter in Adobe Photoshop Elements® software to simplify some of the shapes. Because the drawing didn't lie completely flat on the scanner bed, a bit of unexpected value difference showed up in the black border as well as in the white background with the computer software version. Those value differences seemed more interesting to the design than the solid black and white as I'd intended. I played with those subtle difference and emphasized them somewhat for the cartoon. Thus, what happened by chance when the drawing was scanned became part of the design of the finished tapestry.

to come together as you analyze your thoughts. Put things into the places they seems to fit in the chart as you consider the three questions: *what, why,* and *how.* Don't worry about sentence structure, spelling, or grammar—freely write to spill out ideas without censoring anything you jot down.

Another way to explore and help clarify thoughts about a potential tapestry design can be done by using a graphic representation, somewhat like a spiderweb chart, tree chart, or concept- or mind-mapping framework. If you're not sure about the forms these might take, a quick internet search using those key words will take you to many sites where you'll find examples. While those are often used in business or scientific fields, for design purposes putting ideas down in words and seeing relationships among ideas they express can be a way to quickly analyze and sort out possibilities.

There are almost endless paths to follow when you look around and think about *what* to weave, consider *why* to weave it, and then figure out *how* to go about it. Before moving on to several suggestions that could be used as idea starters, you might want to list thoughts about ideas you currently have for a potential tapestry. Use the questions of *what, why, and how* and fill in a chart like this one with as many things as you can think of that relate. Don't limit yourself at first to deciding what may be "weavable"—just pour out the ideas. The *how* will begin

For instance, I used a version of a spiderweb chart to develop an idea for a tapestry to use in a postcard exchange, called "Here and (T)here," sponsored by the American Tapestry Alliance in 2019. In this exchange, each registered participant was randomly paired with another tapestry weaver somewhere in the world. Each wove a small tapestry postcard and mailed it to the partner weaver. Afterward, an online exhibition of all

What? Why? How? Make a blank chart to fill in or to copy. Let your own thoughts, wishes, and ideas about tapestry flow.

Spiderweb chart exploring ideas about a particular project for which to design a tapestry the postcards was held at the American Tapestry Alliance website. My starting point was that I wanted to make an image related to the theme, so I put the title for the project in the center. Around that I put words and simple phrases that began to occur to me. For instance, I wanted to represent my home in Dahlonega, Georgia, USA, as the "Here." Key ideas I wanted to include were the nearby Appalachian Mountains, and the discovery and mining of gold in this area in the 1800s. I also wanted to have natural dyes from my surroundings used for the yarns.

Although there isn't a right or wrong way to make a diagram of this sort, usually the main question or problem will be central. Thoughts that arise or questions to be answered will branch from that. Some of those points will have other links. Bit by bit, you'll see an overview of the many ideas that are developing about the central idea or objective. More refinement can then take place once you have clearly seen what you want and the ways you may go to get there.

IDEA STARTERS— SETTING THE STAGE

These suggestions are ones you may find useful to kick-start your thinking about what to weave. I'm calling them idea starters, and you could also think of them as design prompts. Of course, you may already have many ideas bouncing around in your mind, and you're ready to begin. Sometimes it may even seem you have too many ideas and are having a hard time deciding which one to choose for a tapestry. However, if you occasionally feel at a loss for the next tapestry idea, one or more of these approaches may take you to the next point—designing and weaving tapestry that you feel good about.

Keeping an ongoing design sketchbook or journal in which you jot down thoughts related to design planning is a good practice to begin and maintain. Digital record keeping is also a way to have ongoing notes of ideas and images that arise, either to share with others or for your own use only.

Supplies and materials for these studies are the same as assembled before for earlier design explorations.

Before listing the suggestions, I want to say this about drawing and painting in image creation. In workshops when I mention using this as an option for tapestry cartoon planning, occasionally someone says, "But I can't draw!" I always reply that one of the things to keep in mind is that you do not have to render realistically to make good designs! You certainly may

make exciting and vibrant images through many means other than drawing or painting. However, I'd encourage you to explore doodling, random mark making, and free experimentation with an assortment of drawing and painting materials. Give yourself permission to play with materials and see how far you can push a medium as you explore it. As with many things, the more you do it, the more comfortable and confident you'll become.

If you do feel you'd like to improve your drawing and painting skills, you may want to work your way through several of the exercises in the Betty Edwards books *Drawing on the Right Side of the Brain* and *Drawing on the Artist Within* to find inspiration and encouragement. Another very valuable resource for ideas if you feel insecure with drawing or painting abilities is Steven Aimone's book *Expressive Drawing: A Practical Guide to Freeing the Artist Within*. Aimone encourages everyone to understand that "whether you're working from a reference or not, you're filtering the experiences of your life to produce a new reality that is uniquely your own." He goes on to say, "There's no need to . . . make it perfect, or make it look like this or that. It's purely about your own expression."[35]

Taking courses in basic drawing and painting may also be options you want to explore. Those may be found in many places, from local colleges or universities to short workshops at art and craft centers, such as those mentioned in the "Resources and References" section.

Of course, if you feel comfortable with drawing and painting, no matter the style you choose to work in—representational, abstract/expressive, or nonobjective—you might adapt almost any artworks made by those means into cartoons for tapestry. If you always keep the thought of allowing the image to be guided by a "weaverly" approach foremost in your mind as you move to a tapestry design, almost anything is possible.

EXPLORING DESIGN PROMPTS AND IDEA STARTERS

FINDING IDEAS FROM PHOTOS

Photographs give us access to almost any image we'd want to use for inspiration. Of course, the internet holds millions of potential reference photos, but I strongly encourage you to use your own photos whenever possible. Your memories of capturing the image in a particular place and time will enhance your connection with the tapestries you might design based on the photos. If you do need to refer to images other than your own, be sure to respect the copyrights of the creator.

1. Browse through photo images you've collected and select two or three you particularly like.
2. Use the L-shaped cropping tool from earlier explorations (see page 178) to select and crop a portion of the image. Alternatively, use digital means to zoom in and crop the photo.
3. Analyze what you find appealing about this selection. Shapes? Colors? Something else?
4. Make notes or sketches, take photographs, or scan details.
5. Make color studies based on the design source, using yarn wrappings, painted swatches, or collages of colored papers.
6. Weave a small sample based on one or more of the studies.

OBSERVATION— FINDING IDEAS FROM LIFE

Working from observation to find images for artworks is a time-honored tradition. One can look to expansive views, as in landscapes, or study figures of people or animals from life. Smaller and more intimate groupings of common, everyday things are often chosen as still-life compositions. Even individual objects become wonderful design references and potential tapestry ideas. These idea starters will focus on individual items first, then move to suggestions about ways to use the initial study with more complexity of design.

1. Assemble several small natural objects to use as sources for design (leaf, twig, feather, pebbles, etc.). Choose one to begin with. You might do similar studies for all of the things you collected.
2. Sketch or photograph the object and continue expanding the design effects with the following suggestions.
3. Simplify to reduce the detail and stylize the image. You might try zooming in by using cropping methods suggested earlier. A good way to simplify is to place a sheet of tracing paper over the image you've made by sketching or photography. Then draw only the most critical outlines. If the original has close values that are hard to see through the tracing paper, use a transparency sheet and wet- or dry-erase marker as in earlier explorations. If you prefer to work digitally, various image-editing software on computer or graphics tablets would be useful for simplifying.
4. Several variations of the simplified version may be explored, using other sheets of tracing paper or transparencies. Possibilities to try include repeating the image several times in different ways, and also flipping the image to give a mirror image.

5. Explore how a border could be used to enhance the image. You might make several different sizes of borders on separate sheets of tracing paper and overlay these onto the design. Could part(s) of the image break out of the border at the side(s)? Look back at Robbie LaFleur's tapestry *Great-Grandmother with Chickens* on page 59 to see how she used a border in her design.
6. Design a cartoon based on your study. You may find tracing paper, transparency sheet, or transfer paper helpful to develop the cartoon.
7. Weave a small sample from your study, possibly making it of a section rather than the whole image.

Explore the light and shadow of simple objects. A piece of fruit sitting on white paper is a good place to start.

Light and shadow can offer a dynamic way to enhance a representational image. Imagine the effect of incorporating a suggestion of form by the way you've observed and represented light and shadow as seen in the real world. Look back at how Mary Cost used bold light and shadow contrasts in each of her tapestries shown (pages 43, 57, and 67). Even though she's reduced details of the buildings and surroundings, one can see the three-dimensionality of the forms she presents. A good way to start finding ways to use these effects in your own tapestries is to observe light and shadow with simple forms.

1. Set up a small, simple natural object on white paper and place a light source nearby so that the object casts shadows. You could try a stone, a piece of fruit, a snail shell, or a seashell.

2. Alternatively, rather than a natural object, fold a strip of cardstock paper and place it on a white background to see the shadows created with a strong sidelight. A strip about 2" wide by 6" or 8" long is a good size to use. Fold it across the width once at some place and stand it on the white background.

3. Photograph or sketch the objects and shadows. Notice the several steps or layers in the shadows and show these as defined shapes.

4. What are the colors you see in the shadows? We often think of shadows as gray, but notice how much color there may be in the cast shadow of the object. Could you exaggerate this for visual effect in tapestry?

5. Observe the object and the shadows on its surface (called form shadows). Those shadows also create shapes, and the placement of those help define the shape. Rounded or curved objects will have a different transition of shadow across the form than the folded paper will. You'll notice distinct edges at the fold where the shadow and the light meet. With rounded forms, the transition from light to dark will be more gradual.

Explore light and shadow by making a single fold in a sheet of cardstock. Place it on a white piece of paper, shine a light on one side, and see the great variety of shadows cast, made possible by one simple fold in the cardstock.

6. As you study the shadows and shapes made by those, think of ways to use colors other than gray to create the shadows. Consider how you'd show the sharp distinction between light and shadow as you'll see with the folded paper in tapestry. Then think about ways to make the subtle shadow transition of a rounded form in weaverly ways.

7. Take a look at one of my tapestry diary pieces on page 175 to see how I've used shadows with two simple kinds of things: sticks and stones.

NOTICING THROUGH NOTAN: A STUDY OF LIGHT AND DARK

Arthur Wesley Dow introduced the concept of notan in the US in the late nineteenth and early twentieth centuries, describing it as a Japanese design concept. It is often discussed as a concept of balancing the light and dark areas in the composition. According to artist and author Dianne Mize, notan means "dark/light" and is a way to reduce the observed into "an underlying simplified pattern" of only dark and light area. Dianne shows several examples of how she uses notan in her own work in her book *Finding Freedom to Create*.[36] Doing an internet search for the term "notan" will lead you to many fascinating examples, both historically and in current use. Learning to see the distinction between areas of darkness and lightness in any scene is helpful to designing interesting compositions.

1. Try notan by first drawing outlines for a group of small thumbnail-scale squares or rectangles on one or more sheets of white paper. (Thumbnail sketches are small and quickly done versions showing an overview of what's being observed. A template for small squares to copy can be found in appendix C.)

2. Use a marking pen with a wide tip or a small brush and ink. Subjects for the notan studies might be found within the landscape. For instance, maybe you'll come across groupings of trees, a fence, or several lawn chairs that offer interesting possibilities of design. As you study the scene, observe the dark and the light areas you see. Now, simplify everything that appears as medium to dark in value into an area of black. Let everything else that is medium-light to the lightest value be represented by the white of the paper.

3. Sketch in the dark values with the wide tip of the marking pen or with the ink. Don't try to render details; simply show where the dark and the light areas are. As an example, see the way Joann Wilson used a couple of small notan thumbnails for tapestries on page 136.

MAKE THE MOST OF GRADATIONS OF COLOR OR VALUE

Gradation or gradual changes to make color or value shifts may be beautifully done with yarn. In painting, gradations are achieved by colors gradually being blended from one to another, making an almost invisible transition point between the changes. In yarn, the more strands you can use as weft bundles, the smoother the transitions can be. Feeling confidence in several ways to make color gradations can definitely enhance your tapestry design choices. Look back at Rebecca Mezoff's beautiful use of color gradation in her tapestry *The Space Before Knowing* on page 34.

1. Try a color gradation from light to dark and from one color to another, using strokes of colored pencils that blend from one to the other, little by little.

2. Next, try a similar color gradation with yarn by wrapping strands around a folded strip of cardstock. Tape ends of the yarns at the back to hold them in place while wrapping on. How many strands of weft in a bundle can you use as you move from one side to the other to make the gradation as smooth as possible to the eye?

3. Try the same color gradation in a woven strip. If you use three strands, weave for a few passes with all three wefts of the same color. Drop one of the colors from the strands and add the next color in the transition into the bundle. Weave a few passes, then drop one more of the first color and add another of the second color. Weave a few more passes, then use three of the second color. If you have small wefts, the more strands you use as you make the change from one color to the next, the smoother the gradation will be. Look back at Mary Alice Donceel's three different color gradation samples on pages 111 and 112 to see effects of several weft strands together for the transitions.

4. Color or value gradation in landscape, for instance, may suggest depth or distance. Consider the effects of atmosphere or time of day on color value and intensity. Observe the differences in quality of color in hue, value, and intension of foreground, middle ground, and background in the landscape. Notice, also, the way the transition of the sky color goes from lightest in the far distance, at the horizon, to more intensity overhead. Possibly do a representation of these observations either with paint or in yarns.

Color gradation using twelve hues from the color wheel, selected from two-ply wool. Warp: 12/18 cotton seine twine warp, sett at 6 epi. Weft was used blended four strands together. 16.75" × 2". *Woven by the author; Chris Dant, photographer*

EXPERIMENT WITH COLOR TRANSITION WITH HATCHING

Use hatching or hachure to create color transitions between two shapes. Hatching and hachure are done with the meet-and-separate method and are traditional ways for creating value changes or transitions between color areas. Take another look at Elizabeth Buckley's tapestry *Molten Beneath Strata* (page 23) to see her use of these methods; also, notice the way Kathe Todd-Hooker has used these techniques to create the subtle shadows of the large flowers in her tapestry *Nasty Ladies unite! Do it now before it's too late!* on page 39.

If you haven't used hatching or hachure before, you might want to take a look at the basic information about the technique in appendix A.

1. Try hatching to make a "blurred" edge between two colors. This may work best if the hatching distance between the passes is small and the colors of these two areas are close in value. Smaller setts will also give more opportunity for hatching to cause this visual effect.
2. You might want to compare this blurred edge with a sharp edge that would result when the same two colors were used side by side, with either a slit between or an interlocking method used.
3. Use hatching to create what could appear to be a third shape between two colors. This may work best if there are longer spaces between the turns of the passes, so that the horizontal lines of the passes will define the shapes.
4. Use hachure with at least three passes to create third and fourth color/value effects between two colors.
5. Try both hatching and hachure using straight vertical edges and also with curving edges. You may find it helpful either to make a cartoon or to ink onto the warps as you do curved edges between the two colors. A simple line drawing can indicate the turn points for the passes. For instance, with hatching, two lines made vertically some distance apart can be used to define places for the turns of the passes. With hachure, three or four lines can be used to indicate your turning points, depending on how many passes are being made in the hachure. A similar approach can be used for curved edges that move upward.

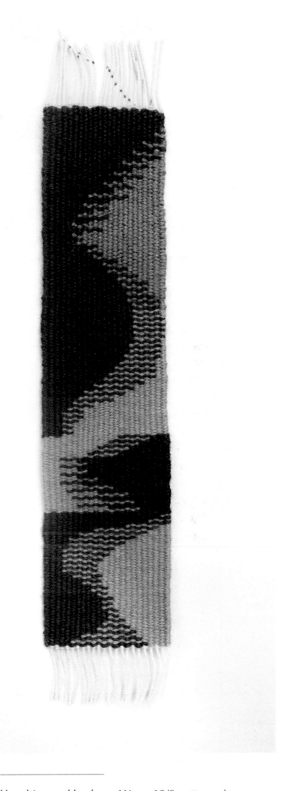

Sampler of hatching and hachure. Warp: 12/9 cotton seine twine, sett at 8 epi. Weft: Norwegian two-ply worsted used four strands together. 10" × 2.5". *Woven by the author; Chris Dant, photographer*

6. Use hatching or hachure in irregularly placed turn points to suggest movement of grass, clouds, or water. Look again at Joan Griffin's tapestry *Swept Away* on page 69 to see how she's used many variations of these methods.

7. You will find that the smaller the warp size and the closer the sett used with hatching and hachure, the smoother the color and value transitions will be. Larger warp and wider sett will have different effects and possibly not yield transition effects as successfully unless the tapestry is very large in scale. But they will instead give bold horizontal linear effects, if that's what you want.

LOOKING AT INTERVALS— THE SPACES BETWEEN SHAPES

The visual spaces between shapes in a composition can create dynamic visual effects. These intervals can, in fact, become the design focus. Think of intervals as being related to positive and negative, or figure-ground relationships. Janet Austin has used this effect with great impact in several tapestries, including the ones shown in this book: *Anticipation*, page 44, and *Another Forest Through the Trees*, page 65.

1. As you saw in Janet's tapestries, nature is a good place to discover interesting arrangements of space among similar shapes. Try several thumbnail sketches of tree trunk placement. Don't be detailed with these; simply place vertical marks of approximate width difference as you see in the trunks in varying spaces as you're observing.

2. Where else might you find simple shapes that are similar in some way and show a variety of distances between them? Can you find interesting arrangements of intervals in human-made things? What about placement among buildings in a city block? Or take a look around in a grocery store at the varying sizes and arrangements of packaging on the shelves. Perhaps the yarn cones sitting in your weaving studio right now are placed in interesting intervals.

3. Create a range of intervals by using black or dark-gray paper cut into strips of varying sizes. Arrange them either horizontally or vertically on a white paper. Move them around to see the interaction between the positive and negative. This is similar to the positive and negative exploration done with the element of shape earlier.

4. Try a symmetrically balanced arrangement where both sides, or top and bottom, match in numbers of strips and placement between.

5. Do an asymmetrical arrangement in which the spaces between the strips are varied, but in such a way that you create a visual balance.

EXPLORE LANDSCAPES, SEASCAPES, CITYSCAPES, CLOUDSCAPES, AND OTHER SCAPES FOR DESIGN IDEAS

Scape is an interesting word. In its definition as a scene or a view, it's usually used as a suffix with another descriptive word such as *land* or *sea*. Artists have used views of various scenes in many ways for centuries. As you looked through the tapestry artists' works in Part One, you saw several examples of land-, sea-, sky-, and cityscapes.

1. Consider different kinds of scenes or views in whatever version of "scape" you want to create. Any medium can be used to explore this idea. Painting loosely with watercolors is a quick way to simply indicate masses of land or sea and sky/clouds. Think about the three distinct divisions that allow us to experience a sense of space on a flat surface, mentioned earlier: foreground (the area that's close to you), the middle ground (partway between near and the most distant things), and the background (most distant areas). Another point noted earlier in the explorations of the element of space: differences of brightness or intensity and also value of colors in each of these land mass areas.

2. Another method to use is paper collage suggestive of a chosen scape. For instance, you might try an abstracted cityscape by using cut-paper shapes of various sizes arranged in an overlapping way. Collage is a good way to simplify major masses of land, sea, or sky as well. If you use both cutting and tearing to make shapes, you'll have a contrasting type of edge as a result. The hard-cut edges adapt themselves to the constraints of tapestry quite well as distinctly separate shapes with horizontal, vertical, or diagonal edges. The softness and irregularities of torn edges offer possibilities for using eccentric weft, pick and pick, hatching, or hachure for transitions between shapes.

3. Look for colors and textures in found papers that could be used along with solid colors. You might also want to paint papers in a variety of ways to use along with the other papers. One way to do that is to mix acrylic paint in colors you want, making a fairly thin consistency that can be brushed on easily with a wide foam brush. Make as many variations of color as you want, changing the mixture slightly after painting each sheet. For instance, move from yellow to green by gradually adding a small amount of blue each time. Don't worry about the irregularities that may show up in the painted sheets—these will give additional texture effects to the collages.

4. Simplify the "_____scape" image, thinking about how different proportions could be used to enhance your idea. Try several versions based on the same selected design idea. For instance, if it's a landscape idea, perhaps the sky will dominate the composition in one example while the land area will fill most of the space in another.

LOOKING AT INTERIORS AS DESIGN STARTERS

Just as artists have often used scenes of landscapes as subjects, they also have used interior spaces for closer views of life. Pat Williams has often placed figures within interiors in her tapestries; one of those, *The Beginning*, is shown on page 72.

1. Look at edges of shapes within the interior space and size relationships among walls, doors, and windows.
2. Observe the corner of a room and see how the edges of the walls as they meet the ceiling will appear as diagonal lines of different angles. This will give a sense of linear perspective that will lead the eye to the corner where the two walls meet. In addition to the visual movement in the lines, do you also see a change of value in the flat surface of the walls? Is one darker than the other? Showing both the way the lines seem to converge at the corner and the value change observed in the walls can create a sense of three-dimensional space in the composition.
3. Consider simple arrangements of objects in a room—chair, table, and lamp, for instance. Possibly arrange a few objects into a small still life.
4. Could you simplify these into basic geometric shapes, perhaps by using cut-paper collage, and arrange them on a background? Think about the positive and negative shapes and spaces between and around these shapes.
5. Look at the notan, or the dark/light arrangement you will find in the interior of a room, and possibly make several thumbnail sketches by using the wide-tip marker or small brush and ink.

WHAT DO YOU SEE BY ZOOMING IN (OR OUT)?

Photographers and videographers often make use of zooming in or out on a scene to emphasize something or someone. Why not try this idea in designing for tapestry?

1. Take a broad view, then move in more closely, and finally very close. You might try this with a landscape, by first taking in a wide view of the whole. Next, from the same place, select a view that is concentrated more on the middle-ground area. Finally, show a very detailed view of something in the foreground. You could record these views by sketching or by photographing the scene several times, with different emphasis each time.
2. Consider how you could combine these views within one composition, possibly overlaying parts in rectangular or square "snippets."
3. Rather than zooming in, think about the same view with a different scale for the overall composition. How much more detail could be included in the same design if the scale of the piece were larger?

TRY A VARIETY OF INTERPRETATIONS

Sometimes the most obvious approach isn't necessarily the best one. Let's say you want to make a tapestry of a flower. Your first impulse might be to take a photograph or make a drawing to work from. Your first representation of the flower might turn out just right. But many times, jumping into the tapestry with the first design attempt doesn't let you explore the image more deeply. Spending a bit more time with in-depth visual research (more photos, sketches, etc.) can often yield even more successful results. As a way to enhance your experience with the image, try interpreting or representing a design source in several different ways:

1. Make written notes about the quality of the colors (dark, dull, light, intense, etc.) and the ratio or amount of colors within the design source.
2. Make a yarn wrapping or paper collage in stripes, based on the colors and ratios of the colors you've observed.
3. Use thumbnail sketches quickly done with pencil or paint to show directional lines and movements observed in the image. Are these angular and geometric? Organic and flowing? A combination?
4. Make a more representational version of the image by drawing from the design source, or using tracing paper or a transparency sheet to copy from a photograph you've made, finding the main outlines within the image.
5. Try several cropped views within the image, each time isolating a feature you feel is important about the source. Take a look at all of these. Does one seem to best represent your intention and thoughts about the subject? Or do they all hold potential design ideas? Could you do one or more tapestries based on these views?

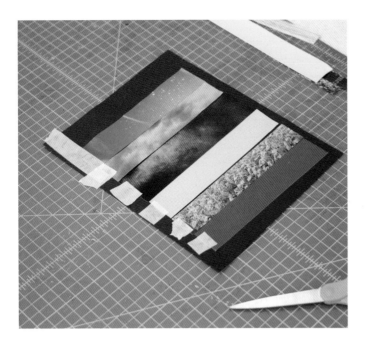

EXPLORE PAPER WEAVING AS A DESIGN STARTER

Weaving with paper strips offers another interesting method for developing tapestry design ideas. This can give an almost random seen/not-seen effect as strips weave in and out of each other. A paper weaving can be quite complex when completed. It may be best to crop into the overall design to find interesting compositional areas. Here are several suggestions for ways to approach paper weaving.

1. Look through discarded magazines or print out photos onto copy paper to find two photos to use for cutting into paper strips for weaving. These might be related in subject or quite different. Colors could also be similar or strongly contrasting. For instance, you might use a landscape as one photo and a cityscape as the other. Rather than looking for particular imagery, you might search for overall color or patterning; print ads in glossy magazines often are great sources for paper-weaving strips.

TOP RIGHT Paper weaving. Next, weave strips across as weft. The strips of warp and weft can be the same or different widths. *Joann Wilson, designer; Chris Dant, photographer*

TOP LEFT Paper weaving. Step 1: cut strips from a variety of papers and place together side by side; tape down to a background sheet. These strips are the warp. *Joann Wilson, designer; Chris Dant, photographer*

BOTTOM Paper weaving. Use a cropping tool to shift around over the paper weaving to find interesting designs as possible tapestry cartoon ideas. *Joann Wilson, designer; Chris Dant, photographer*

2. Cut one photo vertically into multiple strips to serve as the warp. Cut the second photo horizontally for the weft strips. The strips for both warp and weft could be any width, but at least 1" wide would be good. The strips could also be of different widths.

3. Tape the warp strips at the top edge of a sheet of paper large enough to hold all you want to use. Place them so they are just slightly apart to allow the weft strips to easily slip into place.

4. Weave with the second set of strips, using the plain-weave sequence of over and under, sliding each one up toward the top taped edge of the warps. Instead of plain weave you could also weave in any sequence of over-under that you'd want to try. Once you've filled the warp strips with the weft strips, use small pieces of double-sided tape under the edge of each weft strip to hold it in place on the background sheet.

5. Use the L-shaped cropping tool to find an interesting arrangement of shapes, colors, and textures. You might photograph or scan it, or enlarge it to use for a tapestry cartoon.

6. The overall paper weaving as well as any cropped areas is a composite of images that, while abstracted from your original, still retains much of the essence of the design source.

MAKE A "STRING QUILT" AS A DESIGN STARTER

Find inspiration in a traditional quilt-making technique. String quilts are done by sewing strips of fabric, one by one, diagonally across a square of background material. The excess length of the strips (the strings) is then trimmed off at the edges of the square. Many of these fabric squares are then assembled in different ways to create larger, overall patterns of diagonals, triangles, or diamonds. For a paper version of a string quilt, use a background paper that's about 8" by 8". That square will be filled with strips of paper, edges trimmed, and then be cut into small parts to be reassembled in different ways.

Small tapestry underway with a cropped section of a paper weaving as the design inspiration. *Joann Wilson, designer and weaver; Chris Dant, photographer*

1. Select from a variety of papers, combining papers with imagery, such as photos or text, with solid colors. From these, cut an assortment of strips in several different widths.

2. Arrange strips diagonally across the 8" square background and glue them down. You can piece strips together to make them wide enough to reach across from corner to corner, if needed. You might try an alternation of contrasts as you place the strips: dark/light, bright/dull, warm/cool, patterned/solid. Cut off the overhanging strips at the edges to make the square even.

3. Glue down so that each strip is well secured to the background paper, because you're going to be cutting the larger square into several smaller ones.

4. Flip the paper over and mark four columns and four rows each 2" wide, to make a grid of sixteen 2" by 2" squares.

5. Cut out the squares and reassemble them on a second background sheet.

6. As you put them together, try different arrangements to give diagonals, triangles, or diamonds. Once you like a pattern, glue it into place. Alternatively, try different pattern arrangements and photograph each time to have a variety of resulting designs.

7. Try cropping into a section of the overall design to find potential tapestry ideas, as suggested for the paper weaving.

8. Notice as you arrange the sixteen squares that you may sometimes not get them exactly aligned. The background paper you're placing them on could be showing at the edges. This might add to the design effect—take a look at that as you work, and maybe enhance it by putting the squares intentionally out of alignment.

MIX IT UP! EXPLORE MIXED MEDIA

Mixed-media methods are literally that—you would be using a combination of mediums to create the design. In fact, I've described several mixed-media approaches in the design prompts above. Here are a few other suggestions to add to those already mentioned. For instance, you might begin with a "failed" watercolor as the background onto which you'll draw with another medium. Or maybe you'll cut up other artworks and rearrange them into a collage on which you then draw or paint. Why not add fabric or possibly even use stitching, either with sewing machine or by hand, to "draw" lines and make textures? Really, anything goes with this means of creating images. I encourage you to be bold with your explorations; experiment, discover, mix things up—you might be quite happy with the designs you'll develop this way!

1. Paper string quilt. Background square is filled with assorted paper strips placed diagonally across. *Mary Jones, designer; Chris Dant, photographer*

2. Trim edges of the strips to meet the edges of the background square. *Mary Jones, designer; Chris Dant, photographer*

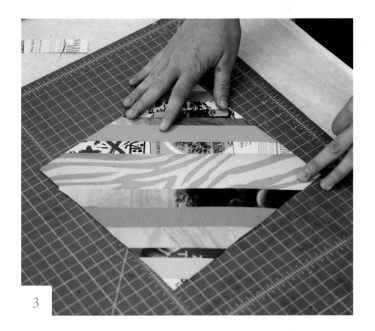

3. Finished square, filled with diagonal strips and ready for the next step. *Mary Jones, designer; Chris Dant, photographer*

4. Measure an even grid on the back and cut into smaller squares. *Mary Jones, designer; Chris Dant, photographer*

5. Rearrange the smaller squares into a new pattern. Try several options before deciding on the final version. *Mary Jones, designer; Chris Dant, photographer*

6. Move the cropping tool over the completed version to find interesting compositions for possible tapestry design. *Mary Jones, designer; Chris Dant, photographer*

DESIGN APPROACHES— A FEW EXAMPLES

In workshops I've been gratified by the eagerness with which participants try out different methods and ideas being presented. One of the wonderful things about being a teacher is being able to see each person's unique responses to design challenges. I asked four people who've taken several workshops with me to contribute some of their design approaches and resulting tapestries. Enjoy having a look at the ways Dorina Scalia, Nancy Nordquist, Joann Wilson, and Allie Dudley have investigated a few of the possibilities for design development.

COLOR IN THE LANDSCAPE AS INSPIRATION

Observations made in the landscape may offer inspiration for designs. One doesn't have to try to represent the source perfectly accurately, however. In fact, the landscape is so rich with details that sometimes it's overwhelming to know where to begin.

Take a look at how Dorina Scalia has used a photo of flowers and foliage. First, she made a collage of the overall scene, simplifying and abstracting the shapes. Then she began to analyze the new composition by cropping into several areas of the larger design to make smaller collages. Once she'd selected several areas to work from, she began to do color wrappings with available yarn. Her abstracted collages then led to a couple of small tapestries.

About her approach, Dorina says:

> First off, when I take a photo I am really thinking about composition and almost abstracting the image right from the start. From there, I begin the collage almost to remove the "subject" and begin seeing shape, form, and color. Next, the photocopy and its manipulation are used to take the image another step away from the original, allowing me once again not

TOP Dorina Scalia. Photograph that served as the design inspiration for many studies using tissue paper collage. *Courtesy of Dorina Scalia*

ABOVE Dorina Scalia. Initial tissue paper collage based on the photograph in image 196. *Courtesy of Dorina Scalia; Chris Dant, photographer*

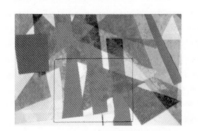

to be influenced by the image but to see another dimension. Then I use the viewfinder to zoom in on sections I feel are esthetically pleasing . . . and adaptable to weaving.

The landscape is a fertile source for ideas and imagery. We observe what's around us all the time. Often, we take photos of what we see around us, and those can be starting points for tapestry designs. Other great starting points are sketches or paintings made from observation and also memories of the land around us.

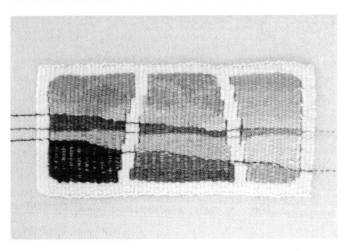

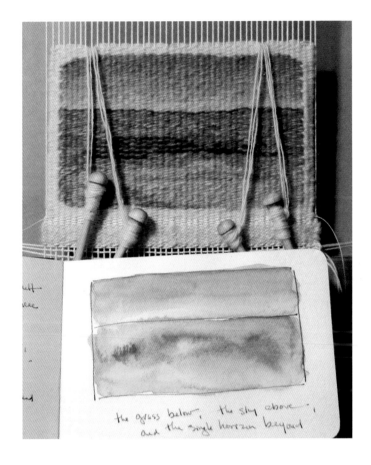

OPPOSITE LEFT Dorina Scalia. Several studies developed from the initial tissue paper collage, including selections cropped from the original, and yarn wrappings. A small tapestry based on one section is included in this group, as well as the cartoon used for the weaving. *Courtesy of Dorina Scalia; Chris Dant, photographer*

OPPOSITE RIGHT Dorina Scalia. Second small tapestry and design inspiration developed from the larger initial tissue paper collage. *Courtesy of Dornia Scalia; Chris Dant, photographer*

LEFT Nancy Nordquist. *The Grass Below*, 2016. A small tapestry in progress, from design based on her watercolor sketch. The quotation noted in her sketchbook is from John Madson, *Where the Sky Began. Courtesy of Nancy Nordquist*

TOP RIGHT Nancy Nordquist. Sketches for *Loss* along with the tapestry in progress. 2019. *Courtesy of Nancy Nordquist*

BOTTOM Nancy Nordquist. *Loss*, 2019. Tapestry: 9.25" × 15.25" × 0.5". *Courtesy of Nancy Nordquist*

Nancy Nordquist has worked both with observation and memories as approaches in designing for tapestries.

For these tapestries, Nancy sketched and made notes about the memories of the prairie landscapes of her childhood.

These are only two of many watercolor sketches and small tapestries she's made that are based on her sketchbooks and journals. Another of Nancy's tapestries and the watercolor sketch for it are shown on page 10. For that tapestry, she chose to simplify the background and the details of the trees to make a more "weaverly" image to work with.

Nancy says this about the way she approaches her design process:

> When I sketch, I try to simplify and put down only the most significant aspects of what I am looking at or thinking about. I deliberately work small and fast in order to keep the image simple. I try to make notes to help me remember what I was experiencing—date, time, weather, what I was thinking. When I look at the images with weaving in mind, usually one thing really stands out—a line, color, shape, or idea—and I use that as the main element of the tapestry, and everything else has to work with that element.

Keeping small sketchbooks, as Nancy Nordquist does, is an excellent way to quickly record ideas about the landscape. Notes about the temperature, the time of day and the quality of the light and shadow, the sounds you hear . . . all of those can be useful enhancements to your memories about the place later when you go back to the sketch as a reference.

NOTAN—A STUDY IN DARK AND LIGHT

Take a look at the page of notan studies by Joann C. Wilson. See how effectively she's reduced the landscape in this group of notan sketches to the essence of the shapes, and she did all of these in around thirty minutes or less. She didn't spend time with details—after all, the small thumbnail size didn't have space for that. The brush-tip marker she used made bold strokes and filled in dark areas easily, helping her simplify details as well. Later she selected two from the group to weave into small tapestries. Both of those show an interesting balance of the dark and light areas. Even simplified to a few bold, black-and-white areas of design, the little tapestries deftly describe to us selected views of a landscape.

LEFT Joann C. Wilson. A page of small notan studies done while at a class at Florida Tropical Weavers Guild. This was one of the design challenges the author presented to the group of class participants. *Courtesy of Joann C. Wilson; photography by the author*

ABOVE Joann C. Wilson. *Lakeside Oaks*, 2015. Tapestries: 4.25" × 4.25" each, mounted on 12" square. These two tapestries were designed from two of the small notan studies. *Courtesy of Joann C. Wilson; Chris Dant, photographer*

OBSERVATION OR MEMORY

In my mind I see an image of the Flint Hills tallgrass prairie in autumn, the big bluestem grass, wine-red, rising above the richly diverse flora and fauna of the prairie. This is like a snapshot, roughly torn into pieces but held together by the horizon, that magical place where the land meets the sky. As accelerated climate change threatens the continued existence of various species of plants and animals, what will be lost?

—Nancy Nordquist,
writing about her tapestry *Loss*

COMBINATION OF WEAVING TECHNIQUES

Allie Dudley innovatively combined two techniques in this landscape: wedge weave and rya. Allie describes her process:

This piece grew out of an exploration of wedge weave as a way to create a landscape. I love pile, and during our workshop at John C. Campbell Folk School, Tommye suggested combining wedge weave with rya knotting. I created the cartoon for this piece by outlining of several layers of mountains directly on the warp with a marker.

Rather than working all the way across the weaving with every pick, I worked wedge weave in sections as normal, adding an oblique row of rya knots after every few passes. The cartoon outline allowed me to see where I needed to change color, which was very helpful when working in wedge weave. The rya also let me experiment with color blending, as I could easily change the weft color several times in one row.

In another weaving shown on page 173, Allie combined traditional overshot weaving, using very fine warp threads sett at 36 epi, with a small area of rya that she wove within the body of the warp. For the rya area she hand-manipulated groups of six warps together to allow enough space for the thick bundles of weft she used in that part.

TOP Allie Dudley. *Rya Wedge Weave*, 2018. Wedge weave side of a tapestry woven in a combination of wedge weave and rya: 7" × 7.5" × 1". *Courtesy of Allie Dudley; Chris Dant, photographer*

BOTTOM Allie Dudley. *Rya Wedge Weave*, 2018. Rya side of a tapestry woven in a combination of wedge weave and rya: 7" × 7.5" × 1". *Courtesy of Allie Dudley; Chris Dant, photographer.*

Part Four

Look at What You've Designed— and Move Ahead

A METHOD OF CRITIQUE | CARTOONS—LOTS OF OPTIONS
FINISHING AND PRESENTATION SUGGESTIONS

> It is the uniqueness in each of us that defines our purpose for being here. . . . Preparing ourselves is the easy part. We have available to us multiples of resources from which and from whom to study craft and composing. All we need to do is to start doing.
>
> —Dianne Mize, from *Finding Freedom to Create*[37]

Eventually the time will come to sit at the loom and make tapestries. Maybe you'll find great pleasure in the designing stages and spend much time with those endeavors. Or instead you might feel that having the yarn in your hands and passing it through the warp as the tapestry grows is where your greatest enjoyment lies; you want to begin weaving as soon as possible. Both ways are right. You will come to understand the best one for you, I believe. Making tapestries is ultimately your best teacher; you must "get there by going there," as I once told a class. In the journey you'll find you will make design decisions and you will also create tapestries.

Next, let's consider ways to really look at and think about the images you're working with, until you've made a design you feel good about. Following that will be information about several methods for making a cartoon. When the tapestry is woven, the final stages of finishing and presentation will be considered as you prepare it for its place in the world.

A METHOD OF CRITIQUE

You've decided to invest time and energy into making a tapestry. You've chosen your subject, and in doing that you've answered the question of *what* will be made. Possibly you've also decided *why* it's something you'll find rewarding to design and weave. Most likely, you've made decisions about the best methods to use for weaving this particular piece—the *how* of the making. Before beginning the tapestry, now is a good time to look at the design with a critical eye. Make changes before beginning or, if the tapestry is underway, honestly appraise its visual impact—is it matching up to your expectations? If not, what could be modified at this stage to make it most effective? Once you've completed the tapestry, it's also good to step back to see it with fresh eyes. How do you think someone else will respond to it?

Art criticism is a way to assess the impact of visual work, whether it's your own or the works of others. The thought of critique may seem intimidating. Stories (and possibly your own past experiences) of brutal and negative critiques of one's artwork may be lingering in your mind. If you've found your way into tapestry making but haven't had prior art instruction, you may feel you can't use a critical approach to your own work or to that of others, but you can. It isn't hard. After all, you've just learned more about the elements and principles of design; you've approached reasons for and ways/styles in which art images may be made. You have knowledge of the skills and tools necessary for making tapestry. With those abilities, you have what you need to engage in valuable and insightful critique of tapestry.

A couple of authors whose work you might like to read if you become interested in learning more about art criticism methods are Terry Barrett and Edmund Burke Feldman. Feldman's method of art criticism is one that many museum and art educators use as a guide. He lists four separate considerations; as you go through these, it's helpful to jot down your responses.

CONSIDERATIONS FOR ART CRITICISM: FELDMAN

- Describe
- Analyze
- Interpret
- Evaluate

1. DESCRIPTION

a. In this step, what do you see? You'll mention the subject. Perhaps it may represent something, be expressive, or possibly be nonobjective. Consider the overall design and the elements used (lines, colors, textures, etc.). Describe the chosen format (square, rectangular, shaped).

b. If it's a completed tapestry or artwork of any kind, note what materials have been used as well as the presentation method, if that's important. Also make note of the techniques used. In other words, take stock of everything that's evident in the artwork.

c. When you look at the work of someone else, do the same things as for your own artwork. Add the artist's name and the title of the work, the date, the size, and materials, if those are known, especially if you'll be writing about the work in your journal or possibly for publication.

d. It might also be important to note the context for the work. Is the artwork by someone who is in the early learning stages of skill and technique? Or is the work by an experienced artist? What is the function for the work? Is it hanging in a public setting, or is it for personal enjoyment?

2. ANALYSIS

a. Next, think about how the elements are brought together into the overall design. For instance, how are the colors used in the composition? Is there a high- or low-value key to the color, or evidence of color contrast of some type?

b. Is there a clear focal point, or are there several areas of emphasis? If so, how does the design cause you to look in certain places or directions?

c. Does the work show balance and, if so, is it symmetrical or nearly so? Or is the design one that is asymmetrically balanced? How do the elements and their placement come together to create the effect of balance?

d. Do you see contrasts of the elements in some way?

e. Is your eye directed into and through the design?

f. Add any other thoughts that relate to how the elements and principles appear to be used in the work to enhance the overall composition.

3. INTERPRETATION

a. On the basis of how the elements and principles are used, does the work present a mood or feeling?

b. Are there visual clues to follow to grasp the idea or narrative, and what are those?

c. Does the process of looking closely through description and analysis suggest a title? How does the title fit with the work?

d. Keep in mind that interpretations aren't right or wrong. Each is largely based on one's experience and personal preferences, but giving the time to look more deeply and closely at how the design is structured and elaborated may enhance your understanding and appreciation for the work.

4. JUDGMENT/EVALUATION

a. Rather than thinking of this as a negative judgmental statement about the quality or value of the work, honestly decide if the elements and principles have been used to enhance the artist's intention. If a pictorial approach was used, was there an implied narrative and did the composition convey the ideas well? Does the work seem to be expressive of mood or give you a particular feeling about the subject? If the purpose is a nonobjective design, have the elements and principles been effectively used to engage the viewer with the work?

b. Whatever the style or intent, is the overall composition effective? Are there things that might have been done differently with the design to make the impact more successful?

c. You've also noticed how the techniques have been used. You will be able to make some evaluation of the level of skill that's evident, as well as the care that was used in the making—the technical excellence.

d. This is where the response of "I like it" or "I don't like it" might now be made, and you're better able to say, "This tapestry (or other artwork) is good because . . . ," with reasons for making the claim based on criteria about design fundamentals and technical aspects of making. Likewise, if you feel the overall design and technical quality are weak, you've taken time to look more closely before coming to your conclusion: you have thought beyond personal preference.

e. If you are using these steps with your own work, whether tapestry or other artwork, perhaps you've noticed ways you might improve the next piece. Or perhaps you're assessing the strong and weak points in a design prior to moving to the tapestry, if it's a cartoon you're planning. If you're considering the work of someone else, you've respectfully given enough time to carefully look at and think about what the artwork shows you.

Thoughtfully looking and analyzing what's been done in your own artwork usually gives you clear ideas about what may need to be changed. Likewise, by taking time to look at the design in a new way you may find you're pleased with the result.

When you look carefully at your own work and that of others with certain criteria in mind about the strengths or weaknesses of aspects of the design, you are using one process for critique that Barrett notes in his book *Crits*. In assessing the work this way, you're recognizing that "interpretations are not so much right, but more or less reasonable, convincing, informative, and enlightening."

Barrett has additional thoughts about interpreting artwork. He also notes the description step as one that's important. When moving to the stage of interpretation, he suggests that these points should be considered: Subject matter + Medium + Form + Context = Meaning.[38] He elaborates his ideas by listing several "Principles of interpretation for critique."[39] Here are a few of those:

PRINCIPLES OF INTERPRETATION FOR CRITIQUE: BARRETT

- Artworks are always about something.
- To interpret a work of art is to understand it in language.
- Feelings are guides to interpretation.
- The critical activities of describing, analyzing, interpreting, judging, and theorizing about works of art are interrelated and interdependent.
- Artworks attract multiple interpretations, and it is not the goal of interpretation to arrive at single, grand, unified, composite interpretations.
- There is a range of interpretations any artwork will allow.

- Meanings of artworks are not limited to what their artists meant them to be about.
- Interpretations are not so much right, but more or less reasonable, convincing, informative, and enlightening.

It is thought provoking to read and reflect on Barrett's principles for interpreting artworks. After all, if you've chosen to weave tapestries, you *are* creating artworks. You may have very specific intents for the images and the way you've chosen to weave them. However, it's especially important to remember this notion of Barrett's: "Meanings of artworks are not limited to what their artists meant them to be about." This is something we all need to keep very much in mind when we're designing and weaving tapestries. What someone else sees and appreciates in your work might not necessarily be what you'd intended. Each of us brings our own experiences and emotions to any visual representation. Understand that that's the case, and accepting it is one way we come to terms with how our tapestries will be understood by viewers. Barrett's book *Crits* is one that can be very helpful to becoming comfortable with using a positive, critical eye for assessing your own tapestries and those of others.

Next, I'll go through the four steps mentioned both by Feldman and Barrett in an analysis of a couple of my works, one a preliminary design and the other a completed tapestry. I'll begin with an image in which I'll point out what seemed to be weak in the composition, and those qualities that wouldn't translate well into tapestry. I'll note ideas that this gave me for the design that was finally used for a tapestry.

MY OWN CRITIQUE OF A DESIGN IN DEVELOPMENT

This is one of several drawings and paintings based on photographs I'd taken as fiddleheads emerged in the spring. My goal of doing this series of studies was to develop the ideas into a weaveable image for tapestry.

1. FIRST, THE DESCRIPTION STEP

The medium is acrylic paint. The shapes are both painted and stenciled from real leaves. The format is a vertical rectangle, its length almost twice the width, with overall size 48" by 26". The design is based on a close-up view of the forest floor with fiddleheads and fern fronds. Two fiddleheads are shown as spiral shapes in the top third of

that varies from intense near the center to light at the top. Dark, dull blue-green is seen in the lower area, extending from the left to the center.

Many small, indistinct, leaflike shapes create the overall background pattern.

The larger, narrow shapes lean toward each other from opposite sides. The long diagonal stem of the central fiddlehead seems to visually merge at its upper right with a similar width of dull dark green in the background that continues to the upper right. This gives a diagonal movement extending from near the lower left to the upper right corner.

2. NEXT COMES THE ANALYSIS STEP

The focal point / emphasis is the two spirals of the fiddleheads in the upper third of the composition. The stems of both lean toward the right, but the spiraling movement of the fiddleheads takes the eye around to the left. This helps counteract the movement, but the placement of both so close together in the upper left part of the design makes the whole thing somewhat unbalanced, showing neither symmetrical nor asymmetrical stability.

The multiple leaflike shapes throughout the composition create an overall pattern that is busy and confusing.

The movement set up by the center fiddlehead's stem and the medium-dark shape touching it at the upper right seems to take the eye up and out of the design in an awkward way.

Tertiary complementary colors of dull red-orange and dark blue-green are used throughout the background. The fiddleheads and fronds are dull yellow-greens in dark, medium, and light values. The overall color scheme is a contrast of warm and cool colors.

The space is mostly flat, although the visual weight in the background is at the bottom, with the darker bluish green that strongly contrasts with other color values in the design.

the rectangle, beginning with long narrow stems at the bottom left of the design. Several other nearly vertical shapes move from bottom to top, representing plant stems with many leaves extending out from each side.

Several values of green are used, all muted or neutral in tone. The primary background color is a dull red-orange

Tommye McClure Scanlin. Acrylic paint and graphite on unstretched canvas, 2008. One design possibility for a tapestry based on fiddleheads.

3. INTERPRETATION

The many small shapes of leaves throughout the background suggest an abundance of growth. Fiddleheads are found for a short time in the spring of the year, and thoughts of nature's cyclical renewal are echoed in the composition.

Making the two fiddleheads larger and out of scale with the fern fronds surrounding them puts the emphasis on the spiraling shapes. This enhances the concept of abundant new growth.

4. FINALLY, THE JUDGMENT/ EVALUATION STEP ARRIVES

Although some of the ideas I was trying to convey about the abundance of new growth in spring are in the design, I felt there were enough things visually wrong with it to not use it as is. However, it seemed that the two fiddleheads used in combination with background ferns could be simplified and made into a stronger design.

Thinking about the design further, I felt that the placement of the fiddleheads could be adjusted to improve the balance of the composition by moving them apart. Both still could be used at the left side, but by shifting the position the eye could find balance more easily.

The leaves and stems of the background could be simplified, with the right side having mostly fern fronds, and fiddleheads taking up the left area. This made for a simpler, stronger composition and more weaveable shapes.

Another change could be made in the overall design format. The images could be placed within a border with an organic, irregular edge. Some of the shapes could extend outward into the border to enhance a sense of growth and expansiveness without the multiple, visually confusing background shapes.

Changes in the colors were needed to enliven the composition. I felt it was too murky and uninteresting as it was, lending nothing to the concept of lush new growth.

Now, let's look at the finished tapestry that was woven after trying several more design versions.

MY OWN CRITIQUE OF A TAPESTRY: *SPRING PROFUSION*

1. DESCRIPTION

This is a tapestry titled *Spring Profusion*. It has a vertical format, 30" high by 23" wide, and sett at 8 ends per inch. It's woven with wool. Multiple strands have been used in the weft to make blends of colors. There are almost no solid, unmixed colors throughout the tapestry except in the bottom and top border areas. The tapestry was woven with the design turned 90° to the warp direction.

There is a balance of warm and cool colors throughout the design. There are complementary colors in the border, where the violet in the bottom parts makes a transition into pale yellow at the sides, the top being entirely pale yellow. The violet is light in value, so the color transition between the two colors is a smooth gradation. There are only a few areas of dark value: dark red-orange near the right lower area that extends almost to the left side, and a few darker leaves in a stem at the right.

The central part of the design is made up of stylized and simplified organic shapes: two spirals suggesting fiddleheads are at the left side, and on the right side there are tall stems filled with multiple leaves. A few leaves extend out into the border at the top and on the right side. A few other thin vertical shapes are behind the main objects.

There are various greens in the dominant shapes, ranging from light and bright to dark and dull. The background is made up of a dark, dull red at the bottom that makes a transition into pink/orange, and then violet and darker greens as it moves toward the top. Some of the dark, dull red is repeated in several small places within the main shapes.

The background is indistinct, showing the use of hatching as transition between color areas. Because of the direction the tapestry was woven, the hatching technique gives a pattern of thin, vertical lines of irregular height. There are some wavy lines in the background weft, indicating places where eccentric weft technique has been used.

There's a small geometric shape in the lower right corner within the red-orange that is different from the organic shapes; it is in low contrast to the background and isn't easily noticed.

Tommye McClure Scanlin. *Spring Profusion*, 2008. Tapestry: 31" × 24.75".
Collection of Thomas E. Scanlin; Chris Dant, photographer

2. ANALYSIS

During this step I want to consider how the overall design is composed. I notice that the contrast between the warm and cool colors helps emphasize the importance of the central features—the two fiddleheads and the many leaf/stem shapes. The overall color effect is high key, with mostly light and medium values. The dark values of deep red-orange and darker green are used in smaller amounts but give weight and draw attention to different parts of the composition, acting as counterpoints to the brightest areas.

There is a clear focal point in the largest fiddlehead. It attracts attention because of its bold spiral shape, the size difference, and its placement just slightly left of center. The color is also lighter and brighter in that shape. The second fiddlehead pulls attention away from the center to the upper left. To counter those movements, the multiple leaves seen in the stems at the right cause the eye to move back over to that area.

All the shapes at each side lean slightly in the direction of one another and toward the central area. Both the fiddleheads slightly move toward the right, while a couple of the leafy stems curve around the top and behind the fiddleheads.

Although both sides have different shapes, they fill the areas similarly in their vertical placement and are also related in color. This gives a nearly symmetrical balance to the composition.

The almost obscured geometric design in the lower right gains significance by being different from the more organic lines and shapes in the rest of the tapestry.

3. INTERPRETATION

The fact that fiddleheads appear in the springtime allows one to infer that this is a composition about new growth. Making the fiddleheads the dominant feature in the composition and enlarging the scale places emphasis on a tiny emergent form found only for a fleeting time in the forest floor in the spring of the year.

The way the stem and leaves extend out of the central area into the right side and top border suggests expansiveness and growth. The border has an irregular edge as it meets the interior and enhances the dominance of the organic shapes within the tapestry. The idea presented is of growth that spreads beyond boundaries.

Because of its difference from the rest of the design, the small geometric shape at the lower right suggests a symbolic element such as a signature or weaver's mark.

The title, *Spring Profusion*, lets one know that renewal of nature in the springtime is indeed a valid interpretation for the tapestry.

4. JUDGMENT/EVALUATION

After looking closely at the factors that have been used in the composition and the resulting interpretation of the image, I feel that this tapestry has successfully met my goals in designing and weaving it as a celebration of the cyclic renewal of nature.

As you make a habit of looking critically to describe, analyze, interpret, and evaluate what's happening within a design as it's being developed, it will soon become second nature to scrutinize both its strengths and its weaknesses. Various solutions to the design problems will come to mind in the process. The more you keep your options open before deciding on the final image, the stronger your finished work can become.

All in all, looking thoughtfully and carefully at your own tapestries and those of others will give you a deeper understanding and appreciation both for the works and those who create them.

CARTOONS—LOTS OF OPTIONS

Cartoons—not just for laughs! The term "cartoon" has meaning beyond the comedic or satirical definition often associated with it. In fact, making cartoons as a stage of design work for tapestry, as well as for fresco and other painting methods, has been done for hundreds of years. The cartoon was, and still is today, a full-size image on which the final work is based.

When European tapestry was primarily done to weave large-scale, mural-sized pieces to hang on the walls of castles and churches, it was not the work of a single person. The weavers of the tapestry were skilled craftspeople who executed the designs created by an artist in another medium, usually painting.

The term "cartoon" is derived from the Italian *cartone* (literally, a large sheet of heavy paper), meaning a drawing with a full-scale design for execution in another medium. A patron would commission an artist to design a tapestry to be executed by a tapestry workshop. The artist would make the cartoon, usually with paint on either fabric or paper, as a full-scale version of what was to be woven. The cartoon was often used more than once to weave an edition of tapestries based on it. Valuable cartoons may have been passed through several decades of use until they were worn out. Nevertheless, several of the artist Raphael's cartoons still exist and are housed at the Victoria and Albert Museum in London.[40]

Although cartoons were used extensively in European tapestries to plan often-quite-elaborate pictorial images, many cultural traditions do not employ this means for designing and weaving tapestries. Textiles woven in the southwestern United States, for instance, often follow pattern and design traditions passed through generations of weavers. The weavings show variations and elaborations of "weaverly" methods in bands of horizontal lines, shapes made side by side vertically or woven along diagonals. These geometric characteristics are found worldwide and across time in many kinds of weft-faced weaves.

In addition to the weavings of the southwestern United States, notable examples are seen in Middle Eastern kilims; African Kente cloth; Norwegian *lynildvev*, or lightning weave, and *rutevev*, or square weave; and textiles of the ancient Andes.

Traditions aside, in the twentieth and twenty-first centuries there has been an almost grassroots movement of people becoming interested in tapestry making, whether as art medium for a professional artist or as an engaging pastime. Most of the time, the artist-weaver designs the images and the cartoons based on those images.

There are many ways a tapestry idea can begin and then become a weaving. Avenues into the design stages have been mentioned in the discussion about *what* to weave, *why* to weave it, and *how* to go about it. Many ideas have been presented in the suggestions for finding design ideas for tapestry. Now, let me describe a few ways those ideas may be turned into working cartoons for tapestry weaving.[41]

Tommye McClure Scanlin. *Hambidge Kiln Bricks*, 2017. Tapestry: 6" × 6" (7.5" × 7.5" × 1" framed). This shows the photograph from which the cartoon was designed, taken by the author, the cartoon on tracing paper, and finished tapestry. *Chris Dant, photographer*

1. First comes the design source. This might simply be a loose preliminary sketch, or it may be an artwork in its own right. In fact, a work created in any medium can become the basis for a tapestry design. Transforming an idea or an image created in another medium into a weaveable design can take many directions.

2. Other decisions to make when developing the source image into a cartoon include the size for the tapestry and the best direction in which to weave it.

3. We'll look at several details about the cartoon itself and what types of materials are suitable for making it.

4. Once the cartoon is completed, you have alternatives about how to use it. You might want to do the traditional method of inking directly from the cartoon onto the warp threads to have the marks as the guide while weaving—if so, what would you use for that? Would you prefer to have the cartoon held in place behind the warp? What about following a gridded design by measuring and counting warp ends as you weave? Each of these methods may be ones you want to use at some point, and it's good to become comfortable with all.

No matter how the original design was created, you'll often need to simplify to make the image suitable for weaving. Always keep in mind that a tapestry inspired by the design source is an artwork on its own merits, done in an entirely different medium. Many characteristics of the medium used for the design source may not translate well into weaving. When creating tapestries, acknowledging and working with the "weaverly" nature of the technique will usually lead to your most successful outcome.

Alice Martin. Cartoon for tapestry designed during tapestry class at Penland School of Craft, August 2019. This was based on cut-paper collage. The inset shows the nearly completed tapestry. *Courtesy of Alice Martin; Chris Dant, photographer*

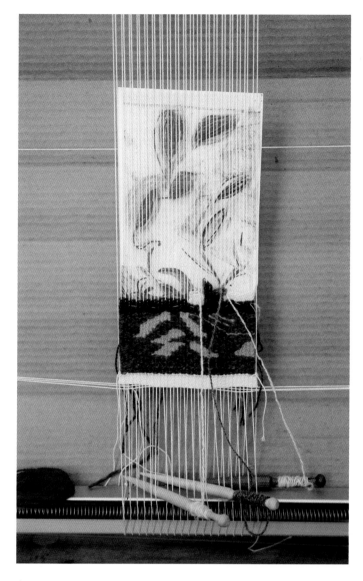

CREATING THE CARTOON

After the design is completed, the next step is to make the actual cartoon. At this point, decide which direction will be the best orientation for weaving the tapestry. Should it be woven with the image upright, going with the warp direction? Or will it be best to turn the design to weave it with the image 90° to the warp?

Robin Beveridge. Tapestry underway, with cartoon placed behind the weaving. The design was created by using vine charcoal for quick sketching. Designed and woven at Penland School of Craft, August 2019. *Courtesy of Robin Beveridge; Chris Dant, photographer*

- Determining the direction in which to weave the image may be based on the visual elements that are dominant in the design. For instance, if you have lots of thin vertical lines and shapes, those are much easier to weave in a horizontal direction as passes of weft, rather than as thin lines moving upward along the warp direction.

  Another factor that may determine the direction in which to weave the image is the size of the loom available. Perhaps you want a piece that is wider than the loom will allow. If the image were turned sideways for weaving, would the length of warp on the loom give the width needed?

- Most of the time, an outline drawing to show the edges of shapes will be easiest to follow as the cartoon because the outlines are easier to see through the warps as guides for weaving. How will you convert your original design source into outlines, and how will you make the cartoon the size you want to weave?

  If the tapestry is to be small and if your design from which you want to work is also small, you can possibly make a tracing directly from it to convert into a line drawing for the cartoon.

  It may be, however, that the design is made in a medium you can't easily trace over—say you've used oil pastels or chalk pastels for a drawing you want to use. Tracing over either of those would transfer some of the medium to your cartoon paper.

  One solution might be to redraw the outlines of the design directly onto the cartoon paper with permanent marker, using the original as reference as you draw.

  Another option is to photograph the original and use a home printer to make a copy that you can then use to trace from for the cartoon.

  Before doing the tracing, you may want to check to see if you can use the printed copy from the original as the working cartoon. Sometimes that can be done, but it's often hard to discern the edges of shapes if the design is in full color or gray scale. If that's the case, make the outlines from the print by putting tracing paper, or transparent or translucent drafting film such as Mylar®, over the image and draw the lines with a permanent marker. Put the original design nearby for color reference as you weave.

  For larger cartoons, several ways to enlarge will be discussed shortly.

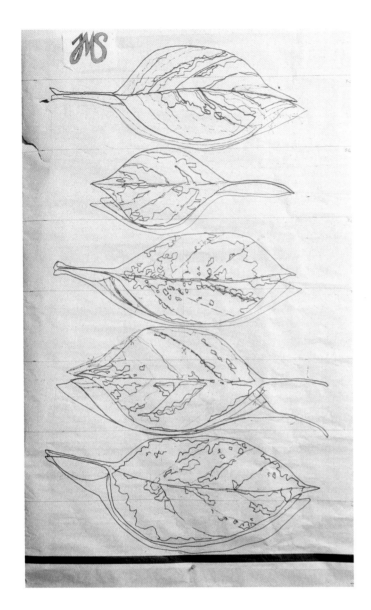

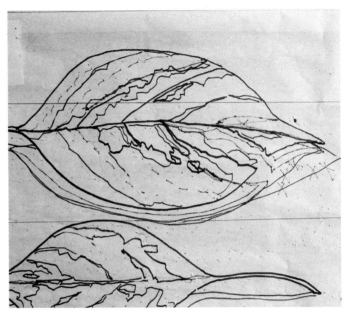

MATERIALS FOR CARTOONS

Bogus paper, kraft paper, or layout bond paper all are good choices for making larger cartoons. Rolls of these are usually available in 36" or wider widths and many feet or yards long.

Transparent or translucent polyester film such as those available from Grafix® are useful both for copying the image and being used as the cartoon. This is available as sheets and as rolls, several inches wide by many feet long.

Tracing paper can also be used for cartoons, although it can be torn more easily than the other papers.

Permanent marker in a couple of colors will be handy.

Depending on how you make the cartoon, some of the previous tools could be useful: pencils, eraser, ruler for drawing a cartoon to scale, for instance.

When it comes to using cartoons, there are several materials you could use. If you want to do inking onto the warp, a water-resistant ink and either a dip pen or small brush, or a permanent laundry marker, would be used. For stitching on a cartoon, curved needle and regular sewing thread are needed. If you want to use magnets, small ones about $5/16$" diameter by $1/8$" thickness are sufficient for holding most cartoons in place.

Use a permanent marker to draw the outline onto a cartoon. If you need to make corrections as you draw, use a different color of marker. With large cartoons it's helpful to have a series of horizontal lines drawn in a different color than what's used for the image, across the width of the cartoon, perhaps every 6" or so. A center vertical line drawn through the cartoon is also a useful guide for ensuring that the cartoon stays squared with the weaving.

ABOVE LEFT Cartoon drawn with permanent marker on white kraft paper. Additional length is added at the bottom for ease of attachment behind the warp (the blue horizontal line near the bottom is blue painter's tape holding on the extra length). *Design by the author; Chris Dant, photographer*

ABOVE RIGHT Detail of the cartoon. Red horizontal lines every 6". These are useful for keeping the cartoon aligned and helping keep track of woven progress. Corrections made, with old contours marked with Xs. Tiny holes over the surface result from stitching the cartoon on as the tapestry was woven. *Chris Dant, photographer*

Be sure to allow for extra length of an inch or so at the bottom and several inches at the top, depending on the size at the loom. The extra few inches provides space to attach the cartoon to the beginning and allows support for the upper part at the end.

MAKE THE CARTOON THE SIZE YOU WANT—SCALE THE IMAGE UP OR DOWN

Your original design may be the size you want for the tapestry; if so, then you're ready to move forward by doing one of the methods mentioned before. However, your original image may be larger or smaller than the desired tapestry size. How do you convert to the size you'll want to use for the cartoon?

The traditional way to scale an image either up or down and maintain the same aspect ratio (the proportional relationship between the height and width) is by redrawing, using the original as the guide. By doing this you will maintain the same proportions of width to height as the image is enlarged or reduced to the size needed for the cartoon.

DOING THE MATH

1. First, calculate the aspect ratio needed between the original and the material for the cartoon. Measure the dimensions of the original design. For instance, perhaps you have an 8" by 10" image. One option is, of course, to weave an 8" by 10" tapestry. In that case, simply make a cartoon directly from the original.

2. However, let's say you want the tapestry to be larger. You could easily increase both width and height two times to have a 16" by 20" tapestry. Or increase by more than two times in both directions to make it yet larger. If, for instance, you want it to be four times the size of the original design source, measuring the length of each side and multiplying each by 4 would give the new dimensions. You can also make it smaller. To be one-half the size, the original lengths of each side would be divided by two, making it 4" by 5". In doing these calculations, you're using a ratio of 1:X, with 1 representing the dimension you have and X being the unknown dimension. From this you can determine not only the size you want the tapestry to be, but also the size you'll need to make the cartoon.

3. But what if you know only one of the finished tapestry dimensions before beginning? Perhaps you want the tapestry to be 30" wide. In that case, how long will you make the

tapestry to proportionately match the original design of 8" by 10"?

4. First decide, on the basis of the design, which direction to weave the image. That tells you which dimension is the width, and which is the height, for the enlargement.

5. In this instance, let's imagine that the image will be woven in the warp direction, with a desired width of 30". The original image is 8" wide by 10" high. The width of the tapestry will be 30". Your remaining question is to find the variable: How long to make the tapestry? You'll do a simple equation that will keep the 1:X proportion by cross-multiplying to find the variable:

$8/10 = 30/X$

$8X = 300$

$X = 37.5$ inches

This makes the enlargement 30" wide by 37.5" long, and the proportions of the design have remained the same.

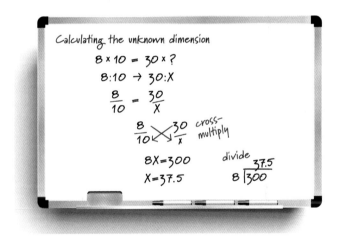

Illustration by Margo Booth, whiteboard image done with Adobe Illustrator® in iStock.com

WORKING WITH A GRID TO RESIZE FROM ORIGINAL TO CARTOON BY HAND

1. To scale the cartoon by hand to either a larger or smaller version, you'll need a grid with a 1:X ratio both for the original and the cartoon. For instance, once again think about an 8" by 10" original image as the design source. If you want the tapestry to be twice the size, or 16" by 20", you'll want a 1:2 ratio. To maintain the aspect ratio, place a 1" by 1" grid over the original design, and a 2" by 2" grid over the paper that's large enough for the cartoon.

2. Next, carefully copy what's seen in each square of the grid, overlaying the original, smaller image into the grid drawn on the larger cartoon paper.

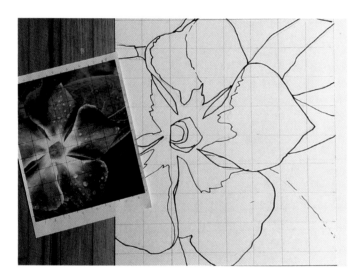

3. It's easy to draw the grid marks onto the cartoon paper with a ruler or yardstick and pencil, but how will you place a grid over the original without drawing on it? If it's small enough, you can place a transparency sheet over the original and draw the grid lines onto it, using a dry- or wet-erase marker. You can also use clear vinyl from rolls you could purchase at a fabric store, if the design is larger than the 8.5" by 11" of most transparency sheets; draw the grid lines on the vinyl with dry- or wet-erase marker.

4. You could also photograph the original design, then print it on letter-size or legal-size copy paper and draw the grid marks over it to the size proportion you'll need for scaling up or down as you make the cartoon.

5. Once the design is scaled up, by using pencil to draw into the larger squares, you can go back over the lines with permanent marker and erase out the pencil and grid marks, if you want.

6. For making a cartoon smaller than the original design, the same process would apply. Let's say you want it half the size of an original image of 20" by 45". That makes the needed cartoon size 10" by 22.5", a 2:1 ratio. The grid over the original would be 2" by 2" squares, and on the scaled-down cartoon paper you'd make a 1" by 1" grid. Draw into the smaller grid, following the larger image. Finish up with permanent marker lines.

RESIZING WITH AID OF DIGITAL MEANS

1. Software: You can also enlarge the design with image-editing software that will allow you to make the image the size you want. Then, one by one, crop sections from the original to open into a new file in a size capable of being printed with a home printer. Reassemble and tape the sections back together for the cartoon.

2. Large-format printing: Another option is to make a digital file, either from the original or a line drawing of it, by scanning or photographing it. The preference would be to use a line drawing from the original, since that will be easiest to use as the working cartoon. The digital file can be taken to a print service for enlargement with a wide-format printer. Most have the capability of printing on a paper size up to 42" wide by many feet long. This is usually relatively inexpensive, but it is a good idea to check prices first.

3. Projection: Enlarging with a computer or digital tablet and projector is another possibility. This is an easy way to zoom up to the desired cartoon size. For this method, pin or tape your selected cartoon paper to a wall, then mark out the dimensions of the size for the enlarged image, making sure to allow for margins at top and bottom several inches beyond the image length.

Project the design within the marked edges and draw the basic outlines with permanent marker. Stop occasionally, turn on the overhead light, and check the line drawing to see if you've included the details you want.

PUTTING THE CARTOON TO USE

There are several ways you can use the cartoon as a guide for your tapestry, and you may want to try each method to see which you prefer. In fact, you may find you will use all of these from time to time, depending on circumstances.

Inking onto the Warp

1. A traditional way to use a cartoon was as a guide for inking marks onto the warp threads. Those marks would then be followed for the weaving in almost a "paint-by-numbers" way. India ink was a medium used, with a sharpened stick or bamboo pen nib as the tool.

2. If you choose to ink onto the warp, be sure you have waterproof ink. If you're using black, you might also dilute it a bit with water so the mark is not quite so dark. Instead of a bamboo nib you might try a dip pen with nib, or a small pointed brush. Take care that you don't splatter droplets of ink onto woven areas! In fact, you might pin pieces of muslin or old towels at front and back of woven areas as you do the marking. Allow the ink to dry thoroughly before weaving.

3. Inking onto the warps can also be done with a permanent laundry marker. Try to use a light hand when inking, to lessen the possibility of staining through light colors of weft. You might want to test for potential staining by the marker, even though it's supposed to be permanent. Make some marks with it onto cotton cloth or scraps of warp threads and let it dry completely. Then wet it thoroughly and blot with white cloth or a paper towel to see if there's any ink bleeding or staining—if so, don't use the marking tool.

4. When inking, the warp ends need to be flattened so that the cartoon and the marks that are being made on the warps are accurate. If you're using a frame loom with one open shed, temporarily close the shed by weaving a strand of weft through the opposite pick shed and near the top of the warp, pull it taut, and tie it from one side of the frame to the other. If using a loom with a shedding device, simply leave the sheds closed.

5. Put the cartoon behind the warps and hold it closely in place. To do this, it's handy to use bankers' clamps, sewing or quilters' clips, T pins, or even clothespins to attach the bottom margin of the cartoon to the warp. If using a frame loom, a couple of strings placed behind the cartoon from the bottom edges up to the top of the opposite sides in an X will keep the cartoon close to the warps. The design needs to be close so that the lines of inking will be as accurate as possible.

    On a larger loom a similar method can be used, with a couple of strings behind the cartoon and attached to the lower edge of the tie-on area and the upper part of the loom in an X.

6. For ease of management of a large cartoon, it can be cut into narrower strips 6"–8" high across the width of the weaving. Place the sections one by one, as needed, behind the warps when inking on, holding them in place with pins or clips.

7. Start from one side and dot the warp with the ink at the point where a line of the cartoon intersects with it. Do this from the top to the bottom of one warp, or from the bottom to the top, before moving to the next warp and repeating, marking where the cartoon line coincides with the warp. Be careful not to smear the ink with your hand as you go along. Work from warp to warp until the section is inked.

8. Once the first marks are on, go back to each one and ink again, this time rolling the warp slightly back and forth with your fingers to make the mark all the way around to encircle each warp end. This is done because the warps will shift position as you weave, sometimes putting the ink marks at the back and making it hard to follow. Let it dry thoroughly before weaving over the inked area. You might like to complete a section, a few inches high across the width, at the end of a session at the loom, so it will be thoroughly dry and ready for weaving the following day.

April Price is inking from a cartoon onto a warp during a class at Penland School of Craft, August 2019. *Courtesy of April Price; Chris Dant, photographer*

Attaching the Cartoon by Stitching It in Place

1. You may find that stitching the cartoon in place behind the warps is preferable to inking on. For one thing, it's quicker to do, and there is no chance of ink marks bleeding through the surface from warps. For stitching on the cartoon, regular sewing thread and a curved needle are used.

2. Weave up a bit first so that you'll be able to make the first attachment of the cartoon. The amount you've used as the header will usually be all that's needed for the first line of stitches to be made. If you plan to have a turn-back or hem, the stitching can be done into that once it's woven. You've allowed for a margin of an inch or so at the bottom of the cartoon, and this gives a place for the first row of stitches as you begin the attachment. Use bankers' clamps, sewing or quilters' clips, clothespins, or T pins to hold the bottom of the cartoon until you have the first row of stitching done.

3. Near the top and behind the warp, you'll want to have some way to support the cartoon so that it stays in place as you weave. On larger looms there may be a couple of hooks at each side behind the warp, into which a support bar can be placed. The top of the cartoon with the longer margin allowance will hang over that. If your large loom doesn't have

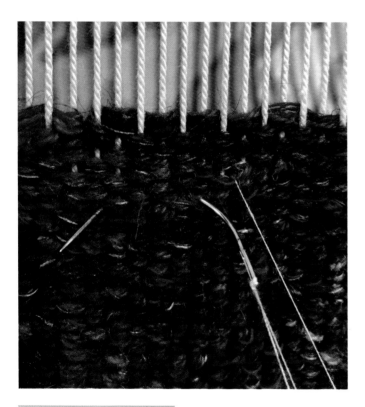

Detail of stitching a cartoon behind tapestry. Curved needle and sewing thread can be used for this.

hooks or a cartoon support bar, you can suspend a dowel or a length of ½" PVC pipe with a couple of pieces of cord at each side behind the warp as the support bar.

4. An alternative to using a supporting bar for the cartoon is to stretch a piece of sturdy cord from one side of the loom's frame to the other behind the warp, tying it tightly at each side of the loom. The cartoon can then drape over the cord. This method of holding the cartoon up is especially useful for a smaller loom that may be sitting on the table or held in your lap.

5. A needle and regular sewing thread can be used to stitch the cartoon to the tapestry. If your tapestry is narrow enough that you can reach around easily from one edge to the back, a regular straight sewing needle will be fine for doing the stitching. However, on wider pieces it will be impossible for one hand to be behind the cartoon to help guide the needle. In that case, a curved needle becomes a useful tool. The curved needle will let you stitch through the front of the tapestry, into the cartoon at the back, and to the front again in one sweeping push.

6. Use a wide running stitch to attach the cartoon to the weaving. Pull firmly with each stitch to bring the cartoon paper as close to the warps as possible. Hold the tension on the thread with one hand while you push the needle through for the next stitch, and then pull the new stitch tight. At the end of a stitching area, tie the thread to itself at the last stitch.

7. Stitch on every few inches of height. In detail areas you may want to keep the cartoon attached within about ½" of the top of the weaving, since that keeps the lines of the design close to the weaving area.

8. Be sure to clip out lower rows of sewing thread after you've reattached the cartoon farther up. This is especially important if you have a loom with a cloth beam around which you'll be winding the tapestry as you weave—you do not want the cartoon to wind onto the cloth beam with the tapestry. Also, if you're using a continuous warp on a frame loom that will be shifted around as more warp is needed, you certainly don't want the cartoon to be trapped between the frame and the tapestry when moving the warp down.

9. If by chance your cartoon gets askew, but your tapestry is turning out all right when you notice it, don't panic! If you do see that you'll be running into trouble with the image if you continue as is, cut the stitches out, shift the cartoon, and reattach it. Moving from the center out to either side when attaching the cartoon usually lessens the chance of the cartoon paper getting out of position, especially if the tapestry is wide. This is where measurement or alignment marks on the cartoon come in handy, as seen in the detail on page 148.

10. Remember that the stitch line doesn't have to stay level. In fact, if you build your tapestry shape by shape so that the top of the edge is always irregular in height, stitching on of the cartoon should follow the edge within about ½". It will meander up and down, but that's what it should do to keep the lines of the cartoon close to where you need them as reference while weaving.

Attaching the Cartoon with Magnets

An alternative to stitching with needle and thread is to use small magnets to hold the cartoon to the tapestry. Use two magnets at each attachment point, one at the back behind the cartoon paper and one on the woven area of the tapestry (not on empty warp threads). Several pairs will be used across the width, placed about 2"–6" apart depending on the width of the tapestry. You don't need large or extremely powerful magnets for this method of attaching a cartoon.

WARNING: These small magnets can be dangerous, and if swallowed can be lethal. Be sure to keep them away from small children and pets. Additionally, individuals with pacemakers or internal medical devices should not handle strong rare-earth magnets, according to several Material Safety Data Sheets.

Joan Griffin. Detail of *Swept Away*, tapestry shown earlier on page 69. Joan has attached her cartoon with magnets. Also notice her references for color and shapes attached above the weaving. *Courtesy of Joan Griffin*

WORKING WITHOUT A CARTOON

Of course, you may choose not to use an actual cartoon from which to work, but rather to build shapes on the loom as the weaving progresses. After all, following a cartoon is only one approach to making tapestries. The cartoon is just an assistant to the creative problem-solving you'll constantly be doing as your tapestry grows. Your goal always is to make the tapestry a "weaverly" work of art. It will be one that could not have been done in any other medium, as Silvia Heyden has reminded us: "In order to be meaningful, tapestry must find its own identity."

FINISHING AND PRESENTATION SUGGESTIONS

At last, your tapestry is woven! As you began, perhaps you made decisions about finishing and presentation methods you wanted to use. After all, every one of these stages will add to the viewer's overall experience of your tapestry. A few of the methods you may select for these last steps must be planned for in advance. Let's consider a few approaches and factors to consider for each.

The tapestry is a piece of fabric, after all. It has unique characteristics of surface qualities that make it quite different from a painting or a work on paper. As you know, textiles often are hung so that the flexibility of the fabric is evident in the display. It could be that your first decision is whether you want the tapestry to hang freely from the top edge, as textile pieces—especially larger ones—frequently are presented. Or would you rather have it mounted onto a rigid background. Maybe you want to use a frame for it. And it could even be that the hanging device is an important factor in the overall design concept of the tapestry.

To some extent, the method you choose may be based on the size. Small tapestries are often more visually effective if they're mounted onto a rigid backing rather than floating against a wall as a small bit of cloth. Larger tapestries also may be mounted onto a rigid background.

I'll describe a few of the ways I've used for finishing and presentation with my tapestries. There are certainly other approaches to the ending steps, and many of the books about tapestry technique cover an assortment of methods. You may also want to take a look at the several suggestions at the American

Tapestry Alliance website.[42]

Often the question arises about the way the back of the tapestry should be finished off. Should you hide the weft tails or leave them exposed? You'll find there are many opinions about the "right" or "best" way to do that. As with many things in tapestry, the way you choose depends on several factors. If you've decided to hide the weft tails, you may taper the ends, if a single ply. If the yarn is plied, you might unravel and overlap new ends as they're entered. In some instances, it may be that you'll choose to insert the wefts up into the tapestry, to run alongside warp ends. This works fine if you're using fewer strands of wefts and if your warps are wider apart.

However, you may find that you have multiple changes of the weft all over the tapestry, giving hundreds of tail ends. Perhaps you've used several strands together to make up your wefts so that you can mix colors, textures, or both as you weave. Those many ends will be almost impossible to thread into the body of the tapestry beside warps. Not only would it be almost as time consuming as weaving the tapestry, it could cause the tapestry surface to bulge or wrinkle as too much weft goes into too little space. Then there are some techniques that are done in a way that allows the weft to float from one spot to another across the back. Double-weft interlock is a method that makes a ridge on the surface as it's being done, and is usually used when the tapestry is woven from the back. When that interlock is used, the fabric is definitely not smooth on both sides.

Keep in mind that there are valid reasons for using either approach—leaving weft tails at the back or making both sides equally smooth. Different historical and cultural traditions adapt methods to suit their purposes. If you've learned from someone who's accustomed to a particular way of handling it, and you like the way you've been shown for dealing with weft tails, certainly continue to use that way. If you'd like to try a different approach—why not do so? Whatever works for you both in the physicality of doing the job and also the aesthetics of what you desire is what you should do.

No matter the method of finishing the tapestry that you may choose, the weaving needs to be secured. Starting and ending with a half hitch, as described in the tapestry-weaving basics in appendix A, will give you confidence that the wefts aren't going to shift as you complete the last steps. If you choose not to use the half hitch, just be sure the last few picks will stay in place until getting to your preferred way for securing the weft.

Next, hems or turn-backs may be used, or you might choose a method where the warp ends become part of the final appearance of the tapestry. Another question that may come up, especially if you have a background in fabric weaving, is whether to "wet finish" a tapestry. Wet finishing refers to washing the woven textile after it's off the loom to help the fibers settle into place within the weave structure. Typically, this isn't a part of finishing for tapestry weaving. However, sometimes steaming or blocking might be done, depending on the yarns used. Jean Pierre and Yadin Larochette have written about the pros and cons of steaming and blocking, as well as other finishing ideas, in *Anatomy of a Tapestry: Techniques, Materials, Care*. Let's consider a few of these options.

1. If a hem or turn-back is your choice, plan for and weave an allowance for it both at the beginning and the end of the tapestry. The length of the hem may vary; on smaller pieces, around 1" may be fine; on larger pieces, 2" or more will probably be best. The warp sett and overall thickness of the tapestry may serve as a guide in judging how deep to make the hem; for instance, a dense cloth would need a wider turn-back so it wouldn't be too bulky at the edge.

   If you use multiple strands of yarn as the weft, you might consider using a few fewer to weave the hem area.

   When you weave a hem, making slits every few inches across the width helps ensure that the edges of the bottom or top of the tapestry don't draw in at the hem. The slits will act sort of like clipping or notching a seam would if you were sewing a garment.

   Additionally, you may want to put in a row or two of soumak at the top of the hem, before starting the major part of the weaving, then a corresponding one when ending, just before the hem. The soumak will serve as a line where the fold-back is done, and helps hide any tiny bit of warp that could show at the fold.

   You may want to trim the warps to an even, shorter length of about ½" before turning the hem back. You can also trim them after stitching the hem, but usually this is easier to do beforehand. Sharp scissors are important for trimming warps. You can also use a rotary cutter, straight edge, and cutting mat for this.

   The hem may be attached to the surface of the back of the tapestry with small catch stitches by using regular sewing thread, carefully slipping a tapestry needle under a weft as you move along to make the stitch.

   You could also take the stitch through to the front, around one warp and to the back again, making sure to hide the thread between wefts. Don't pull too tightly when doing this, to keep the face of the tapestry from showing dots from the stitches across the width.
2. Instead of using a hem or turn-back, you might consider a method that acknowledges the presence of the warp as a part of the design. Warp endings such as overhand knots, a half-Damascus edge, and woven-edge finishes allow the warp to be noticeable, if that's appropriate for the effect you want.

   You might even decide that the warp should be exposed as fringe, and consider a braid of some kind to group the warps. Many of the warp-finishing methods shown in Peter Collingwood's book *The Techniques of Rug Weaving* can be used for tapestry.

RIGID MOUNTING OPTIONS

For a rigid mount the basics consist of having either a frame or a solid surface that will be covered by an inner layer of thin, soft fabric (cotton flannel, for instance). Next, an outer layer of fabric is stretched onto the mount, and the tapestry is stitched to that. Either a hanging device is put on the back of the mounting surface, or the tapestry is placed into a frame and made hanging-ready.

Foam Core Board

A good rigid mounting solution for smaller sizes up to about 18" is to use foam core board as the background over which to place the fabric covering. Foam core boards larger than around 18" may show effects of some bowing over time due to humidity. Foam core is available in archival quality, if preferred. Cutting the mounting board from this material to any size is easy to do with a utility knife.

The color and type of fabric covering for the mounting frame or board will be a choice made depending on what you want for the overall effect of the tapestry. Just like selecting a color for a mat to use with a flat artwork, this can enhance or detract from the work. When making the decision about the mounting-fabric color, consider if you will use the mounting to help visually straighten the selvedge. If you will, then you might want to choose a value or tone of color for the mounting fabric that is similar to the majority of the colors seen at the edges of the tapestry. Keep in mind that often, a neutral color is a good pick for almost any tapestry.

Similarly, if you've used a method of end finish where the warp ends are seen, as in half-Damascus edge or overhand knots, do you want the warp color to stand out against the background fabric or not be so noticeable? Possibly you'll want to lessen the contrast by using a mounting fabric similar in color and value to the warps. As an example, cotton canvas or duck cloth is a good mounting choice that's visually compatible with the color of natural cotton seine twine. Linen warps are well suited to being mounted on linen fabric of similar tone.

1. Cutting foam core board in preparation for making a mounting board for tapestry. This is ½" thickness being used.

2. An inner layer of cotton flannel is first attached to the foam core board by stapling it in place.

3. Trim excess width once the fabric is attached. Clip the corners closely for the inner fabric to reduce bulk.

4. Measure mounting fabric and trim to about 2" wider on all sides to ensure enough to pull to the back and staple.

Demonstrated by Allie Dudley, studio assistant at the tapestry class, Penland School of Craft, August 2019, taught by the author. *Photographs by Chris Dant*

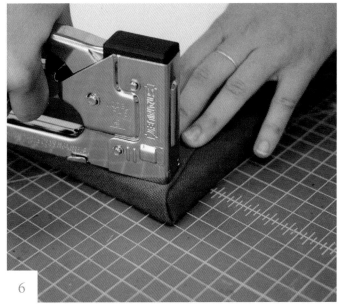

5. Neatly tuck and fold each corner.

6. Staple the folded corners before finishing the third and fourth sides. If you need to readjust as the last of the sides are done, the edge staples may be taken out and the fabric refolded at the corners.

7. Place the tapestry onto the mounting board and align it to the edges as you want.

8. Stitching the tapestry on the mounting board with a curved needle and sewing thread

9

10

All the fabric you use should be prewashed and the outer fabric pressed; the flannel inner layer will smooth out when stretched onto the frame and stapled, so it doesn't need to be ironed.

The photos beginning on the preceding pages show several of the steps for mounting with a rigid backing, using foam core board.

Materials used included ½" foam core board, self-healing cutting board, a utility knife with fresh blades, a metal edge ruler, a pencil, a staple gun and staples, fabric for the inner layer (cotton flannel), fabric for the outer layer, a mat board slightly smaller in size than the foam core board dimensions used for covering the back, craft glue and container, a wide foam brush, wax paper, a stack of books to use as weights, a few T pins, a curved sewing needle, sewing thread, and a push-pin hanger.

Cut the mounting board and cover with an inner layer of flannel. This is shown in **photos 1, 2, and 3**.

1. For the mounting board, ½" foam core board was used. The size of the board in this instance is approximately an inch larger in height and width than the tapestry and will allow for a ½" margin around the piece. The mounting board is measured and then cut, using a fresh blade in the utility knife. A self-healing cutting mat is quite helpful for this process, as is a metal yardstick.

2. Measure the fabric pieces about 3"–4" larger than the mounting board, to give you enough allowance to pull to the back and staple in place. The inner layer of cotton flannel is used first. Lay the prewashed fabric flat on the work surface and smooth with your hands. Place the board centered within the fabric.

3. Use a staple gun and ¼" staples to first attach the fabric at one side, beginning in the center and stapling out to one edge. Go back to the center and staple to the other edge. Smooth the cloth toward the edges as you go, but don't pull it crossways. Putting the staples at a diagonal will lessen the chance of ripping the fabric when pulling across in the stretching step.

4. Next you will attach the opposite side. Again start in the center, and this time, while moving to the edges as you staple, also pull across to stretch and smooth the cloth. Do the same as before by stapling out from the center to the edge, putting the staples diagonally.

5. Move to the third side; smooth toward each edge as you staple from center out, first one direction and then the other.

---

9. The back of the mounting board can be covered with a piece of illustration or mat board, cut slightly smaller than the board. Use diluted craft glue spread with a wide foam brush for this. Work quickly so the glue stays tacky.

---

10. While glue is damp, place the board on the back to cover the edges of the fabric and hides the staples. Put wax paper as a barrier on top of that and add weights. Let dry overnight.

6. Last, go to the fourth side and pull, stretch, and smooth as you staple the cloth, starting in the center and working out to each edge in turn.

7. When all four sides are attached, pinch the fabric together at each corner and trim straight up to cut away the excess cloth up along the edge, and then cut straight across. You'll wind up with an angled cut that takes out the excess fabric. Trim the edges of this inner fabric around all four sides so the excess width is removed.

Cover the board with the outer fabric layer. This is shown in **photos 4, 5, and 6**.

The mounting fabric in this instance is a commercial cotton plain weave in a color that works with one of the colors in the tapestry. It has also been washed, dried, and steam-pressed (there was no need to press the flannel under the layer, since it smoothed out as it was attached).

1. Begin on one edge and, as before, start at the center; smooth and staple as you move to about 1" from the edge, placing the staples at an angle as you go. Leave that corner area unattached at this stage.

2. Go to the opposite side and pull across as you start at the center once again, stapling, stretching, and smoothing to each edge in turn. As with the first side, leave a bit at the edge without staples at this point.

3. Do the third and fourth sides the same way.

4. Next, clip excess fabric out in a rectangular shape along one side near each corner, then fold the edges over and staple at the back. This step is a bit tricky—you'll want to pull the corners tightly and smoothly to make them as neat as you can. Staple these folds down. Check the front to be sure all the fabric is smoothly stretched. If you need to pull on some areas to smooth it out and add more staples, do that now. Once the face of the mounting fabric looks even and smooth, you're ready to stitch on the tapestry.

Stitch the tapestry to the fabric-covered mounting board. This is shown in **photos 7 and 8**.

Lay the tapestry onto the mounting board and pin it temporarily in place with T pins. The mounting board, in this case, is about 1" larger than the tapestry in overall size to give a ½" margin showing around the edges of the weaving. If your tapestry is slightly different in width from top to bottom, place it as evenly within the mounting board as you can.

1. Use a curved needle to stitch the tapestry to the mounting fabric, moving around the edges. Select a color of sewing thread that will be as compatible with the edge colors as possible. Similarity in value or tone is fine; you don't have to have an exact color match. If, by chance, the colors are extremely different in areas around the edges, you can change the stitching color at those places to better blend in. On pieces with the warp showing at the edge, the stitching color may be changed to the warp color.

2. As you attach the tapestry, let the curved needle slip through the mounting fabric and anchor into the inner layer of fabric. It will travel up about ¼" and then come out between the first and second warps. When you bring the needle out, tug just a bit to conceal the sewing thread between wefts, but not so hard as to "dimple" in the tapestry. Take the needle directly across and into the mounting fabric again, where you'll take another stitch under the fabric and up to the next point of attachment to the tapestry.

3. Stitch around all four sides, changing colors if necessary. Hide the beginning and ending of the thread under the body of the tapestry.

Cover the back of the mounting board and prepare for hanging. This is shown in **photos 9 and 10**.

After stitching the tapestry in place, the back of the mounting board may be covered with a piece of mat or illustration board to hide the raw edges of fabric and the staples. Cut this board just slightly smaller than the mounting board so you won't see the edges when the piece hangs. You could also put this backing board in place before stitching on the tapestry, if you want to.

1. For this process, wax paper is helpful to protect the surface you're working on as you glue up the backing board. Put down two pieces of the wax paper, each large enough for the mounting board to be on one and the backing board on the other.

2. Put the backing board on the work surface, and brush slightly diluted craft glue over the entire piece, using a foam brush. Work quickly so that the glue stays moist.

3. Put the mounting board on the other piece of wax paper close by, facedown and with the back showing the edges of the cloth, and the staples exposed. At this point you can put the back covering on, either with the tapestry already stitched on or you can stitch it in place once the backing is adhered and the glue has dried.

4. Once you've coated the backing board with glue, immediately flip it over and lay it across the back of the mounting board, covering the raw edges of the fabric and the staples.

5. Put a sheet of wax paper slightly larger than the board on the back to serve as a barrier to keep any bits of glue from your weights. Place something heavy, such as a stack of books, on the mounting board. Leave it overnight, and when you uncover it the next day, all should be fine, with the back ready for the hanging device.

6. Pushpin hangers are a good solution for hanging because they'll penetrate through the mat board backing and into the foam core. This is an easy method to use and should stay in place, but if you want a bit of extra security for the hanger, you can put a dot of glue on the pins as you push them into place.

The tapestry mounted onto the background fabric-covered board may be put into a frame, if desired. If you choose that method, put the hanging device at the back of the frame rather into the mounting board.

Wood Frame as Mounting Option

A wooden frame of any size could either be cut and assembled at home, if you have the equipment, or made to order by a frame shop. You can also buy artist stretcher strips in separate pieces and put together a frame. However, the artist stretcher strips will limit you to standard available lengths and may not be exactly what you need for a particular size of tapestry. This is where having the means to custom-adapt the frame size is good. As you're looking for frames that might be available, you'll find that a rigid frame is usually called a *strainer* and is different from *stretchers* that you can find at an art supply shop. The stretchers have the ability to tighten up loosened artist canvas by having thin wedges of wood tapped into the spaces at the back corners of the frame, and strainers have firmly fixed corners. Either of these options is fine for the mounting frame.

There are a couple of approaches to using either a strainer frame or one made from artist stretcher strips.

1. With one approach, the inner and outer layers of fabric are pulled firmly over the frame and stapled in place, and a large zigzag sort of stitch is used to hold the tapestry against the fabric face. These stitches go from the back to the front, around one warp, to the back, and then diagonally to another stitching point. The stitches would be hidden in the weft, if attaching this way, and should not pulled too tightly to cause the tapestry surface to dimple. The edges of the tapestry can also be stitched on, as described with the foam core board.

2. Another way to prepare the mounting frame is to first cover it with a piece of archival board cut to the same dimensions, and then stretch the inner and outer fabric over that. This gives a firm, rigid base for the tapestry to rest against rather than having only the open space of frame behind the mounting cloth. Depending on the size and weight of the tapestry, without the rigidity of the underlying board covering the frame, after time the mounting fabric may become a bit loose. This looseness will sometimes let the tapestry sink somewhat to show the edges of the frame.

For the wooden frame with a rigid base option, use the same method as described for the foam core board for stretching the fabric and stitching on the tapestry.

3. If you're mounting larger tapestries, say over 36" or so across, you may want to brace the frame with extra crosswise pieces.

Allie Dudley, *Roses*, 2019, tapestry.
Allie Dudley, photographer.

Once the tapestry is mounted on the background, it may be used as is, by adding a hanging device to the back, or it could be taken one more step to be framed in some way. If you choose to place the tapestry behind glass, as if it were a flat artwork on paper, be sure the glass doesn't press down against the surface of the weaving. Framing without glass is an alternative that will allow the tapestry's texture to be appreciated. Deeper frames, such as shadow box or floater frame types, work well with both ways of presentation. See a floater frame used with the small tapestry shown on page 145.

D rings and picture-hanging wire attached at the back edges of the frame would be used for hanging.

FREE-HANGING OPTIONS

Maybe you would prefer to have your tapestry hang loose, suspended along the top edge. This is a traditional way that many textiles of all kinds are presented, and is a good approach for larger pieces. Keep in mind that gravity will be working on the textile when you are hanging it freely, so the direction that the tapestry was woven should be considered. If designed so that the warp is turned in the horizontal direction when finished, any slits will be pulled downward with the weight of the wefts. Anticipating this, you may want to stitch the slits so that the joins are from a warp to the adjacent warp, either as you weave or afterward. Another solution would be to use interlocking techniques throughout the weaving so that the weft joins are as strong as they could possibly be.

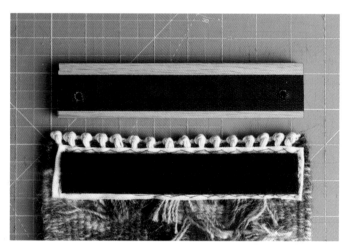

LEFT Loop side of Velcro® brand hook-and-loop fastener is attached to a cotton twill tape, first with basting stitches (*red thread*). Final stitching is done with a catch stitch (*gray thread*) to hold the Velcro to the tapestry. *Chris Dant, photographer*

TOP Loop side of a hook-and-loop fastener is shown at one end of the tapestry, and warp ends at the opposite side. The warp finish used overhand knots, with warps then put to the back in groups and stitched in place. *Chris Dant, photographer*

BOTTOM The hanging bar and top of the tapestry. *Chris Dant, photographer*

Methods for hanging from the top edge include weaving a turn-back at the top and stitching it to the body of the tapestry to make a channel into which a rod can be inserted, or sewing a sleeve or casing of another fabric at the top back and inserting a rod or batten, or attaching the loop side of a hook-and-loop fastener to the back and the hook side to a wooden bar or batten. There is also a magnetic slat system used in many museums as a solution for hanging large textiles. This option is expensive compared to others but is worth investigating, since it may be what you're looking for, especially if the tapestry will be permanently installed somewhere.[43]

Some people choose to put a liner at the back of a free-hanging tapestry, while others prefer to leave the back without liner. In place of a stitched-on lining, some museum conservators recommend having muslin or a polyethylene plastic sheet placed on a wall that is wooden or on an outside wall that might be prone to moisture.[44]

The method described below is one I've frequently used for larger tapestries. The process is similar to that shown in diagrams at the "Hanging Textiles" page from the George Washington University Museum / Textile Museum website.[45]

Materials used were cotton twill tape or carpet webbing; hook-and-loop fastener; sewing machine with regular sewing thread; straight pins or thin T pins; regular sewing needle; buttonhole thread; tapestry needle; scissors; ruler; wooden batten (poplar for low resin quality), approximately ½" by 2" or 3" and whatever width is needed to be about ½" narrower than the width of the tapestry; staple gun and staples; and possibly D rings and hanging wire. You might also want to seal the wood batten with a couple of coats of polyurethane before attaching the hook side of the fastener to it (this serves as a barrier against acid in the wood).

The twill tape or carpet webbing should be slightly wider than the hook-and-loop fastener so you'll be able to stitch through that and not the loop fastener when attaching it to the tapestry. Measure out the tape to be about 1½" wider than the tapestry. You'll fold back each edge of the tape when you attach it, to give a clean finish.

1. Stitch the loop side of the hook-and-loop fastener onto the twill tape with a sewing machine. Sew around all four sides, and if it's a wide piece, you may want to also stitch a couple of lines through the middle part to be sure it's held flat against the tape.
2. Position the twill tape about ¼"–½" down from the top edge of the tapestry. Make sure it's also about ¼"–½" away from each side of the tapestry.
3. Pin into place and then baste it down, using regular sewing thread and a sewing needle. Once the basting stitches are

in, you can take out the pins and let the basting thread do the work of holding the tape in place until it's permanently stitched on.

4. As you attach the twill tape by hand, it's helpful to put the tapestry facedown, with the end you're stitching the twill tape onto, at the edge of a table. Use a catch stitch (sometimes called a herringbone catch stitch) to stitch the twill tape onto the tapestry with a tapestry needle and buttonhole thread. To do this, go through to the face of the tapestry, around one warp, then back to the reverse to bring the needle up through the tape, ready to make the next stitch.
5. Let the catch stitch zigzag along the edge of the twill tape as you move across. Especially on larger pieces, if you start at the center and first move to one side, then from the center to the opposite side you'll have less chance of the twill tape shifting slightly forward as you go.
6. Attach the twill tape at the top first and then at the bottom, making sure that with each stitch the thread is taken to the face and around a warp, burying the thread between wefts as it comes to the back again. The stitches can be made about ¼" apart. Don't pull the stitch so tightly that you make a dimple on the face. Clip the basting stitches out after finishing with the catch stitch.
7. Prepare your hanging bar by sanding it and giving it a couple of coats of water-based polyurethane varnish, if you wish. This will seal the wood to avoid possible staining or acid migration onto the tapestry in the future; be sure to let it dry thoroughly before stapling the hook side of the fastener strip onto it.
8. D rings can be placed on the back of the bar, or eye screws in the ends, to use for hanging. Alternatively, before putting the hook strip onto the bar, you might drill holes into the wood that can be used when hanging (see photo on page 161). Afterward, use an awl to punch through the drilled holes to open up a space in the hook strip.

For hanging, the bar is placed on a wall and the tapestry is applied to it, matching up the hook and loop sides of the fastener.

OTHER FINISHING SOLUTIONS

Many other solutions may be found for finishing and presentation. For instance, take another look at the wrought-iron frame designed and fabricated specifically for Nancy Crampton's tapestry by her husband, which was mentioned on page 27. Expediency and cost are certainly factors to consider when deciding on what direction you want to take. Also think about the convenience of finding supplies, although now almost anything can be purchased online; there's no need to drive all over town looking for a particular size of twill tape, for instance.

With the final steps for my own work, I like to keep two things in mind. One is that I want anything I do to the tapestry to be reversible. If I don't like a mounting method sometime later, or if for some reason it's gotten damaged, I can easily remove the tapestry and remount it. The other thing is that everything I do to the tapestry in the finishing-and-presentation method I choose becomes a factor in how the whole thing is viewed. If I've designed a tapestry successfully and woven it well, I surely don't want to botch all of that by the way I hang it!

What does the future hold for your tapestries once you've woven them? Maybe you're making them for your home, and for family and friends. Perhaps you'll be designing and weaving for exhibition and sales purposes. There will be times when tapestries will need care and cleaning. Keep in mind that these are only suggestions—I am not a trained textile conservationist, but I have used these methods safely with my own tapestries. Use your best judgment about whether any of these suggestions would be appropriate and safe for you to use with your tapestry.

Removing dust with a gentle vacuuming could be done occasionally. If you have a tapestry hanging freely, check the back periodically to see that insects haven't taken up residence there. If you're storing tapestries that are free hanging, roll them around either a cardboard tube that's covered with clean cotton muslin, or cover a pool noodle (those cylindrical, firm foam shapes used by kids) with a muslin layer. Roll with the face of the tapestry out (not in)—that way, when it's unrolled any slight curl of fabric will be toward the wall. Cover the rolled tapestry with another clean muslin piece, either tie around the bundle with cord in a couple of places or pin with safety pins, and store flat. Smaller tapestries could be stored in archival boxes wrapped in acid-free tissue. Find companies that offer these items by searching for textile conservation supplies on the web. One is Conservation Support Systems, https://conservationsupport-systems.com/main.

If, by chance, the tapestry needs to be cleaned with water, do it with cool water and without soap, if possible. However, remember that dyes used for the yarns might bleed or run, and dark colors might stain onto light areas if that happens. Also, if the tapestry is woven with a variety of yarn types, you might find that some fibers shrink while others don't when handled this way. If you need to use a cleaning agent, Orvus WA Paste is one of the things recommended. But use only a little. Find a container large enough that you won't have to fold or wrinkle the tapestry—your bathtub might be the best for larger pieces. Rinse carefully several times and very gently squeeze out water. Absorb excess moisture by blotting with towels, and dry flat on other towels, out of the sun. All textiles can suffer sun damage, so it's best not to hang tapestries near windows for lengths of time, if possible.

The more extensive methods you could use for care of tapestries are beyond the scope of this book. However, if you do an internet search for textile conservation, you'll find several sites that offer information. Notice whether the site is from a museum or other organization that has a conservation department—those will likely be the ones from which to find the best information. You might also like to read about the conservation methods for tapestry discussed in the book mentioned earlier, *Anatomy of a Tapestry: Techniques, Materials, Care* by Jean Pierre and Yadin Larochette. Yadin's training in textile conservation, as well as the fact that she is the daughter of renowned tapestry artists Jean Pierre Larochette and Yael Lurie, gives her definitive knowledge of methods for care of tapestries for current and future generations.

Looking Ahead—What Comes Next?

> [I]t is this very *lack* of speed, this steady slow progress onward that is part of the spirit of tapestry and its place as a living art form. And the peculiar glow and lustre inherent in the heavy weft—the soft but firm tapestry cloth is more than physical contrast to the material hardness of our world. Above all, the order of growth on the loom emerges in the completed tapestry with an underlying rightness of purpose, control, freedom and fantasy that has a special place in a world of frantic and complex pressures.
>
> —Archie Brennan[46]

I was fortunate within a few months after retiring from my university position to be able to take an eight-week concentration class with Archie Brennan and Susan Martin Maffei at Penland School of Craft. At that point I'd been weaving tapestries for thirteen years—yet there was so much I didn't know. That experience, with their guidance, opened up ways to help me refine my understanding of tapestry techniques. In addition to learning more about techniques for weaving, I saw two master teachers in action. Each day they worked individually with every person, and there was also a group activity of some kind—a discussion, demonstration, drawing session, or question-and-answer time. Many of the times in the group sessions, Archie would talk about tapestry and the purpose for this curious activity in our world today. His musings were based on decades of tapestry making, and the wisdom of his words moved me greatly. I left the session with my head full of inspiration about tapestry, as well as a desire to share what I was learning—and what I felt was a model, from their examples of teaching style, for how to proceed.

I began soon afterward to teach tapestry workshops myself. The ideas and design explorations found in this book have been part and parcel of that particular work in progress for many years. As I collected materials in preparation for writing, I went through past handouts I'd developed for classes, notes to myself as I evaluated workshops that were underway, and journal entries about my own tapestry work. In the review, I saw recurring themes. For instance, I've often wondered if this is *good* enough—is it the best way to explain something to students or to tackle an idea in my work? I've revisited concepts time and again, often keeping the basic premise but changing something to—I hope—make it more coherent and a better example, or to flesh it out more.

When I was at the university in the first year of art study, one of my professors made the statement to the class that we would make the same painting over and over, all our lives. At first I didn't understand what she was talking about. Now I believe the point she was making was that each of us has a unique voice. Every single one of us would have a way of handling design, composition, and image that we would continue to rehash and refine as the years went by. That's certainly the case with the ideas I've just written about. I hope that the assorted ideas and explorations I've presented here will encourage you to seek, find, and continue to refine your unique voice for design, composition, and image in tapestry.

One more thing before ending—I'd like to encourage, even challenge, each of you to adopt a daily practice of tapestry making. Whether you do it in the way I choose to or not doesn't matter. What does is that you weave daily.

As I'm writing this, I'm halfway through the tenth year of what I call my tapestry diaries. Each year I dedicate a loom to a warp for the diary. Every day I weave a small amount for the day. A larger image completed each month is sometimes incorporated into the whole tapestry, yet the daily bits of weaving are small. As each tapestry diary is unrolled at the end of a year, the 365 small areas of weaving are there as a record of the passing of each day. When I don't have time to work on larger tapestries, this small daily devotion keeps my tapestry skills honed. My tapestry diary for 2018 is shown on page 175. I've written more about my tapestry diaries in a few places that are listed in the notes.[47] If a daily commitment to a bit of tapestry isn't for you—that's fine. Nevertheless, whether it's doing a daily sketch or writing in an ongoing journal, I think you'll find that devoting a little time to making something, even something small, each day will be rewarding. You may find in the process the spark that ignites into the flame of creativity in your hands, illuminating what you see with your eyes and feel in your heart.

Happy designing and weaving to you!

Acknowledgments

It would be impossible to give credit and thanks to everyone I've encountered through the years who have given me encouragement in this incredible journey of learning and sharing. I say incredible because becoming a teacher was the furthest thing in my mind when I was a child. Circumstances led me into the field, and great mentors kept me there. Those mentors not only gave me insight into the processes for making things but also showed me that often sharing with others is the best way to learn.

Guidance from beloved teachers including Bob Owens, Edwina Bringle, Archie Brennan, and Susan Martin Maffei has been helpful to me in ways too numerous to mention. Artists Ken and Terri Bryson, Molly Elkind, Rebecca Mezoff, Sarah Swett, and Pat Williams have read versions of this book and offered much-needed advice.

Terri and Ken Bryson have also given their time and expertise in photography, editing, and arranging details with other Atlanta-area tapestry study group members to help make this all come together. Chris Dant, assistant professor of visual art at the University of North Georgia, has done an amazing job with photography of work in progress by my students at Penland School of Craft, as well as of many design explorations, tapestry samples, and larger tapestries.

Patrick Horan helped explain to me a simple way to calculate sizes when writing about cartoons. Both he and his wife, Noel Thurner, who introduced me to the wonderful yarns from Norway, have been important to my creative life and in many other ways for decades.

Margo Booth in Dahlonega led me through the final stages of manuscript preparation with gentle, precise, and knowing guidance. A special note of gratitude goes to Margo in the memory of her husband, Jimmy Booth. Margo spent much time working with me during what turned out to be the last weeks of his life as she assisted me through the manuscript details.

Sandra Korinchak, senior editor at Schiffer Publishing, has given me support from the beginning when I first submitted the idea for the book through to the end. I couldn't have gotten this finished without either Margo or Sandra. My appreciation goes to Brenda McCallum who took my words and images and beautifully designed them into these pages.

Students continue to amaze me with their willingness to participate in exploring ideas and trying things out. I appreciate that Allie Dudley, Nancy Nordquist, Dorina Scalia, and Joann C. Wilson have allowed me to use examples from designs and tapestries they've either done or begun in some of my workshops.

Participants in my last class at Penland School of Craft in 2019 were gracious to allow Chris Dant to photograph them as they worked, and to provide several examples for the book. Thank you so much, Theresa Ballaine, Robin Beveridge, Deborah Carroll, Allie Dudley, Annette Harrison, Mary Jones, Alice Martin, April Price, Sofia Pujol, Holly Wilkes, and Joann Wilson, for taking part in the class and trying out many of these ideas.

Becca Pontes, a visual art major at the University of North Georgia, worked with me to set up the pipe loom for photography. My intrepid niece Megan Smith Noble put in hours of work to sort out index details.

I'm especially appreciative to my colleagues in the Atlanta-area tapestry study group who took on the challenge of weaving samples of many of the ideas presented here: Terri Bryson, Mary Alice Donceel, Nancy Dugger, Deb Gottlieb, Izumi Hubbard, Mary Jane Lea, Dinah Rose, and Sarah Thomsen. Thank you, thank you, thank you!

My admiration and gratitude to these artists who have generously allowed me to present, with their works, beautiful examples of a few of the many ways design fundamentals play a role in contemporary tapestry: Janet Austin, Nicki Bair, Archie Brennan, Elizabeth Buckley, Barbara Burns, Don Burns, Mary Cost, Nancy Crampton, Jane Freear-Wyld,

Heather Gallegos-Rex, Joan Griffin, Lyn Hart, Barbara Heller, Betty Hilton-Nash, Susan Iverson, David Johnson, Robbie LaFleur, Connie Lippert, Mary Jane Lord, Susan Martin Maffei, LaDonna Mayer, Rebecca Mezoff, Erin M. Riley, Michael Rohde, Kathy Spoering, Becky Stevens, Sarah Swett, Kathe Todd-Hooker, Linda Wallace, Sarah Warren, Sue Weil, and Pat Williams.

Thank you to the family of Silvia Heyden, who allowed images of her tapestries and also her words to be part of this effort. I was fortunate to meet Silvia several years ago when she opened up her home to members of Tapestry Weavers South and showed us scores of her tapestries. She also wove for us as we watched—quite a special treat. Later I was able to take part in a brief workshop she arranged near her home in Durham, North Carolina. Although my own work is quite different in style and approach than hers, the inspiration and learning that came from those experiences remain with me still.

My appreciation goes to Billy Collins and his publisher, the University of Pittsburgh Press, for use of his poem "Horizon" from *The Art of Drowning* (© 1995). Joann Wilson is the one who first introduced me to the poem several years ago, and I've used it ever since as an example as I talk to students—one more thing I must thank Joann for, in addition to the many "What if . . . ?" questions she's brought up in workshops!

Steven Aimone kindly allowed me to quote from his book *Expressive Drawing: A Practical Guide to Freeing the Artist Within*. I've been fortunate to be a student in several of his workshops, and those have always been amazing—as are his books.

Dianne Mize gave permission to quote from her book *Finding Freedom to Create*. I've known Dianne for many decades and admire the way she's shared with thousands of students through the years, and she continues to do so in her widely followed newsletter and videos.

I have quoted from Archie Brennan at the start of my "Looking Ahead" comments, with gratitude both to Susan Martin Maffei and Sharon Marcus for their permission on his behalf. That quote, from the *Tapestry: The Narrative Voice* catalog for the 1989–1991 exhibition coordinated by Sharon Marcus, is just one example of Archie's insightful writing about tapestry. Archie's words have inspired and guided me for many years—I have notebooks from past workshops, filled with his comments, and reread them often. It was with great sadness I learned that Archie had passed away on October 31, 2019. The many people that he touched will always miss him. But what a legacy in tapestry he's left for us all.

Thank you, Rebecca Mezoff, for writing the foreword and for being a guiding light for so many tapestry weavers around the world! Your work in the field of tapestry education is truly a beacon.

I'm grateful to the artist residency locations both of the Hambidge Center and the Lillian E. Smith Center, where I spent several weeks at different times during the two years of working on this book. These centers have enriched my life, as well as the lives of many, for decades, and I treasure each time I'm able to be at those beautiful places.

Support from friends and family, particularly my husband, Thomas, has been what's often kept me going when I've gotten discouraged. They've helped me see that a new day brings a fresh start, with the bright promise of morning waiting to be fulfilled—much like weft threads filling the warps of tapestry.

APPENDIX A

Tapestry-Weaving Basics

Tapestry weaving is both simple and complex. The most basic description is that it is a fabric woven with wefts that cover the warp in discontinuous ways to create designs. It's made of the simplest of all weave structures, called plain weave, which takes weft threads over and under warp threads in an alternating sequence as they're woven.

Despite the over-one, under-one simplicity of the weave structure, there is complexity in many aspects of tapestry weaving. It begins with the subtle differences of thread tension in both warp and weft that can be problematic if not controlled. Then there's the fact that the image one designs may not be easily interpreted through the technique, requiring adjustments or adaptations. Added to that is the time it takes to make a tapestry. It may seem that mastering the necessary skills is impossible, but approaching it with study, diligence, and practice can lead you into the many joys found in the weaving of tapestries.

Equipment and Tools

- Loom: A loom of any type can be used for tapestry, from the simplest of frames you build yourself to more complicated pieces of equipment you might purchase.

  Directions for building a frame loom from galvanized pipe are given following this section in appendix B. In addition to a loom, you'll need a few other things:
- Warp: You'll want something strong and resilient for warp. Cotton seine twine, linen, and wool are possibilities.
- Weft: Almost anything can be used for weft. Smaller yarns may be grouped to make the weft larger, if needed. Usually, you'll want the weft to be able to pack easily to completely cover the warp.
- Scissors
- Bobbins, needle, beater: Tapestry bobbins and a tapestry needle or two are options, although your fingers might be all you want to use to carry the weft. A beater for the weft also is an option. A kitchen fork can serve this purpose.

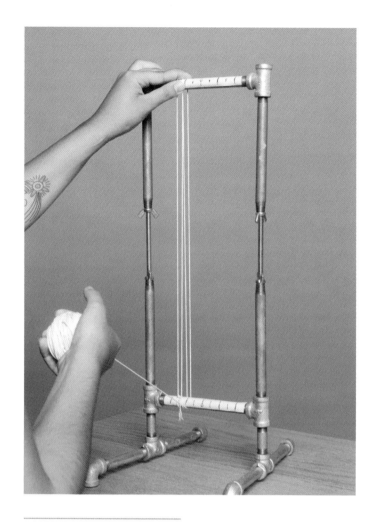

Small galvanized pipe loom being warped by University of North Georgia student Becca Pontes. *Chris Dant, photographer*

Preparing for Weaving

There are several ways a warp may be set up for tapestry; some depend on the type of loom that's being used. My discussion here assumes that you can set up a warp on your loom and weave tapestry techniques. However, I'll mention a few things that might be helpful, beginning with a suggestion about how to determine the number of threads per inch to use: the warp sett.

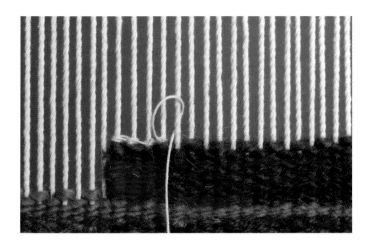

First step of half hitch used to secure weft at beginning and end of tapestry. *Chris Dant, photographer*

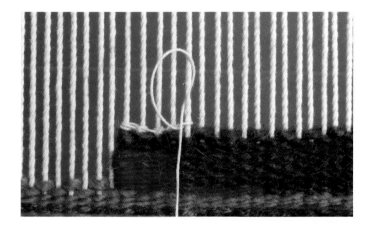

Second step of half hitch. Each warp in sequence will have these two steps done across the width. *Chris Dant, photographer*

Master weaver Archie Brennan offers a way to gauge the warp sett in his article "The Space between the Warps."[48] He recommends wrapping the selected warp thread closely within 1 centimeter on a ruler. Count the wraps and use that number as the number of warp threads needed *per inch*. This is called the warp *ends per inch* (abbreviated as epi). He notes that this is a starting place for what might be considered a "classic" warp-to-weft spacing for tapestry, and goes on to discuss why one may sometimes want to vary from that.

At the beginning, after a header is woven, it's good to use half hitches to secure the weft of the tapestry as it begins. This is also done at the end of the tapestry. In my own work, I do

this step no matter what other end finishing method I plan. With the half hitches in place, the wefts are secure and there's no chance of the last picks beginning to unravel before the final steps are done. The half hitches may be done with a small seine twine, buttonhole thread, or even regular sewing thread.

Meet and Separate: A Basic Technique for Building Shapes as You Weave

Tapestry is created by weaving different shapes, and those can be complex or simple. Shapes may be built up independently in decreasing ways or made row by row, with the wefts changing across the width of the weaving as the shapes are made. In either instance, the *meet-and-separate* method can be used.

The direction in which the wefts travel is important when using meet and separate. In this method, wefts should travel *opposite* each other *in the same shed*, along the same row or pick. This ensures that the plain-weave sequence is correct for every pick that lies in the common row, allowing the plain-weave structure to be maintained. This is important when the design shifts to cause shapes to be woven on top of others. This is the essence of the meet-and-separate method—that wefts will be in correct sequence with each other along a shared row, no matter how many wefts are in place.

Tapestry maker and teacher Archie Brennan describes this when he says there are two questions to ask and answer for meet and separate:

(1) *On what shed do I begin?* Answer: on the opposite shed of the weaving below.

(2) *From what side do I begin, left or right?* Answer: from the opposite direction from the weft used for the existing shape that is in the same shed.

If there is no shape in place, then the new shape can begin on the left or the right, but the next adjoining shape must follow the answer above.

Another way to think about the opposition of wefts in the same shed is this: At the meeting point, as the adjacent wefts turn back to make the second pick of the plain-weave sequence, each adjacent weft will either be going *over* (on top), or *under* (behind) the warp around which it turns. This puts the wefts in either a high or a low position on the adjacent warp threads.

The two picks of plain weave make up a *pass* in tapestry, the complete sequence of the weave structure.

Detail of two wefts in meet and separate. Left side shows the low (valley) turn, with weft behind the warp at the edge of the return. Right side is a high (hill) turn, with weft going over the warp at the edge of the return. *Chris Dant, photographer*

The key to using this method is making sure to have the wefts in the correct direction as they meet and separate in the common shed. There are ways to correct the order if you get out of it, and you will as soon as another shape is used within the same shed. "Is this so bad?" you might say. Yes, because it can cause you to not be able to pack the weft sufficiently to cover the warp, since the weft will be double the thickness where it overlaps. One solution is to change the direction of one of the original two wefts as the third one is entered.

Shapes may be woven by building *descending* or *decreasing* shapes first, then filling in beside the shape with the next color. Stepping back or dropping out warp threads with each pass allows this to happen. The number of warps involved and the position of the weft as the turn is made will give different angles to the shape, and a degree of smoothness or "steppiness" to the edge of the shape.

Shapes may appear to be angular or curving, but both effects are created by weft turns made in steps. Think of the steps as pixels in a digital image. The closer the sett of the warp, the smaller the visual steps will be, and the eye will "read" the edge as being smoother.

Alternatively, rather than building shapes individually, each color could be used in the common shed, with the other color brought to meet (or separate) with it, all the way across the row. In this way, the tapestry will grow row by row or pick by pick. Some weavers prefer to weave in this way. Regardless of your preference for way of working, the theory of meet and separate remains the same—at each pick, or one-half of a complete tapestry pass, colors will either be meeting or separating in the same shed.

Hatching and Hachure: A Way to Blend Colors and to Create Other Shape Areas

Hatching and *hachure* are interchangeable terms for traditional methods of blending colors between shapes. The technique includes a small sequence of passes that interact or alternate with each other. In Renaissance and Baroque period tapestries, this method was often used to show shadows, folds of drapery, the roundness of forms, and the illusion of transparency. The method can be based on using meet and separate.

First let's consider one weft traveling in a long pass and then a shorter pass, to be followed by a second color that meets and separates at each turning point of the first.

As the passes of weft pack into place, horizontal lines are created. Often, the use of more passes for the transition points between the two colors is what's described as hachure. It's really simply hatching with more passes being used.

In this example, the dark-purple weft first moves to the left in a long pass, then makes a shorter pass. Two passes (or four picks) of dark-purple weft are in place. Next, the bright-red weft moves to the right to meet and separate from each point where the first weft turned, in two matching passes. Following

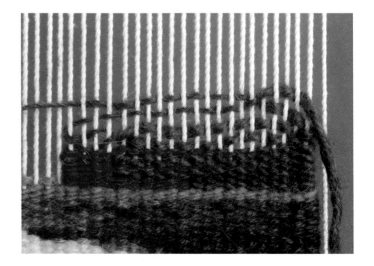

Expanded view of meet and separate, set up to do hatching. *Chris Dant, photographer*

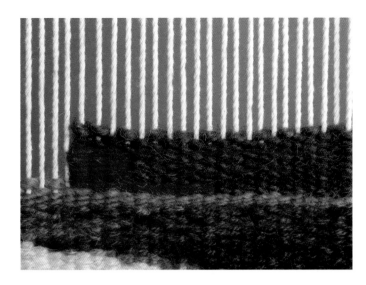

Hatching in place. Notice the "third" value between the left and right sides, created by the pattern of horizontal lines made by the hatching. *Chris Dant, photographer*

that, the dark-purple weft is taken to the left in a long pass, followed by a short pass. The bright red again meets and separates with both passes of dark purple. When woven into place, with the wefts closely packed to hide the warp, horizontal lines of dark purple and bright red will alternate in the middle area between the solid areas of dark purple on the right side and bright-red weft at the left side.

For more complex hatching three or four passes of one color are made, for instance one being long, the next medium, and then one shorter in length. The second color then meets and separates at those passes.

The points where the weft turns are done may stay in the same position, making vertical separations of design areas. They may also move from side to side, either staying the same number of warp threads apart, or shifting and varying the position of the turning points as the tapestry grows upward.

Wonderful effects may be created using two colors only and taking advantage of the beauty of meet and separate as used with hatching.

Adding Shapes

Once other shapes/colors are added, the meet-and-separate orientation of the original two colors will be thrown off. One or the other of the first two colors will interact correctly with a new color. The other will be in the wrong direction to maintain the plain weave without having an overlap of weft as shapes begin to move around.

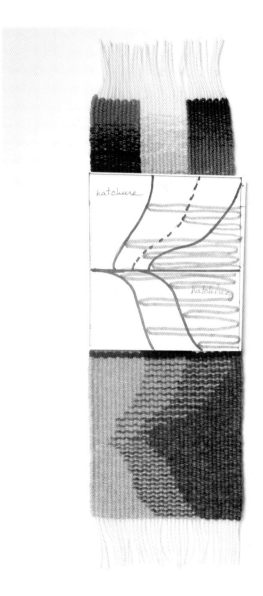

Sample of hatching and hachure used with curving edges. The diagram above the woven sample shows the movements the weft takes at the turns, not the actual number of passes in the tapestry. *Chris Dant, photographer*

One way to correct this, as mentioned before, is to change the direction of one of the original two colors. This may be done by ending it, then restarting it from the opposite side of a shape in the same shed. This will put all three of the colors in a correct meet-and-separate sequence.

Kathe Todd-Hooker gives clear diagrams to show several other solutions to this dilemma in her book *Tapestry 101*, when she describes fixing the bobbin order.[49]

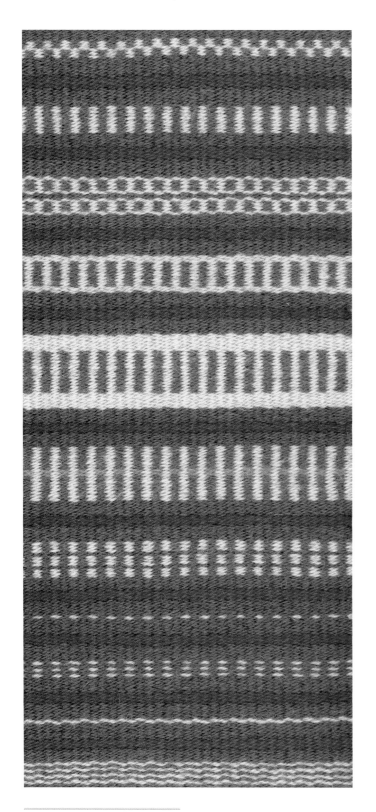

Other Methods: Pick and Pick, Soumak, Twining, Rya

Unlike meet and separate, these methods will not necessarily maintain the same sequence of weft as they are used. In fact soumak, twining, and rya aren't strictly weaving methods. I'm only briefly describing these techniques because in-depth information about all of them can be found in various references. One source in particular that gives excellent diagrams and discussion of these methods is Peter Collingwood's book *Techniques of Rug Weaving.*[50]

PICK AND PICK

When weaving with pick and pick, each of the two sheds of a plain-weave pass is woven with a different color. This will create a vertical line that runs along alternate warp threads when continued in the same sequence, over and over.

The vertical line can be shifted to the other warp by making two sequential picks (or a whole pass) of one of the colors, then returning to the alternation of the two.

Dots or spots of color can also be made using pick and pick. The dots can be made to show up either on alternating warps or on the same warps.

To make alternating dots, follow two picks of one color with one pick of a second color and then return to two picks of the first color.

Dots will align above each other when three picks of the alternate color are placed between the contrasting picks.[51]

You might want to experiment with making dots larger and smaller, combining them with vertical lines of pick and pick, and with more solid bands of color. Any of these effects could also be used within shapes as well as across the whole width of a tapestry. Add varying color for one of the picks into the mix, and you'll soon see that this simple method can quickly become visually very complex.

At the edge of the pick-and-pick area, the way the wefts are interlocked will be a bit different depending on whether there is an odd or even number of warps being included. In *The Techniques of Rug Weaving*, Peter Collingwood gives extensive diagrams of different ways to handle the edges when using pick and pick.[52]

Detail of pick-and-pick sampler, showing some of the variety of effects of the two wefts used in alternation

SOUMAK

Soumak is a way of wrapping weft around warps that gives a supplemental float of yarn across the surface. It is often used in combination with weaving where two or more picks of plain weave are placed between rows of soumak.[53] The number of warps involved in the wrapping will be a factor in how textured the surface will become when soumak is used in an overall effect. Look back at the detail of David Johnson's soumak tapestry *Transformation* on page 36 to see the texture possibilities of this method.

Soumak can also move out of the horizontal direction to become like drawing on the surface. The method of flying shuttle, as seen in Coptic tapestry, is structurally very similar to soumak.[54]

In "Finishing and Presentation Suggestions," on page 155, it was mentioned that a line of soumak is sometimes used at the bottom and top edges of tapestry at the turn-back point before the hem. The float of yarn that happens with soumak is helpful in hiding any bit of warp that could possibly peek between wefts as the hem is turned to the back.

Peter Collingwood's book also has a great variety of diagrams and descriptions of ways that soumak can be carried out.

TWINING

Twining is done with paired strands of yarn, either the same color or two different colors. The two strands twist between warp threads so that each warp thread is enclosed as the twining moves across. The warp threads remain stationary when twining is done. A variety of pattern effects can be made with twining when two colors are used.[55] Twining along a decreasing or increasing edge built with weaving can help smooth the weft steps somewhat.

Twining may also be done by taking paired strands of yarn across passes of weft in a vertical or angled way. When twining across wefts, the two ends of yarn will exchange places, back to front and front to back. The effect will look a bit like stitching, with the length of the "stitches" depending on the number of passes between the exchange points. This method adds the yarn as a supplemental component to the woven surface.[56]

RYA

Rya is one of many knotted-pile methods that can be found throughout many parts of the world. The name "rya" is mostly associated with Scandinavian knotted-pile rugs and bed

Allie Dudley.
Combination of rya and overshot weaving (*detail*). 2019. *Courtesy of Allie Dudley; Chris Dant, photographer*

coverings. The knot used for rya is called a Ghiordes knot.[57] Passes of plain weave are used between rows of knots; this may be done with tapestry methods to give a distinctive two-sided appearance. Knots can also be used selectively within the overall piece, as seen in the piece by Allie Dudley in which she inserts a small area of rya into a larger body of overshot weaving.

Ending the Tapestry

Secure the tapestry with half hitches at the top before cutting off. The half hitches are done the same way as at the bottom when beginning. There is no need to weave anything else once the half hitches are in place at the top.

The warp ends may be finished in one of several ways. See "Finishing and Presentation Suggestions" on page 154.

Troubleshooting

- *Edges moving inward due to uneven warp tension*: Be sure that the warp is put onto the loom with even tension and stays firm. The warps will draw together more if the tension becomes slack, and this can cause the edges to pull in. Also, if there are areas where one or more warps have less tension, the warp will drift and the weft won't pack level at these points.
- *Warp spacing can change and cause pulling in*: Watch the spacing of the warps closely and correct any moving together or tightening of the warp sett immediately. Often, pulling in at the edges happens because some of the warps away from the selvedge have begun to get too close together.
- *Break large areas of the same color into a more than one weft*: If you're weaving a single color over a large width, you may need to make more than one weft bundle. The more distance over which a single weft source is used, the greater the chance is that pulling in will happen. Weave these separate bobbins or butterflies of the same-color weft in a way that is either regular, as in a diagonal pattern back and forth, or irregularly placed. If in a regular pattern, there will be a chance of the tiny slit at the turn points or cutbacks becoming visible. You may like this because it can create beautiful subtle patterning within solid areas. If you don't want to notice the turn points or cutbacks, however, staggering them in irregular ways will make them less noticeable.
- *Warps that tend to spread apart*: You're probably not pulling the wefts tightly enough in areas. Try to slightly tighten up each weft pass until the warps pull back into the spacing needed. The weft tension needs to be constantly adjusted throughout the weaving. Another thing that may cause this is that the weft is too large for the warp sett. In that case, you'll also notice that the weft doesn't completely cover the warp.
- *The edge of the weaving or a shape within the tapestry is building up too high*: You are probably getting too much draw-in at the selvedges or the edges of the shape, making the warps pull closer together. Watch the spacing at the turns from the very beginning and correct any pulling in that may be seen.
- *The edge of the weaving is sloping down*: Take care that the last few warp ends at the selvedge or at the edge of a shape don't begin to spread too far apart. Make the selvedge turns of the weft firm, not too tight and not too loose.
- *Surface of the tapestry is showing vertical ribs*: Another thing to watch out for is "ribbing" of the surface. If you begin to notice vertical lines on the face of the tapestry, maybe showing up over only a few warps in areas or over many, this indicates that the weft tension isn't the same in both sheds. The weft is being pulled more tightly in one direction than the other. Be sure that each pick of weft undulates around the warps rather than lying straight in the shed. The warp should move very little back and forth as the wefts cross over and under it; instead, the wefts should "snake" around the warps.
- *There is wrinkling or buckling to the surface*: Most likely there is too much weft being packed into too little space between warps. If it hasn't happened before in the weaving, are you in an area where there are many small shapes being used side by side? Try to make the turns between shapes firm; smaller shapes may need a bit more weft tension than larger shapes. The weft may also be larger than needed. Visualize the space between warp threads and the turn of two wefts between those two warps—each weft should take up one-half of the space between those two warps.
- *Shapes are "squashed" and distorted*: Remember that the weft of the tapestry will be pushed down, packed, and compressed by the weaving that builds above previously woven areas. If you're following a cartoon, be sure to weave slightly above the top of a shape or edge. How much above? That depends on sett, thickness of weft, and how hard you're beating. Notice the amount of compression that occurs and try to compensate for that. It may be as much as ¼".
- *Circular shapes seem to have "ears"*: This relates to the point above. Rounded edges are woven with different numbers of passes used at the warps involved. These passes make steps up or down, rather than smooth curving edges. When weaving circular or curving shapes, the sides need to be woven tall enough to compensate for the compression that will happen as the weft packs down. The sides may look high enough as you begin weaving the top of the curving shape, but then will

flatten as weft is packed above. When weaving a circle, it's a challenge to estimate how tall that side area must be. Because the contour of the circle as woven is really a series of stairsteps, the more warps involved in forming the circle, the more convincing the shape will appear.

- *Diagonal shapes are too jagged or stepped*: The angle may be being made on a high turn more often than on a low. When weaving, two low passes visually will appear to equal one high pass. As the angles of the diagonals increase, the number of passes at each turn must increase, making steeper angles appear more stepped. Sometimes the steps can be somewhat smoothed in appearance by twining along the edge or by using soumak.

Moving Forward with Tapestry

This has been a very basic introduction to a few of the steps in making tapestry. If you're an experienced tapestry weaver, you are well versed in all the preceding information. For those who are new to it, I highly recommend face-to-face study at a workshop or class, if one is available to you. That's not always feasible, so I'd also encourage you to read a how-to book (or many), watch a video about the making of tapestry, perhaps join online conversations about tapestry in social media, and check out an organization such as the American Tapestry Alliance for guidance and inspiration. Suggested resources for further information about tapestry techniques are given at the end of this book.

Remember this about tapestry—it's a jealous medium; it likes for you to spend time with it. The more you stay away, the more challenging it will be when you want to return. You'll find your fingers fumbling with threads that once flowed so smoothly into the warps. Your brain suddenly can't wrap itself around the techniques that had felt so familiar. The surface quality of the tapestry is harsh or sleazy and the edges . . . well, would *meandering* be the best word to describe them?

Tapestry Diary—A Year of My Life *is one of an ongoing, yearlong commitment to a weaving I've been doing since 2009. Each year since then, I've started a tapestry with very little preplanning that I call a tapestry diary. In these, I weave a small increment each day, with the color and amount to be done depending on circumstances of time, mood, or other factors I don't (and sometimes can't) predetermine. Just like life . . . one has some sense of plan, but there are always things that come up. I truly believe that "weaving every darn day" in this way has made me a better tapestry weaver. Not everyone wants or needs to do a process like this! But to be a better tapestry weaver one must do the work.*

Tommye McClure Scanlin. *Tapestry Diary—A Year of My Life*, 2018. 62" × 12" × 0.5". Photo © Tim Barnwell

If you want to become proficient in weaving tapestry, then weave it every darn day—even if only a few passes each time. Give yourself goals that are easy to reach. Maybe don't try to finish a square yard of tapestry in a month, but *do* go all out to finish a square foot. In fact, you might challenge yourself with weaving at least a square foot of tapestry in a month's time for a year. You could achieve that in several small pieces, or one that's 12" by 12" in each month of the year.

I'll bet that if you commit yourself to weaving at least that much each month for the next twelve months, you'll truly feel that you and tapestry have become partners. You'll soon find you're saying to yourself and others: "I'm a tapestry weaver."

Appendix B
Simple Pipe Loom to Build

A pipe loom similar to this is shown on page 168.

Parts Needed*

6 – ¼" diameter threaded pipe (called nipple), 6" long each
4 – ¼" diameter threaded nipple, 4" long each
2 – ¼" diameter threaded nipple, 1" long each
4 – Elbows to fit the ¼" threaded pipes
4 – Tees to fit the ¼" threaded pipes
2 – Caps for the ¼" threaded pipes
2 – Threaded rods, 12" × ¼" diameter
4 – Wingnuts to fit the threaded rod

Assembling the Loom

The frame of the loom is built with the six pieces of 6" long nipple.

The top has two elbows joining three of the 6" pieces into a U shape.

The bottom has two tees joining the three remaining 6" pieces into another U shape.

The two 1" long nipples screw into the bottom tees to make the legs.

Screw two more tees on the other end of the 1" pieces. These will hold the feet extensions.

Put the 4" nipple at either end of the bottom tees, placing an elbow on one end and a cap on the other end.

---

*Optional parts—to make leash bar holder:

2 – ¼" tees for the top of the loom
2 – ¼" street elbows to fit the ¼" tees
2 – ¼" threaded nipple, 5" long each (leash hanger)
2 – Caps for the ¼" leash hanger
2 – ¼" diameter dowels (one as leash holder and approximately 8" wide, the other dowel for the open shed, approximately 5" wide)

Optional assembly for the top to install leash bar holder:

Use two tees here instead of the elbows. Those are to hold a 5" leash hanger extension. Screw the street elbows to the top tees, then the 5" nipple to extend forward. Put the caps on the leash hanger.

Note that larger and longer pipes may be used to build bigger looms by using the basics of this extremely versatile plan. Thanks to Archie Brennan for his brilliant pipe loom designs of all sizes that he's inspired hundreds of people to build over the past decades. Other diagrams of his designs for looms are found at his website: www.brennan-maffei.com/Loom.htm.

Sarah Swett describes her many pipe looms in this post from her blog: www.afieldguidetoneedlework.com/blog/galvanized-pipe-looms.

Useful Templates

Template for 2" squares

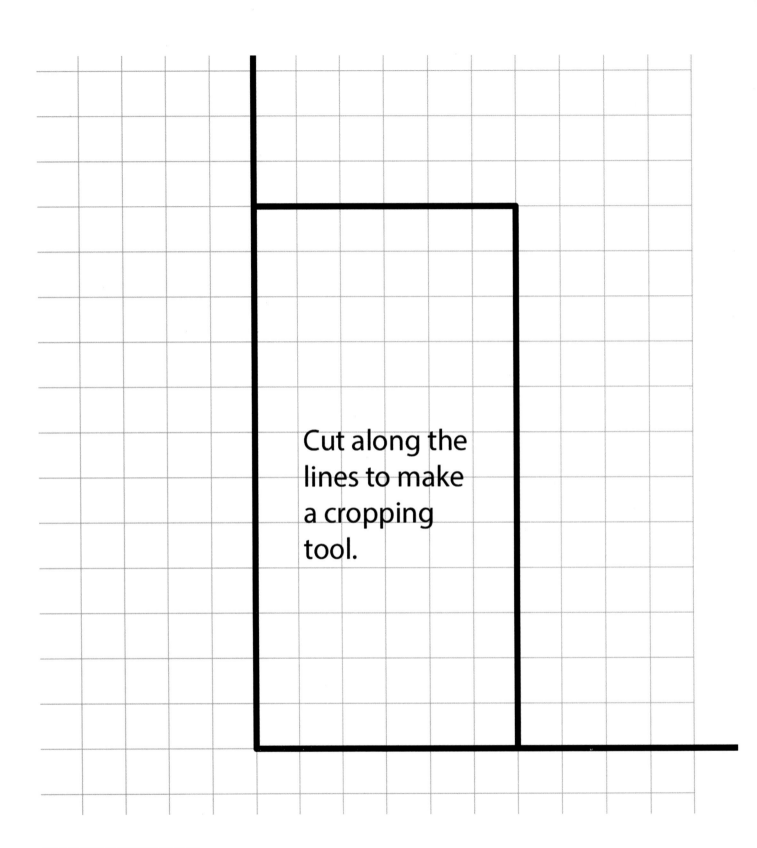

Cut along the lines to make a cropping tool.

Template for L-shaped cropping tool

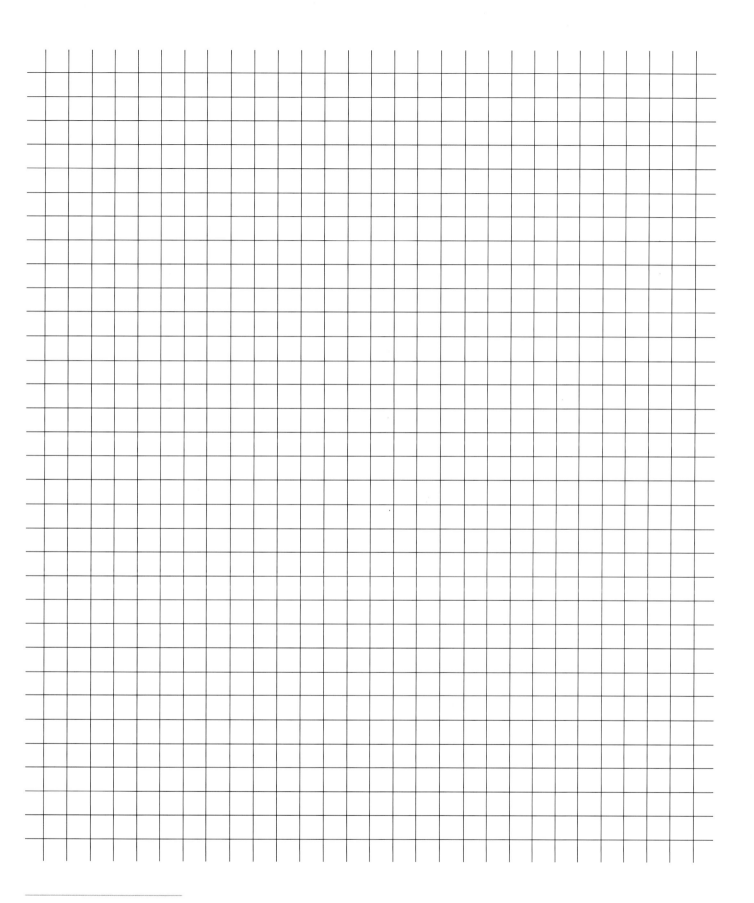

Template for ¼" grid

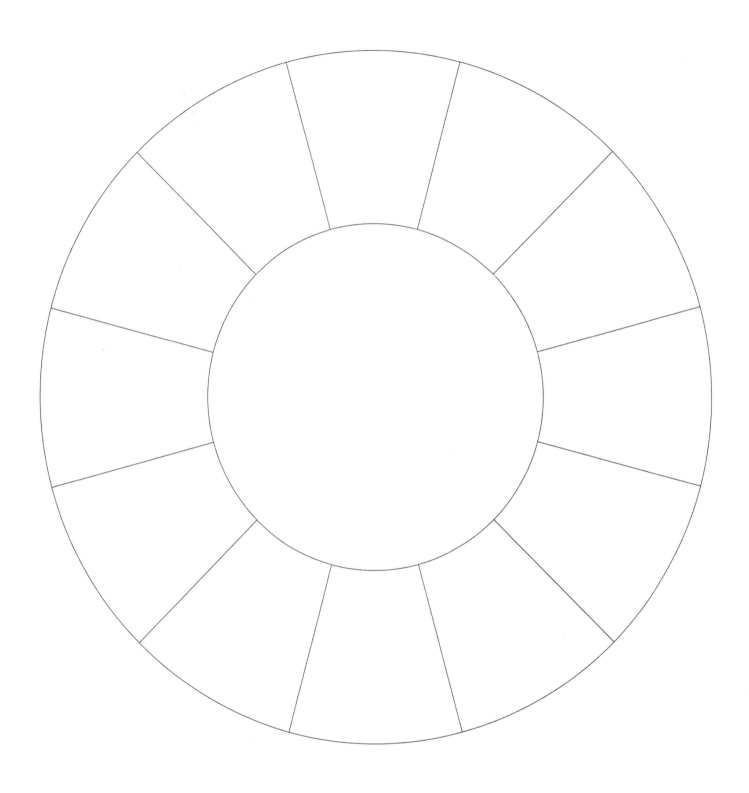

Template for color wheel

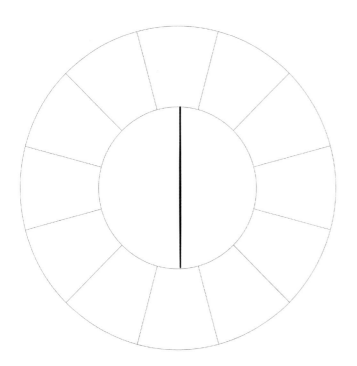

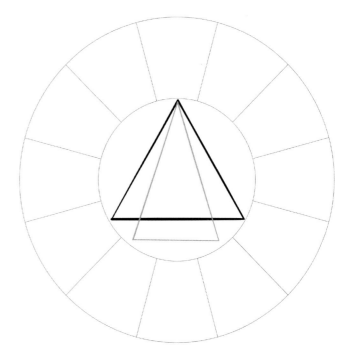

TOP Diagram of complementary pairs. Draw a similar one onto a transparency sheet and rotate to find any complementary pair around the wheel.

TOP RIGHT Diagram for two triads: equilateral triangle and isosceles triangle. Transparency sheets can be made for both. Place one or the other onto the color wheel to locate triads. Rotate to find more.

BOTTOM Diagram for two four-color groups: square and rectangle Transparency sheets can be made for both. Use one or the other to locate four-color groups on the color wheel. Rotate to find more.

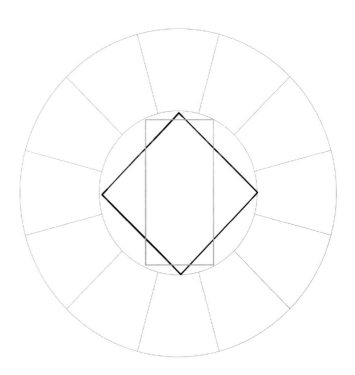

Glossary: Basic Tapestry and Basic Design Terms

Tapestry Terms

Beater—used to pack in weft

Bobbin—holds weft yarn; may be of several types, including Gobelin style or Aubusson flute

Butterfly—bundle of yarn done in such a way that weft may pull out as needed

Cartoon—design from which tapestry is woven; may be attached to the back of the warp

Closed shed (pick shed)—opposite the open shed

Ends per inch (epi)—number of warp threads used in 1". The sett of the weaving.

Half hitch—used to secure weft at beginning and ending of tapestry

Hatching and hachure—methods of meet and separate to give horizontal lines between colors; a shading method

High or low—two positions a weft yarn may take as it makes a turn around a warp on the second pick of a pass. Other terms are hill or full for the high turn, and valley or hollow for the low turn.

Interlock—method of joining shapes by wefts interlocking around each other between warps, including single-weft interlock and double-weft interlock

Meet and separate—method in which wefts travel in opposite directions in the same shed

Open shed—a shed that is permanently held open with a shed rod

Pass—two pick of weft, one in each shed to complete a cycle or sequence of plain weave

Pick—a single trip of weft in a shed

Pick and pick—method for creating vertical stripes in weft-faced weaving, done by alternating different-color picks of weft woven in opposite sheds

Pick shed—weaver-selected shed, picked with the fingers. Also a "down" or closed shed.

Plain weave—simplest weave of over one, under one

Rya—one of the many types of knotted pile

Sett—number of warp ends in each inch of the weaving

Shed—opening through which weft is passed

Soumak—a method of warp wrapping by weft threads. Soumak may also be carried across wefts in a meandering way, to be attached by wrapping around a warp at points; sometimes called "flying shuttle" when used in this way.

Twining—a method of weft exchanging positions from front to back between warp threads in a figure-eight manner. Vertical twining is done by a yarn exchanging positions from front to back of the tapestry, crossing over woven passes of weft; this may be used to "draw" details on the surface of the tapestry.

Warp—the thread on the loom; needs to be strong for the tension of the warp for tapestry

Warp-way stripes—stripes that are created with pick-and-pick method, running in the warp direction

Weft—the yarn or thread used for weaving into the warp

Weft-way stripes—solid stripes or bands of color that run in the weft direction

A more extensive glossary for tapestry terms is found at the American Tapestry Alliance website at this link: https://americantapestryalliance.org/tapestry-education/ educational-articles-on-tapestry-weaving/ glossary-of-tapestry-terms/

Design Terms

Analogous colors—related or side-by-side colors as found on the color wheel. These have a common hue relationship; for instance, red, red-orange, orange, yellow-orange.

Aspect ratio—the relationship between the height and width of a rectangle

Asymmetrical balance—a sense of balance in which visual weight or movements may direct the viewer's eye

Atmospheric perspective—also called aerial perspective. Refers to the change of color intensity and value when seeing space in depth in a landscape.

Balance—sense of equilibrium in the artwork. In two-dimensional compositions it may be created by several means to give the viewer a feeling that all parts are in balance. In three-dimensional works, literal balance is sometimes necessary.

Bezold effect—colors are influenced by background colors. For instance, black or white surrounding colors make a difference of visual impact.

Color—one of the elements of art and design. Variations may be seen in hue (location on the color wheel), intensity (saturation or strength of color quality), or value (degree of light or dark). Colors may be either **additive** or **subtractive**. Additive primaries of red, green, and blue result in other colors when combined; additive colors are used in lighting and computer-based applications. Subtractive primaries of red, yellow, and blue mix to create other colors; these are used with many art media, including paint and dyes.

Color wheel—a diagrammatic way to see the colors of the spectrum in relationship to each other. The color wheel commonly used in practical ways has twelve hues: three primaries, three secondaries, and six tertiaries.

Complementary colors—hues that are opposite each other on the color wheel. When placed side by side at full strength or intensity, the visual effect of each is heightened. When mixed together, either as paint or dye, or in yarn, the effect is to neutralize each other.

Composition—overall design of the space, within which the elements and principles are used

Counterchange—design effect with opposite values in a mirror image. A dark-light checkerboard is a simple example of counterchange.

Design format—the compositional space; includes overall shape of the work

Design fundamentals—basic components of visual art and design that include the elements and principles

Elements of design—components of all art and design. Often included are line, shape and form or volume, value, texture, space, and color.

Emphasis—areas of interest within a composition, sometimes called focal point(s)

Fibonacci series—series of numbers beginning with 0, 1, with each successive number being added to the previous one. For instance, $1 + 1 = 2$, $1 + 2 = 3$, $2 + 3 = 5$ . . . Often used as a designing concept to plan ratio of sizes or numbers of elements within a composition.

Figure-ground—refers to the shapes and the background within the design. Figure-ground relationship means how each relates to the other in placement, size, contrast, etc. Positive-negative is another term used for this idea.

Format—shape, size, configuration of the overall design space

Golden mean—also called the golden section, golden rectangle, or golden ratio. The relationship of parts in 1 to 1.618 ratio.

Hexad—six hues located by placing a hexagonal diagram over the twelve-color wheel. Two combinations are found: all the primary and secondary colors as one; all tertiary colors are included in the other.

Line—one of the most basic elements of art made by a movement of a tool and medium; can give a delineation of edge

Monochromatic—variations of one hue in tints, tones, and shades. For instance, pink, pure red, and burgundy would be variations of the hue red.

Notan—reducing the overall design image to only areas of dark and light

Primary colors—in subtractive colors as used in artwork, including dyeing processes, these are commonly thought of as red, yellow, and blue. The quality of each of the primaries may be "biased" or lean toward warm or cool versions of the hues.

Principles of design—ways in which the elements are used in the overall composition. Often included are balance (symmetrical, radial, and asymmetrical), emphasis, rhythm and repetition, proportion, and variety.

Proportion—relationship of parts to each other or to the whole composition (or both)

Repetition—recurrence of motif or elements. This may be seen in regular or irregular, alternating, progressive, or flowing rhythm of elements.

Rule of thirds—division of design space into one-third areas horizontally and vertically. Focal points or areas of interest are often planned to lie at or adjacent to the intersection of the division lines.

Scale—the sizes of parts within a composition. The scale may be realistic and represent expected sizes, or exaggerated for expressive reasons. Scale also refers to the overall size of the artwork.

Secondary colors—created by combining two each of the primary colors. Red plus blue yields violet; red plus yellow makes orange; yellow plus blue results in green.

Shape and form—on a two-dimensional surface, shapes may be made by outline, washes of paint, and cut bits of paper, for instance. Form is seen as three-dimensional objects with height, width, and depth used.

Space—on a two-dimensional surface, space may be shallow or seemingly deep; overlapping of shapes, color changes to suggest distance, and linear perspective are among ways to create an illusion of space in depth on a flat surface.

Symmetrical balance—also called formal balance. Parts of design are arranged on either side of a central axis, side to side or top to bottom. Radial balance is another form of formal balance, with things arranged around a central point.

Tertiary colors—intermediate colors found between adjacent primary and secondary colors around the color wheel: yellow-orange, red-orange, red-violet, blue-violet, blue-green, yellow-green

Tetrad—four colors found by using a square or rectangular diagram over the color wheel to find orderly relationships. A square diagram would locate three possible combinations of hues: a primary and secondary, plus two tertiary hues, each complements or opposites of each other. A rectangular diagram would locate six combinations of hues: three would contain primary and secondaries, each complements or opposites of each other; three others would contain all tertiary hues, each complements or opposites of each other.

Texture—the tactile quality of surface or the simulation of it in visual ways

Thumbnail sketch—a small, quick sketch in which basic design areas are shown

Triad—three colors selected by using a triangular diagram over the color wheel to find orderly relationships. These may be found by overlaying an equilateral triangle that locates three farthest-apart hues (the primary colors, for instance) and then may be rotated to find any other equally distant hues. An isosceles triangle may locate what's also called "split complement" by pointing out three colors, with two of the three being found on either side of the first color's complement or opposite on the color wheel.

Unity—all elements and principles work in harmony to give an overall feeling of "rightness" to the composition.

Variety—differences among elements and principles to enliven the composition

Appendix E

Resources and References

Selected Resources for Design, Creativity, and Tapestry Technique

Books about Design and Creativity

Aimone, Steven. *Design! A Lively Guide to Design Basics for Artists & Craftspeople.* New York: Lark Books, 2007.

_____. *Expressive Drawing: A Practical Guide to Freeing the Artist Within.* New York: Lark Books, 2009.

Albers, Josef. *The Interaction of Color.* New Haven, CT: Yale University Press, 1963.

_____. *The Interaction of Color.* iPad app, available through the App Store.

Barrett, Terry. *Crits: A Student Manual.* London: Bloomsbury, 2019.

Edwards, Betty. *Color: A Course in Mastering the Art of Mixing Colors.* New York: Jeremy P. Tarcher / Penguin, 2004.

Feldman, Edmund Burk. *Varieties of Visual Experience.* Englewood Cliffs, NJ: Prentice-Hall, 1981.

Hornung, David. *Color: A Workshop for Artists and Designers.* 2nd ed. London: Laurence King, 2012.

Itten, Johannes. *The Color Star.* New York: Wiley, 1986.

_____. *The Elements of Color.* New York: Wiley, 1970.

Kurtz, Carol. *Designing for Weaving: A Study Guide for Drafting, Design and Color.* New York: Hastings House, 1981.

Lambert, Patricia, Barbara Staepelaere, and Mary G. Fry. *Color and Fiber.* Atglen, PA: Schiffer, 1997.

Menz, Deb. *Color Works: The Crafter's Guide to Color.* Loveland, CO: Interweave, 2004.

Mize, Dianne. *Finding Freedom to Create: A Painter's Roadmap.* Bloomington, IN: Balboa, 2014.

Books about Tapestry Technique, Design, and Finishing

Larochette, Jean Pierre, and Yadin Larochette. *Anatomy of a Tapestry: Techniques, Materials, Care.* Atglen, PA: Schiffer, 2020.

Mailand, Harold F., and Dorothy Stites Alig. *Preserving Textiles: A Guide for the Nonspecialist.* Indianapolis, IN: Indianapolis Museum of Art, 1999.

Mezoff, Rebecca. *The Art of Tapestry Weaving: A Complete Guide to Mastering the Techniques for Making Images with Yarn.* North Adams, MA: Storey, 2020.

Russell, Carol K. *Tapestry Handbook: The Next Generation.* Atglen, PA: Schiffer, 2007.

Scanlin, Tommye McClure. *The Nature of Things: Essays of a Tapestry Weaver.* Dahlonega: University of North Georgia Press, 2020.

Sidore, Micala. *The Art Is the Cloth: How to Look at and Understand Tapestries*. Atglen, PA: Schiffer, 2020.

Soroka, Joanne. *Tapestry Weaving: Design and Technique*. Wiltshire, UK: Crowood, 2011.

Todd-Hooker, Kathe. *Line in Tapestry*. Albany, OR: Fine Fiber Press, 2005.

_____. *Shaped Tapestry*. Albany, OR: Fine Fiber Press, 2004.

_____. *Tapestry 101*. Albany, OR: Fine Fiber Press, 2007.

Books about Dyeing

Boutrup, Joy, and Catharine Ellis. *The Art and Science of Natural Dyes: Principles, Experiments, and Results*. Atglen, PA: Schiffer, 2019.

Menz, Deb. *Color in Spinning*. Loveland, CO: Interweave, 2005.

Zicafoose, Mary. *Ikat: The Essential Handbook to Weaving with Resists*. The Weaver's Studio series. New York: Penguin, 2020.

Internet Resources

As we all know, internet resources are constantly in flux. The following links were current at the time of writing. Social media sources have many topic-specific groups that may be followed. Word of mouth often will lead you to sites that will be of interest as they become available.

Several interesting websites for color and other art and design information:

WebExhibits is an online interactive museum of science, humanities, and culture. The information about color is wide ranging. www.webexhibits.org.

ColorMatters is an online resource created by Jill Morton. Many color topics are covered in her website. http://color-matters.com.

Dr. Ron Knott's website about Fibonacci and golden mean is informative: www.maths.surrey.ac.uk/hosted-sites/R.Knott/Fibonacci/fibnat.html.

Kevin MacLeod's website for generating grids of all kinds is very helpful: https://incompetech.com/.

Thousands of images of art and design are available for viewing online. Three are Metropolitan Museum of Art Open Access (www.metmuseum.org/art/collection), Museum of Modern Art online collection (www.moma.org/collection/works?locale=en), and National Museum of Women in the Arts (https://nmwa.org/our-collection).

Tapestry Organizations

American Tapestry Alliance (ATA) is an organization of over 1,000 members as of 2019. Membership is open worldwide. https://americantapestryalliance.org.

> **Educational topics:** Many topics about tapestry technique, ideas, and inspiration may be found at the American Tapestry Alliance (ATA) website, particularly in the ever-expanding Educational Articles section. https://americantapestryalliance.org/education/educational-articles/.

> **Mentoring programs:** The ATA offers mentoring for basic, intermediate, and advanced levels of tapestry. More information may be found at the ATA website, currently at this link: https://americantapestryalliance.org/tapestry-education/apestry-weaving-instruction-mentoring-program/.

Regional tapestry groups in the USA include Tapestry Weavers South (TWS), Tapestry Weavers West (TWW), and Tapestry Weavers in New England (TWiNE). Contact information about those can be found at the ATA website: http://americantapestryalliance.org/NandR/Links.html.

British Tapestry Group—open to membership from around the world. www.thebritishtapestrygroup.co.uk/.

Canadian Tapestry Network—open to membership from around the world. www.canadiantapestrynetwork.com/.

Selected Locations for Further Study in Tapestry or Art and Design

Check out opportunities in your local area. Many community art centers have classes available throughout the year. Colleges and university art programs offer other options for study, either for credit or as audit.

Arrowmont School of Art and Craft
556 Parkway, Gatlinburg, TN 37738
(865) 436-5860
https://arrowmont.org

John C. Campbell Folk School
1 Folk School Rd., Brasstown, NC 28902
(828) 837-2775
https://folkschool.org

Penland School of Craft
67 Doras Trail
Penland, North Carolina 28765
(828) 765-2359
https://penland.org

Other Tapestry Study Options

Video:

Archie Brennan and Susan Martin Maffei instructional videos: "Woven Tapestry Techniques" is available for streaming; information can be found through their website at www.brennan-maffei.com/.

A Weaverly Path: The Tapestry Life of Silvia Heyden, a documentary film by Kenny Dalsheimer. Although this film is about Silvia Heyden's life and tapestries, and not instructional focused, seeing and hearing about her inspiring tapestries is a learning experience. http://aweaverlypath.com/.

Online lessons:

Rebecca Mezoff online learning covers several topics for tapestry, including "Weaving Tapestry on Little Looms," "Warp and Weft: Learning the Structure of Tapestry," "Color Gradation Techniques for Tapestry," "Design Solutions for the Artist/Weaver," and "Four Selvedge Warping with Sarah C. Swett," produced by Rebecca Mezoff Tapestry Studio. https://rebeccamezoff.com/online-learning.

Notes

1. Silvia Heyden, *The Making of Modern Tapestry: My Journey of Discovery* (Durham, NC: Silvia Heyden, 1998), 65.
2. Edmund Burke Feldman, *Varieties of Visual Experience* (Englewood Cliffs, NJ: Prentice-Hall, 1981), 223.
3. Read more from Barbara Burns about the inspiration for and the process of creating *The Little Devil Corset* at her website, https://www.burns-studio.com/category/corsets/.
4. Betty Edwards, *Color: A Course in Mastering the Art of Mixing Colors* (New York: Jeremy P. Tarcher / Penguin, 2004), 15–16.
5. Josef Albers, *Interaction of Color* (New Haven, CT: Yale University Press, 1963), 42.
6. For instance, this website gives simple descriptions of the basics of color theory: http://desktoppub.about.com/od/howcolorworks/ss/Color-Basics-Desktop-Publishing.htm.
7. The term "tertiary" is also used to describe the mixture created between primary and secondary colors. The term also has a different meaning—the mixture of two secondary hues that creates a neutral mix. For instance, mixing orange and violet, green and violet, or green and orange. Albers used a version of Goethe's color triangle to describe the mixing of these tertiaries, in *Interaction of Color*, 66–67.
8. Edwards, *Color: A Course in Mastering the Art of Mixing Colors*, 54–55.
9. Johannes Itten, *The Elements of Color* (New York: John Wiley & Sons, 1970), 72–74.
10. Deb Menz, *Color Works: The Crafters Guide to Color* (Loveland, CO: Interweave, 2004), 25.
11. Albers, *Interaction of Color*, 33.
12. Mary Stewart, *Launching the Imagination: A Comprehensive Guide to Basic Design*, 5th ed. (New York: McGraw-Hill Education, 2015), 58.
13. Stewart, *Launching the Imagination*, 50–51.
14. Joanne Soroka, *Tapestry Weaving: Design and Technique* (Wiltshire, UK: Crowood, 2011), 114.
15. https://americantapestryalliance.org/artist-pages/.
16. https://americantapestryalliance.org/tapestry-education/educational-articles-on-tapestry-weaving/choosing-colors/.
17. https://americantapestryalliance.org/tapestry-education/educational-articles-on-tapestry-weaving/the-simple-short-version-of-colour-movement-in-tapestry/.
18. Feldman, *Varieties of Visual Experience*, 251.
19. Comments on inspiration for *The Farmer's Daughter's Yggdrasil (Tree of Life)* may be found on Robbie LaFleur's blog at this post: https://robbielafleur.com/2019/07/23/underway-tree-of-life-red-river-valley-version/.
20. Feldman, *Varieties of Visual Experience*, 260–62.
21. Susan Martin Maffei describes the inspiration for her tapestry *Sicilian Defense* at her website: http://susanmartinmaffei.com/scrolls#.
22. Michael Rohde's statement about his work with the portraits as well as other inspirations may be found at his website: www.michaelrohde.com/#!/page/504289/statement.
23. Priya Hemenway, *Divine Proportion: Phi in Art, Nature, and Science* (New York: Sterling, 2005).
24. Dianne Mize, *Finding Freedom to Create* (Bloomington, IN: Balboa, 2014), 83–86.
25. Steven Aimone, *Expressive Drawing: A Practical Guide to Freeing the Artist Within* (New York: Lark Books, 2009), 177.
26. Billy Collins, "Horizon," *The Art of Drowning* (Pittsburgh, PA: University of Pittsburgh Press, 1995), 41.
27. Itten, *The Elements of Color* (New York: John Wiley & Sons, 1970), 72.
28. Pantone Studio is one of the palette generators available for mobile devices. On computers, there is Colormind (http://colormind.io/).
29. Thousands of images are available for viewing online. Three sources are the Metropolitan Museum of Art Open Access (www.metmuseum.org/art/collection), the Museum of Modern Art online collection (www.moma.org/collection/works?locale=en), and the National Museum of Women in the Arts (https://nmwa.org/our-collection).
30. Elmer's Re-Stick Glue Stick is good for this.
31. Magic Rub erasers are perfect to use for this but are more expensive than some other types. Rubber-stamp-cutting material may also be used for this exercise.

32. Kevin MacLeod has a website that provides a variety of public-domain downloadable grids, lines, and other patterning shapes: https://incompetech.com/wordpress/.

33. Steven Aimone, *Design! A Lively Guide to Design Basics for Artists & Craftspeople* (New York: Lark Books, 2004), 14.

34. Betty Edwards, *Drawing on the Artist Within* (New York: Simon & Schuster, 1986), chapter 7, "Drawing Out Insight."

35. Aimone, *Expressive Drawing*, 17.

36. Mize, *Finding Freedom to Create*, 84.

37. Ibid., 144.

38. Terry Barrett, *Crits: A Student Manual* (London: Bloomsbury, 2019), 96.

39. Ibid., 105–106.

40. www.vam.ac.uk/collections/raphael-cartoons.

41. Tommye McClure Scanlin, "Idea Gallery: Make a Cartoon and Use it for Tapestry!," *Handwoven*, January/February 2021: 22–25.

42. "Mounting and Hanging Tapestries: A Variety of Solutions," https://americantapestryalliance.org/tapes-try-education/educational-articles-on-tapestry-weaving/mounting-and-hanging-tapestries-a-variety-of-solu-tions/.

43. www.smallcorp.com/magnet-slats/.

44. Harold F. Mailand and Dorothy Stites Alig, *Preserving Textiles: A Guide for the Nonspecialist* (Indianapolis, IN: Indianapolis Museum of Art, 1999), 48.

45. https://museum.gwu.edu/hanging-textiles.

46. Archie Brennan, "Tapestry, a 20th Century Art Form?," essay in *Tapestry: The Narrative Voice*, 1989. Catalog of exhibition of the same name held 1989–91 in seven galleries worldwide, coordinated by Sharon Marcus.

47. Tommye McClure Scanlin, "Threads if [sic] Time—One Day at a Time," *Tapestry Weaver: The British Tapestry Group*, November 2012: 12–15. "Time Warp and Weft: A Celebration of the Passage of Time through Weaving," *Shuttle, Spindle & Dyepot*, Summer 2017, 36–40. "Threads of Time," in *The Nature of Things: Essays of a Tapestry Weaver* (Dahlonega, GA: University of North Georgia Press, 2020), 168–177.

48. Archie Brennan, "The Space between the Warps" https://americantapestryalliance.org/tapestry-education/educational-articles-on-tapestry-weaving/the-space-between-the-warps/.

49. Kathe Todd-Hooker, *Tapestry 101* (Albany, OR: Fine Fiber Press, 2007), 40.

50. Peter Collingwood, *The Techniques of Rug Weaving* (New York: Watson-Guptill, 1968), chapters 6.1 ("Soumak"), 6.4 ("Knotted Pile"), and 13.1 ("Weft Twining"). Collingwood's book is included in the *On-line Digital Archive of Weaving and Related Documents* (www2.cs.arizona.edu/patterns/weaving/books/cp_rug1_1.pdf).

51. Nancy Hoskins, *Weft-Faced Pattern Weaves: Tabby to Taqueté* (Seattle: University of Washington Press, 1992) 37–47.
Hoskins's book has diagrams for many variations of pick and pick patterning.

52. Collingwood, *The Techniques of Rug Weaving*, 103–13.

53. Ibid., 183–203.

54. Dorothy Clews, https://americantapestryalliance.org/fall02newsletter/ATAFallNewsletterpg18.htm.

55. Collingwood, *The Techniques of Rug Weaving*, 463–77.

56. Kathe Todd-Hooker, *Line in Tapestry* (Albany, OR: Fine Fiber Press, 2012), 55–57.

57. Collingwood, *The Techniques of Rug Weaving*, 225–30.

Bibliography

Aimone, Steven. *Design! A Lively Guide to Design Basics for Artists & Craftspeople*. New York: Lark Books, 2007.

_____. *Expressive Drawing: A Practical Guide to Freeing the Artist Within*. New York: Lark Books, 2009.

Albers, Josef. *The Interaction of Color*. New Haven, CT: Yale University Press, 1963.

_____. *The Interaction of Color*. iPad app, available through iTunes Store.

Barrett, Terry. *Crits: A Student Manual*. London: Bloomsbury, 2019.

Brennan, Archie. "Tapestry, a 20th Century Art Form?" In *Tapestry: The Narrative Voice*. Portland, OR, 1989. Catalog of exhibition of the same name held in 1989–91, coordinated by Sharon Marcus.

Cameron, Julia. *The Artist's Way*. New York: Tarcher-Perigee, 2016.

Collins, Billy. *The Art of Drowning*. Pittsburgh, PA: University of Pittsburgh Press, 1995.

Collingwood, Peter. *The Techniques of Rug Weaving*. New York: Watson-Guptill, 1968.

Dow, Arthur Wesley. *Composition*. 13th ed. New introduction by Joseph Mascheck. Berkeley: University of California Press, 1997.

Edwards, Betty. *Color: A Course in Mastering the Art of Mixing Colors*. New York: Tarcher-Perigee, 2004.

_____. *Drawing on the Artist Within*. New York: Simon & Schuster, 1986.

_____. *Drawing on the Right Side of the Brain*. New York: Tarcher-Perigee, 2012.

Feldman, Edmund Burke. *Varieties of Visual Experience*. Englewood Cliffs, NJ: Prentice-Hall, 1981.

Hemenway, Priya. *Divine Proportion: Phi in Art, Nature, and Science*. New York: Sterling, 2005.

Heyden, Silvia. *The Making of Modern Tapestry: My Journey of Discovery*. Durham, NC: Silvia Heyden, 1998.

Hoskins, Nancy. *Weft-Faced Pattern Weaves: Tabby to Taqueté*. Seattle: University of Washington Press, 1992.

Itten, Johannes. *The Color Star*. New York: Wiley, 1986.

_____. *The Elements of Color*. New York: Wiley, 1970.

Kurtz, Carol. *Designing for Weaving: A Study Guide for Drafting, Design and Color*. New York: Hastings House, 1981.

Lambert, Patricia, Barbara Staepelaere, and Mary G. Fry. *Color and Fiber*. West Chester, PA: Schiffer, 1986.

Larochette, Jean Pierre, and Yadin Larochette. *Anatomy of a Tapestry: Techniques, Materials, Care*. Atglen, PA: Schiffer, 2020.

Mailand, Harold F., and Dorothy Stites Alig. *Preserving Textiles: A Guide for the Nonspecialist*. Indianapolis, IN: Indianapolis Museum of Art, 1999.

Menz, Deb. *Color Works: The Crafter's Guide to Color*. Loveland, CO: Interweave, 2004.

Mize, Dianne. *Finding Freedom to Create: A Painter's Roadmap*. Bloomington, IN: Balboa, 2014.

Soroka, Joanne. *Tapestry Weaving: Design and Technique*. Wiltshire, UK: Crowood, 2011.

Stewart, Mary. *Launching the Imagination: A Comprehensive Guide to Basic Design*. 5th ed. New York: McGraw-Hill Education, 2015.

Todd-Hooker, Kathe. *Line in Tapestry*. Albany, OR: Fine Fiber Press, 2005.

_____. *Shaped Tapestry*. Albany, OR: Fine Fiber Press, 2004.

_____. *Tapestry 101*. Albany, OR: Fine Fiber Press, 2007.

Contributors of Tapestry Works and/or Study Samples

Janet Austin, 44, 65
Robin Beveridge, 147
Nicki Bair, 71, 75
Archie Brennan, 16, 58
Terri Bryson, 110
Elizabeth Buckley, 23, 41
Barbara Burns, 29, 72
Don Burns, 32, 43, 58, 67
Mary Cost, 43, 57, 67
Nancy Crampton, 27
Mary Alice Donceel, 111, 112
Allie Dudley, 137, 156–158, 160, 173
Nancy Dugger, 113, 114
Jane Freear-Wyld, 21
Heather Gallegos-Rex, 57, 69
Deb Gottlieb, 114
Joan Griffin, 62, 69, 153
Lyn Hart, 18, 38

Barbara Heller, 41, 60, 64
Silvia Heyden, 9, 12, 17
Betty Hilton-Nash, 27, 50, 67
Susan Iverson, 28, 71
David Johnson, 15, 36, 40
Mary Jones, 132–133
Robbie LaFleur, 59, 61
Mary Jane Lea, 9, 115
Connie Lippert, 26
Mary Jane Lord, 58, 63
Susan Martin Maffei, 29, 56, 68
Alice Martin, 146
LaDonna Mayer, 24, 32, 43
Rebecca Mezoff, 7, 23, 34, 66
Nancy Nordquist, 10, 135
Becca Pontes, 168
April Price, 151
Erin M. Riley, 24, 73

Michael Rohde, 49, 50, 74
Dinah Rose, 116
Dorina Scalia, 134
Tommye McClure Scanlin, 37, 49, 72, 84, 91, 121, 141, 143, 145, 175
Kathy Spoering, 33, 48
Becky Stevens, 18, 74
Sarah Swett, 73
Sarah Thomsen, 117
Kathe Todd-Hooker, 22, 39
Linda Wallace, 25, 70
Sarah Warren, 34, 44
Sue Weil, 27, 65, 75
Pat Williams, 33, 37, 63, 72
Joann C. Wilson, 130–131, 136

Index

Tommye McClure Scanlin, professor emerita, University of North Georgia, is a tapestry weaver and longtime art educator. Her work has been shown widely, and she maintains an active studio practice. Her teaching career spans all levels of students, from youngsters to retirees. In the past 45 years, in addition to university teaching, she has also taught tapestry in short classes and workshops, including at Arrowmont, John C. Campbell Folk School, and Penland School of Craft. Visit her at www.scanlintapestry.com.